TERESA OF AVILA

OUTSTANDING CHRISTIAN THINKERS

Series Editor: Brian Davies OP

The series offers a range of authoritative studies on people who have made an outstanding contribution to Christian thought and understanding. The series will range across the full spectrum of Christian thought to include Catholic and Protestant thinkers, to cover East and West, historical and contemporary figures. By and large, each volume will focus on a single 'thinker', but occasionally the subject may be a movement or a school of thought.

Brian Davies OP, the series editor, is Regent of Studies at Blackfriars, Oxford, where he also teaches philosophy. He is a member of the Theology Faculty of the University of Oxford and tutor in theology at St Benet's Hall, Oxford. He has lectured regularly at the University of Bristol, Fordham University, New York, and the Beda College, Rome. He is Reviews Editor of *New Blackfriars*. His previous publications include: *An Introduction to the Philosophy of Religion* (OUP, 1982); *Thinking about God* (Geoffrey Chapman, 1985); and he was editor of *Language, Meaning and God* (Geoffrey Chapman, 1987).

Existing titles in the series:

The Apostolic Fathers
Simon Tugwell OP

Denys the Areopagite
Andrew Louth

The Venerable Bede
Benedicta Ward

Anselm
G. R. Evans

Teresa of Avila
Rowan Williams

Handel
Hamish Swanston

Reinhold Niebuhr
Kenneth Durkin

Yves Congar
Aidan Nichols OP

Planned titles in the series include:

Berkeley
David Berman

The Neo-Thomists
Gerald McCool SJ

Bultmann
David Fergusson

Karl Rahner
William Dych SJ

TERESA OF AVILA

Rowan Williams

GEOFFREY CHAPMAN

Geoffrey Chapman
An imprint of Cassell Publishers Limited
Villiers House, 41/47 Strand, London WC2N 5JE, England

First published 1991

British Library Cataloguing in Publication Data
Williams, Rowan
   Teresa of Avila—(Outstanding christian thinkers).
   1. Carmelites. Teresa, of Avila, Saint, 1515–1582
   I. Title   II. Series
   271.971024

ISBN 0 225 66579 4 (hardback)
0 225 66547 6 (paperback)

Typeset by Colset Private Limited, Singapore
Printed and bound in Great Britain by
Biddles Ltd, Guildford and King's Lynn

Contents

Editorial foreword

St Anselm of Canterbury once described himself as someone with faith seeking understanding. In words addressed to God he says, 'I long to understand in some degree thy truth, which my heart believes and loves. For I do not seek to understand that I may believe, but I believe in order to understand.'

And this is what Christians have always inevitably said, either explicitly or implicitly. Christianity rests on faith, but it also has content. It teaches and proclaims a distinctive and challenging view of reality. It naturally encourages reflection. It is something to think about; something about which one might even have second thoughts.

But what have the greatest Christian thinkers said? And is it worth saying? Does it engage with modern problems? Does it provide us with a vision to live by? Does it make sense? Can it be preached? Is it believable?

This series originates with questions like these in mind. Written by experts, it aims to provide clear, authoritative and critical accounts of outstanding Christian writers from New Testament times to the present. It will range across the full spectrum of Christian thought to include Catholic and Protestant thinkers, thinkers from East and West, thinkers ancient, mediaeval and modern.

The series draws on the best scholarship currently available, so it will interest all with a professional concern for the history of Christian ideas. But contributors will also be writing for general readers who have little or no previous knowledge of the subjects to be dealt with. Volumes to appear should therefore prove helpful at a popular as well as an academic level. For the most part they will be devoted to a single thinker, but occasionally the subject will be a movement or school of thought.

Together with her contemporary and friend, John of the Cross, Teresa of Avila, the subject of the present volume, represents the highest point of Catholic spiritual writing in the troubled age of the Reformation and Counter-Reformation. She is also one of the founding figures of modern Spanish literature. Her vivid descriptions of her experiences in prayer have long made her an object of intense interest to psychologists of religion.

This book makes use of the most recent historical research on Teresa and her society and provides a full introduction to all her major works. It shows Teresa to us as more than just a chronicler of paranormal states of consciousness. She emerges as a genuine theologian in her own right, with a powerful contribution to make to contemporary understanding.

Above all, Teresa is chiefly concerned to develop a model of Christian life as friendship with God, a God who abandons status and dignity for the sake of human beings. In this book Rowan Williams also shows how all Teresa's major writings concentrate on this incarnational theme. In the final chapter he argues that Christian mysticism is itself deeply misunderstood unless it is seen within an incarnational framework.

Brian Davies OP

Preface

Teresa of Avila is one of the most accessible and attractive of all the great writers in the Christian mystical tradition; but her very human attractiveness and the fascination of her unusual experiences of vision and rapture tend to obscure two salient facts about her. First, she was a woman reacting to a particularly difficult epoch in the history of the Spanish state and Church; and second, she was an independent theological thinker. She lived in a society whose tensions and anxieties were more like those of modern South Africa than Europe in the last quarter of the twentieth century: though she would have recognized all too readily the horrors of Germany in the 1930s, and the threat of resurgent anti-Semitism in the France of 1990. As a member of a disadvantaged and suspect group—Christians of Jewish descent—she had a perspective on her age rather different from that of many of her contemporaries, however hard she tried to be a 'good' member of the institutions to which she belonged. Much of her theology becomes clearer in the light of her background; which is why this book spends some time examining the world in which she lived. But she is also a theologian of the contemplative life, though she does not give that phrase quite the connotations we have come to expect. She is preoccupied with the contemplative's missionary vocation in a way far removed from the individualistic and slightly precious ambience that the word 'contemplation' can suggest.

Looking at Teresa as far as possible in her own terms means some quite close study of her texts. This book cannot claim to be anything like an exhaustive commentary on her writings, but I hope to draw out some continuities in her often diffuse and sprawling works. I am conscious of a profound debt to Teresian scholars, English and Spanish, who have made this task easier. I must also record my gratitude to the Teresian Association in the United Kingdom: invitations to talk to them, formally and informally, about Teresa have helped me to crystallize what I wanted to say about her and to test it out on a group committed to a way of life—as lay contemplatives involved in apostolic work—very close indeed to Teresa's original vision. I must also thank various people for help and encouragement of various sorts: Brian Davies OP, for getting me to write this in the first place; Colin Thompson and Iain Matthew OCD, for many illuminating conversations and much help with books in Spanish; Sister Martha Reeves for constant friendship and stimulus of a rare kind; and my family for their unfailing patience and generosity.

Rowan Williams
Oxford, 1990

Bibliography and Abbreviations

Teresa's works

The most convenient Spanish edition is that in the series Biblioteca de Autores Cristianos (Madrid, 1962); the same series also includes a text of Osuna's *Alphabet* (Madrid, 1972).

The complete translation in English by E. Allison Peers (London, 1946) is supplemented by two volumes of the *Letters* (London, 1951) in continuous pagination (references in the text are given in the form: *Letters*, volume, number of document, page number); the three volumes published by the Institute of Carmelite Studies, edited and translated by Kieran Kavanaugh and Otilio Rodriguez (Washington, DC, 1976, 1980, 1985), do not include the letters.

Quotations are generally made from the Kavanaugh–Rodriguez version, except for the letters (which are from Peers); I have occasionally corrected Kavanaugh and Rodriguez where they give an obscure or misleading version. Their translation is preferable to Peers in terms of liveliness and readability, but tends to the impressionistic at times.

Teresa's works are abbreviated throughout as follows:

C   *The Interior Castle*
F   *The Book of her Foundations*
L   *The Book of her Life*
S   *Meditations on the Song of Songs*
T   *Spiritual Testimonies*
W   *The Way of Perfection*

SELECTED BIBLIOGRAPHY

Historical Background

E. Allison Peers, *Handbook to the Life and Times of St Teresa and St John of the Cross* (London, 1954).

J.H. Elliott, *Imperial Spain 1469–1716* (London, 1963).

Biographies

E. Allison Peers, *Mother of Carmel. A Portrait of St Teresa of Jesus* (London, 1945). A vivid sketch by the greatest of British Teresian scholars; now slightly dated.

Marcelle Auclair, *St Teresa of Avila* (London, 1952). Detailed, slightly novelistic, in some respects out of date.

Efrén de la Madre de Dios and Otgar Steggink, *Tiempo y vida de Santa Teresa* (Madrid, 1968). The fundamental modern resource for Teresa's biography.

Stephen Clissold, *St Teresa of Avila* (London, 1979). A good and clear digest of modern scholarly work.

Victoria Lincoln, *Teresa, a Woman. A Biography of Teresa of Avila* (Albany, NY, 1984). Extremely detailed; but the boundary between speculation and documentable fact is not clearly marked, and there are many very questionable assertions.

A biography by Shirley du Boulay is currently in preparation.

Studies

Alberto Barrientos (ed.), *Introducción a la lectura de Santa Teresa* (Madrid, 1978). Invaluable guides to the individual works, as well as general essays on historical and other themes.

E.W. Trueman Dicken, *The Crucible of Love. A Study of the Mysticism of St Teresa of Jesus and St John of the Cross* (London, 1963). An exhaustive survey of the teachings of the two great Carmelites; an over-rigid application of scholastic categories to Teresa in particular makes some of its judgements debatable, but it remains something of a classic.

Teresian scholarship is at present very productive. Three works that appeared as the writing of this book was nearing completion deserve mention:

Jodi Bilinkoff, *The Avila of St Teresa. Religious Reform in a Sixteenth-Century City* (Cornell University Press, 1989). An invaluable and comprehensive study of Teresa's immediate social background, which brings out the importance of Avila as a centre for religious reform and protest throughout the early sixteenth century.

Noel Dermot O'Donoghue, *Mystics for our Time* (Edinburgh, 1989). Essays on Teresa, John of the Cross and Thérèse of Lisieux, both idiosyncratic and profound.

Alison Weber, *Teresa of Avila and the Rhetoric of Femininity* (Princeton, 1990). A careful reading of Teresa's texts so as to bring out her rhetorical strategy of bidding for authority by adopting the language of female powerlessness, ignorance or frailty, and also the highly ambivalent results of this in her own *exercise* of authority over women. An original and important essay.

Introduction
A biographical sketch

Teresa's family could reckon itself among the minor nobility, and her father was one of the wealthiest men in Avila; but their security was shadowed by the social and racial tensions typical of the Spain of that period, tensions which will be more fully explored in the first chapter of this book. Don Alonso Sánchez de Cepeda appears in his daughter's autobiography as a serious, devout and conscientious man (though the evidence also indicates that he was an increasingly poor manager of his resources). Perhaps the most dramatic testimony to his high principles is provided by Teresa's recollection that he refused to own slaves; she thoroughly approved of his scruples, but they must have marked him out rather plainly as an eccentric among neighbours of comparable wealth and comfort. Teresa (born in March 1515) was one of twelve children: three sisters and nine brothers (the two eldest being the children of Alonso's first marriage). She describes the family as a happy and united one. Certainly most of them remained in touch throughout their lives, though Teresa was not spared the emotional and financial headaches that often attend the lives of large families of unequal ability and attainment. Probably the best-known story of Teresa's childhood is the attempt she made, accompanied by her elder brother Rodrigo, to run away to 'the land of the Moors' in search of martyrdom, at the age of seven. She had been reading too many saints' lives, she says; but there is a hint too of her mother's obsession with romantic fiction and tales of chivalry, a genre of literature to which Teresa in her teens was no less addicted. In her early adolescence, Teresa, by now

1

an extremely attractive girl, pretty, lively and fond of clothes and jewellery, was involved in a flirtation serious enough to cause mild scandal to the town and much anxiety to her father. Teresa herself wryly observes that the fanatical code of honour observed in Castilian families of her class at least guaranteed that she did not compromise herself irreparably. The result was that Don Alonso decided that she needed the restraint of a convent environment, and, aged sixteen, she was boarded with the Augustinian nuns in Avila, where she was to stay for about eighteen months.

This period was decisive for her. Under the influence of a sensible and warm-hearted novice mistress, she began to consider becoming a nun herself, though, as she says, she was still moved more by fear of hell than by love of God. A period of illness, ending with convalescence at the home of a devout uncle with a good library, settled her mind; after much reflection and (quite demanding) reading, she decided in favour of the cloister. Without her father's knowledge or consent, she left home secretly and entered the Carmelite convent of the Incarnation in Avila. She took the habit in 1536.

Her early years in the convent were interrupted by a very serious illness and a further spell of convalescence at her uncle's (where she read *The Third Spiritual Alphabet* of the Franciscan writer, Francisco de Osuna (*c.* 1492–*c.* 1540), a book of great importance in her spiritual development) and at Becedas, where she received some conspicuously unsuccessful treatment for her illness and also underwent an emotionally disturbing experience (which we shall be discussing further in Chapter 2). More ill than ever, she returned to Avila, fell into a coma thought to be terminal, and could barely move for practically three years. At the very beginning of her time as a nun, she had made extraordinary progress in prayer, with many remarkable experiences of intimacy and what she believed to be 'union' with God; but the exhaustion and depression that followed her illness led her to give up private prayer more or less completely for the best part of two years. When she started praying again, she found no perceptible comforts or rewards; no ecstasy or intimacy. Not until ten years later (1554) did she feel her whole self again engaged in prayer—as a result of a sudden confrontation with an image of Christ's suffering.

She had, during these curious, frustrating years up to 1554, something of a reputation for holiness, and the aura of her recovery from (literally) the brink of the grave still hung about her. Her father turned to her (during the period when she had given up private prayer completely) for help with his spiritual life in his last months, and Teresa felt shame at the distance between her reputation and the reality. As we shall see in reading her *Life*, the experience of these years taught her a good deal about how easy it was to deceive oneself and others as to the state of one's inner life; she at least was able to say with some truth that she had never had any real illusions about her poverty and confusion in this period. But after her 'reconversion' in 1554, she was faced with a far more agonizing set of questions about self-deception and diabolical deception. She began to experience once again unusual states of consciousness and to hear voices purporting to give messages from God. It was a time at which religious eccentricity flourished, and Teresa was only too well aware of the many horror stories in circulation about people (women especially) who had succumbed to fantasies induced by the devil. Her inner doubts were made much worse by those to whom she turned for help.

Avila had its share, and more, of religious houses at this time, and was also something of a centre of general religious fervour. It had produced the great John of Avila (1499/1500–1569), 'Maestro Avila' as he was usually known, a formidable preacher and missioner who was still at this time labouring in southern Spain among the rural poor and the urban gentry alike, a man whose influence extended far and wide in the peninsula. At the time of Teresa's crisis, Avila harboured a remarkable layman, Don Francisco de Salcedo, known for his piety, his austerity and his enthusiasm for theology (he attended courses at the Dominican *studium* in Avila); and also another renowned missioner and preacher, Maestro Gaspar Daza. Salcedo was a relative by marriage of the Cepedas, and Teresa not unnaturally sought his advice; he was alarmed by her accounts of her experience and sent her to Daza, who was equally severe and discouraging. Fortunately for her, Salcedo also introduced her to the newest religious community in Avila, the Society of Jesus (approved by the Pope only fourteen years earlier). Here Teresa found support and understanding, a support which the Jesuits generally continued as the years went on. But the strain of all this brought on more illness; Teresa went to convalesce at the home of a fashionable young widow, Doña Guiomar de Ulloa, sister of a nun at the Incarnation convent. As before, the help of sympathetic and sophisticated lay people was crucial in overcoming some of the deep self-doubts untouched by spiritual directors, and the three years she spent with Doña Guiomar proved to be a time of exceptional growth and consolidation.

Her director from 1556 to late in 1559—with some interruptions which caused her great trouble—was the youthful Jesuit Baltasar Alvarez, who was himself to become in later life a spiritual master of some reputation. At first he had been as nervous as Maestro Daza; but it seems to have been a vision of Christ, unexpected and disorienting, which persuaded him of the authenticity of Teresa's experiences. As a young and inexperienced priest, he had a formidable task with Teresa, whose experiences were becoming stranger and stranger by conventional standards—and at precisely the moment when the Inquisition was acting with greater severity towards those practising mental prayer. The Index of forbidden books published in 1559 banned several works in Spanish on prayer, and the whole climate was hardening towards the use of vernacular literature by the 'unqualified' (women and laity). After Alvarez's departure from Avila in 1559, Teresa was faced yet again with hostile clergy. If she had not had strong personal support from the great ascetic, St Peter of Alcántara (1499–1562), who passed through Avila in 1560, support which echoed what she had earlier heard from the Jesuits, especially from St Francis Borgia whom she had met in 1557, she might have collapsed completely. It is to this period that Teresa's much-discussed and portrayed experience of the 'angel with the fiery dart' belongs. She records (L 29.13) that she was 'sometimes' given a vision of an angel standing by her, with an arrow in his hand, with which he pierced her inmost parts; with its withdrawal she felt an exquisite mixture of pain and joy and an intense desire for God. The erotic overtones of this have been a good deal laboured (and Bernini's notorious statue in Santa Maria della Vittoria, Rome, draws them out pretty explicitly). It would be a mistake to see this as representing the essence of Teresa's spirituality; but one can see why an unsympathetic confessor might wonder what was going on, given the fears and prejudices of the day. Far more typical of this period in 1560 was the increasing number of what Teresa came to call 'imaginative' visions of Christ: inner perceptions of Christ's presence clothed in visible shape (she is careful to distinguish them from hallucinatory impressions of an object in front of the physical eyes). She experienced more and more physical disturbance as well—trance and (she believed) levitation. Happily, by the end of 1560, she had found another supportive confessor in the Dominican, Fray Pedro Ibáñez. In the still greater crisis ahead he was to be an indispensable ally; as was his younger confrère, Fray Domingo Báñez, whose acquaintance Teresa made in 1562. He was for a while to take over from Ibáñez as her confessor; in his maturity, he was one of the foremost theologians of the century.

Teresa was convinced that her experiences were not being given just for her own edification. Back in the Incarnation convent, she and a couple of other sisters began to discuss, very tentatively, the possibility of setting up a new kind of Carmelite house, in which the original simplicity and austerity of the Carmelite rule might be observed: a reform along the lines of the renewal that had taken place in the Franciscan Order, among both the male and the female branches. This idea won strong endorsement from Peter of Alcántara and from Ibáñez, who was able to use his influence locally in support of the project. Doña Guiomar promised money for the foundation; but Teresa, though happy to have her assistance in setting up the proposed house, resisted the idea that there should be a permanent endowment. This was to be a considerable bone of contention: Teresa was determined to establish a house in which religious poverty was more than a matter of words, and she was also, as later events show, anxious about the claims on a community that could and would be made by wealthy benefactors. However, she was flying in the face of practically all the conventional wisdom on the subject. Even Ibáñez disapproved of this. But Teresa was wholly convinced that unconditional poverty was what the new foundation was called to, and refused to give way; once again, Peter of Alcántara supported her unreservedly. By the autumn of 1542 authority had been obtained both from Rome and from the Order, though the house was to be under the jurisdiction of the Bishop of Avila rather than the local Carmelite superiors.

Meanwhile, Teresa herself had spent a good deal of time away from Avila, having been seconded by her religious superiors to be a kind of spiritual 'lady companion' to an aristocratic widow in Toledo. In Doña Luisa de la Cerda's house she met several matrons of the nobility who were to figure a good deal in her later life, above all the Princess of Eboli — wife of one of King Philip's most powerful advisers, the virtual Prime Minister of Spain — and also the Duchess of Medinaceli, wife of the Duke of Alba, himself a personage of immense power in the state. But the most significant result of her stay in Toledo was that Teresa began to write an autobiography. She had already composed for Ibáñez in 1560 a brief account of her state of soul and its development; but in Toledo she met an old acquaintance, Fray García de Toledo, another Dominican, who urged her to write a longer narrative. Others may already have pressed Teresa to do the same. Her first draft of the *Life* was finished in June 1562, just before she returned to Avila.

Although the new foundation was secure in the eyes of the Church by the end of 1562, the civic authorities continued to combat it bitterly—a phenomenon which was to be repeated with several of Teresa's foundations. At least two motives underlay this hostility. Foundations without endowment were simply a charge on the generosity of the public, and most Castilian towns had more than enough mendicants as it was. During this period the once prosperous economy of Castile was beginning its long decline: there was an acute labour shortage as the wool trade found itself unable to cope with expanding demand in Spain and its new colonies in America; cheaper foreign cloth began to be imported; rising prices throughout the economy led to dramatic inflation, and the commercial life of Castile began to fall apart. Those who did not rely on rents for income—the people whom town councils largely represented—were highly vulnerable. Traders and shopkeepers in Avila, and later in other cities, complained that an unendowed religious house would be a dangerous drain on everyone's pockets. Moreover, it is worth noting that in 1540 and 1552 Castile had made legal enactments against begging, which were strongly opposed by some of the religious Orders.

The second cause of unease was rather different; we have already hinted at it in noting Teresa's wish to be free of 'debts of honour' to benefactors. An endowed religious house was a clear part of the social fabric. The wealthy provided an income for it, and in return were granted the right to be buried in the community's church and to have prayers said for their interests in life and death. The family tomb was a significant public place for the display of wealth and 'honour' by means of lavish ornamentation and armorial bearings. Teresa did not want to bind her community to this sort of social service, and, as we shall see in later chapters, she had strong feelings on the subject of family pride. Relatively few benefactors would be like Doña Guiomar, willing to provide basic funding without demanding a spiritual stake in the house and a degree of control in the furnishing of its church. Foundation without endowment was, for Teresa, an essential part of her reconceiving of a religious life genuinely at an angle to the systems of secular power. In later foundations, where the possibilities of earning a reasonable income locally were unquestionably slender, she was to be flexible about endowments; but at this first stage it was vital to make a strong stand.

She was successful. By 1565, the new house, dedicated to St Joseph, for whom Teresa had great devotion, had received the first solemn professions of new sisters; and its constitutions, drawn up by Teresa, had been approved by the Pope. Teresa composed *The Way of Perfection* and her *Meditations on the Song of Songs* in the relatively peaceful atmosphere of St Joseph's in 1565–66. But 1567 saw a new development which determined the whole course of Teresa's subsequent life. She was not content to leave the Reform at simply one house; when the Prior General of the Carmelite Order visited her in 1567, she raised the question of further foundations, and received his permission to explore the possibility. Her motives included the strong sense (which never really left her) that the Carmelite life was an essential support to the Church in a time of crisis. More specifically, her knowledge of the situation in America, where missionaries were struggling to convert the native peoples, intensified her longing to take a more active part in mission herself, and to offer to those who could not share in preaching and teaching a way of life in which they could contribute to the Church's life and health. Between 1567 and her death in 1582, she established fourteen houses, from Burgos in the north to Seville in the south. It is a quite extraordinary record of almost ceaseless work and travel.

It is from these later years that the vast bulk of her correspondence comes. However hard pressed by business, she kept up regular and detailed exchanges with friends and family throughout her life, and the letters are still one of the best ways of getting to know her personality. The style of writing evident in virtually all her works — vivid, slightly breathless, full of self-deprecating asides — is most freely itself in these letters, and combines with lively perceptions of things seen on her journeys, comments on gifts sent, motherly fussing about her correspondents' health and diet, and — except briefly in her last illnesses — a pervasive sense of enjoyment. They are astonishingly *confident* human documents; it is not surprising that so many of them were treasured.

The years of the foundations were also years of savage conflict within the Order itself. A clash with the Provincial in 1571 signalled the beginning of the most serious difficulties, though one of its immediate results was Teresa's unexpected return as prioress to her own old convent of the Incarnation in Avila (where the Provincial imagined she might be kept quiet). There she began writing her history of the foundations. Her relatively brief period of stability back at Avila seems to have been an important time of spiritual maturation. Troubles began again at Pastrana in 1574: the now widowed Princess of

Eboli had attempted to test her vocation in the convent there, with disastrous results. Her unstable and dramatic temperament (and the fact that she was still carrying the last child of her marriage) made her wholly unsuited to the conventual life, and Teresa was eventually forced to exercise the authority given her by the General of the Order and abandon the foundation. This made an enemy of the princess, who, in the following year, made trouble for Teresa with the Inquisition. Other troubled or unstable sisters and novices spread scandal in and around Seville when Teresa was there in 1575, occupied with the foundation of another new house. Although the Inquisition was satisfied that nothing untoward was going on, the Order lost patience and commanded Teresa to return to Castile and stay there.

This hardening of attitudes on the part of the authorities of the unreformed branch of the Order coincided unhappily with the appointment of a new papal nuncio to Spain, who arrived in 1577. His predecessor had been cautiously sympathetic to the Reform; but the climate was to change dramatically for the worse, particularly for the friars of the Reform. The first male house following the Teresian ideal had been established in 1568, with the young Juan de Yepes (John of the Cross) and a more senior friar, Antonio de Heredia, as its only members. Other foundations had followed, not without troubles, once again, with unstable characters. Teresa had immense respect for John ('Senequita' she called him, 'my little Seneca'), and had insisted that he be appointed chaplain to the Incarnation convent when she returned as prioress. His influence on her in the years at the convent is very clear in her later writings. However, they had their differences of temperament and opinion, and Teresa seems never to have been wholly comfortable with him. In contrast, Jeronimo Gracián, who joined the Reform in 1572, was to be her closest friend and confidant until she died; her letters to him are particularly lively, funny and poignant, emotionally possessive. Gracián had been authorized, within six months of his profession, to take over the general supervision of the Reform in Andalusia, but had encountered fierce resistance from the local authorities of the Order. The decree which had banished Teresa from Andalusia also revoked Gracián's appointment. A major crisis of authority developed: the king, who had taken an active and supportive interest in the Reform, encouraged the Teresian Carmelites to disobey the rulings of their Italian superiors and the General Chapter; when the new nuncio confirmed Gracián's deposition the royal council overruled him. In these decades following the Council of Trent, there was great tension over whether the reform of the Church should be in the hands of central ecclesiastical authority in Rome or should be left to those who had already initiated it locally, notably the Spanish monarchy. King Philip was making a clear warning statement to a papacy with which he had already had a fair number of diplomatic problems.

But the worst and most scandalous event in this struggle occurred in the winter of 1577, when John of the Cross was kidnapped by the unreformed friars and held incommunicado for nine months. Teresa, in desperation, appealed directly to the king for help: not without good cause, she feared for John's life. Nothing was done, however, until John escaped from his prison in Toledo in 1578 after being treated with appalling brutality. It became clear that something would have to be done to regularize a situation that was now intolerable and indefensible, and the nuncio, under some pressure from the king's council, agreed to appoint independent assessors to help in a settlement; two of them were Dominicans friendly to Teresa. Gradually some sort of resolution began to appear. The Teresian Carmelites were formally separated, once and for all, from the jurisdiction of the unreformed authorities, and, in June 1580, papal licence was given for the setting up of an independent Reformed province. The 'Discalced' Carmelites, distinguished, as the name suggests, by their sandal-shod feet, as well as by their coarse frieze habits and their observance of other austerities laid down in the early rules and constitutions of the Order, now had an assured future. In 1581 Gracián became Provincial of the Reformed houses.

Much suffering lay ahead, for both Gracián and John of the Cross; but Teresa was, happily, spared the knowledge of the further scandalous quarrels that afflicted the Reform after her death. By 1581 she was exhausted and unwell. She had been seriously ill in 1580; and in September 1581 had been elected prioress at St Joseph's in Avila, only to find that the house needed far-reaching reconstruction, in morale and in finances. This wearing task was suspended in 1582 when she left Avila to make what was to be her last foundation, at Burgos: a foundation fraught with difficulties, as it turned out, and requiring all her skills in negotiation and perseverance. She was already suffering from an internal cancer (so modern medical opinion judges), and the conditions of travelling were particularly uncomfortable. She arrived at her foundation at Alba de Tormes, on her tortuous return journey from Burgos, on 20 September. On 4 October she died.

Her lifespan had witnessed extraordinary changes in Europe and in the Church. When she was born, the Lutheran revolution still lay in the future, the main problem of the Inquisition in Spain was residual Judaism, and the newly united Spanish kingdom was still on the edge of Europe. Change was slow despite the dawning realization of what the conquest of central America might mean. At Teresa's death, the map of Europe had already been altered by the Reformation: England was isolated and at odds with Spain; Germany—the Holy Roman Empire—was more fragmented than ever, its principalities divided by confessional allegiances; France had witnessed the atrocities of religious war and bloody persecution. Spain itself had changed from a brashly confident society, receptive to new learning and international exchange, into an inward-looking, defensive and increasingly inefficient state, in which the Inquisition had closed most of the doors to the intellectual life of Northern Europe. The Church at large had undertaken far-reaching reforms, and, in the face of schism and heresy, had acquired a new sense of the urgent need for unity and control from the centre. (Ironically, as we have seen, Teresa was for years the victim of the mindset resulting from this: an ingrained Italian suspicion of reforms undertaken elsewhere and on the initiative of local authorities.) Teresa might well write, as she did in *The Way of Perfection*, of a 'world in flames'. What is perhaps most striking about her is her ability to preserve intact a simple and coherent sense of the requirements of the Christian gospel through all the complexities of her life in the Church, through all the wearing negotiation with secular and ecclesiastical authorities that occupied her almost to her last breath. To understand her as a theologian, as a 'Doctor of the Church' (the first woman to be granted this title—by Pope Paul VI in 1970), we need to look at those factors in her environment that brought out specific concerns and themes for her; such an attempt is the purpose of this book. But ultimately, understanding her as the kind of theologian she was means understanding what it meant to her to be a 'contemplative', which, as she saw it, was essentially a matter of the sustained awareness of living within the movement of God's love into creation through the life and death of Jesus Christ. That understanding, if we may borrow one of her own most memorable phrases, depends on the 'living book' of lives lived in the Christian tradition of prayer and compassion. A written text can tell very little.

1

Purity and honour
Teresa's social world

PURITY OF BLOOD

In 1520, the Court of Appeal in Valladolid heard a case of a sort not at all unusual at the time. A family from Avila was claiming exemption from a new tax imposed by King Charles in the previous year; to establish their right to avoid payment, they had to establish *hidalguía*, noble status. Neighbours from Avila, resentful of such attempts, were able to bring forward a good deal of embarrassing evidence against the family's claim, of which the most conclusive element was a certificate from the offices of the Inquisition in Toledo proving that the family was of Jewish extraction. In 1485, the father of the four brothers entering the petition had made confession to the inquisitors that he had been guilty of 'apostasy': that is, of practising Judaism in secret. He and his sons had been 'reconciled', after doing the public penance required; but the family's good name had suffered irreparably, and they moved not long after from Toledo to Avila. There, it seems (documentation is lacking), they purchased a certificate of nobility, and attained a high level of wealth and public dignity. But local memories (especially in matters affecting social status) are long, and less fortunate relatives of the brothers in Avila were quite willing to come forward and testify to their unrespectable ancestry.

Nonetheless, the suit appears to have succeeded: the court at Valladolid was obviously as amenable to bribery and the sheer weight of a *fait accompli* as the earlier court that had granted the patent to the father of the petitioners. This reflected a rather significant fact

11

about early sixteenth-century Spain. People who had attained 'noble' status had quite often done so by buying their way; and those capable of buying their way would be predominantly from the merchant class. Historically, this included large numbers of Jews, who, as non-landowners in mediaeval Spain, had naturally made their living in trade and commerce.

Early mediaeval Spain had been a patchwork of small states, Christian and Muslim, living in uneasy truce for most of the time; in the Muslim kingdoms a literate and prosperous Jewish population had flourished, producing some of the greatest cultural and philo-sophical achievements of Jewish history. But by the time Teresa was born this had changed beyond recognition. The *reconquista*, 'recon-quest', of territories controlled by Muslim rulers had been slowly advancing for several centuries, and the process had reached its climax in 1492, with the capture of the Moorish city of Granada in the extreme south. The victors in this struggle were the monarchs of Aragon and Castile, Ferdinand and Isabella: their marriage had united the eastern coastal region, with its very important trading cen-tres and international ports, to the great inland plateau of Castile, in geography and population the largest of the old Christian states. By 1492, Spain was effectively a single unit — and a Christian one.

In fact, it was the Church that provided the most important unify-ing force. Although the crowns of the Christian kingdoms were united, the traditions of government in Aragon and Castile were very different, and without a common religious commitment Spain could easily have disintegrated again. But in addition to this there were increasing attempts to rationalize and unify the administration. The Castilian nobility were still wealthy and powerful, thanks largely to the success of the wool trade in the Middle Ages; the towns were relatively weak. Much of the history of Castile between 1479 (when Isabella became queen) and the end of the sixteenth century is intelligi-ble only against the background of the deep tensions that continued to exist between the great magnates, the civic authorities and the new royal bureaucracy. The crown took some steps to strengthen the town councils against the nobles, but the towns themselves were often resentful of the imposition of royal appointees to keep a watch on their affairs. The magnates kept their wealth and prestige, but lost a good deal of their concrete political power.

In Castile, then, the first half of the sixteenth century was marked by social restlessness and hostility on a large scale. In the complex pattern of warring interests emerging in these years, the former Jewish populations were exceptionally vulnerable on all sides. The expulsion of the remaining Muslims had been accompanied by comparable pressure on Jews: they could convert or be expelled. There was no place for them in the kingdom of the 'Catholic Monarchs' (a title bestowed on Ferdinand and Isabella by the Pope in 1492); survival depended on conformity: at least outward conformity.

Fierce anti-Semitism at the end of the fourteenth century had greatly increased the number of *conversos* (or *marranos*, as they were more colloquially known: 'pigs'). But their wealth and influence — increased through intermarriage with some of the old aristocracy, especially in Castile — made them objects of continuing hatred and suspicion from both the lesser gentry and the population at large. After some particularly violent rioting in Toledo in 1449, *conversos* were prevented from becoming members of the city's administration; and in the course of the century that followed, similar decrees were passed barring *conversos* from most of the major religious Orders, from various civic offices, and from the senior colleges at the universities (which provided candidates for high office in Church and state).[1] Thus to establish an impeccable 'Old Christian' pedigree was imperative if one was to gain access to religious and political power, and to more prosaic privileges like the tax exemptions granted to the nobility (who were liable to municipal but not royal levies).

Limpieza de sangre, 'purity of blood', was increasingly an obsession in sixteenth-century Spain. Its very importance meant that claims to *limpieza* would be subject to some very hostile scrutiny, and this was a significant factor in intensifying a widespread anxiety among the higher echelons of Spanish society. One of the most distinguished modern historians of Habsburg Spain writes: 'Since the testimony of even one malevolent witness could ruin a family's reputation, the effect of the statutes of *limpieza* was in many ways comparable to that of the activities of the Inquisition. They fostered the general sense of insecurity, encouraged the blackmailer and the informer, and prompted desperate attempts at deception.'[2] One obvious and common deception to cover the tracks of unacceptable ancestry was changing the family name; which brings us back to the family with whose affairs we began. The Toledan merchant who had done his penance before the Inquisition in 1485 was Juan Sánchez: his sons either dropped the 'Sánchez' (which seems to have been a recognizably *converso* name in some areas) or combined it with their mother's aristocratic style, 'de Cepeda'. Alonso, probably Juan's second son, continued to call himself Don Alonso Sánchez de Cepeda. Widowed

13

after a brief first marriage, he repeated his father's move in marrying into a distinguished Castilian house in his second nuptials: Doña Beatriz de Ahumada came of a family celebrated in stories of the Reconquest. Their third child and eldest daughter was to call herself Doña Teresa de Ahumada until she was forty-seven.

Teresa of Avila was born into a complex and delicate social situation. Don Alonso was an extremely wealthy man whose public status was nevertheless ambiguous: a member of a familiar and much-resented class, the *conversos*, who had purchased *hidalguía*, nobility, through the fruits of vulgar trade and now held up his head alongside those of truly ancient lineage. The *converso* gentleman represented, in the eyes of the old aristocracy, a debasement of the social coinage: resentment was expressed at the way in which the Crown sold patents of nobility in order to raise money rapidly, resentment felt both by the existing nobility and by the ordinary tax-paying citizen.[3] Both groups naturally looked askance at the anomalous characters who crossed the frontier between them; and when these anomalous persons represented another and still more problematic crossing of frontiers—when they were *conversos*—their position became far more disturbing. The social mobility increasingly generated by wealth in the later Middle Ages was producing an adulteration of the ancient order of things. The recently ennobled convert Jewish businessman was in every imaginable way an 'impure' person and, as such, a threat.[4] At the same time, the whole conception of noble status, and the ideas of 'honour' accompanying it (on which there will be more to say shortly), depended on the belief that the king was the definitive image and touchstone, if not exactly the source, of nobility: if the king granted noble status, it could not be gainsaid. But if the king created nobles of the sort who were becoming more and more numerous in the early sixteenth century, if the king *were* indeed acting as the source of nobility, the conception of noble blood itself became profoundly confused. The traditional feudal gradations between king and commoner were being eroded, and with them the rights of the nobility. In Spain as elsewhere in sixteenth- and seventeenth-century Europe the citizen, noble or common, was increasingly confronted with a royal authority not answerable to its subjects. The multiplication of patents of *hidalguía* was only one sign of the general centralizing of power already mentioned; it was paralleled by the appointment of royal commissaries to sit alongside local magistrates and administrators. The social world of Spain, and especially Castile, in the first decades of the sixteenth century was one in which things and persons were more and more 'out of place', away from their proper setting in the immemorial political order. The anomalous, 'impure' person was both more familiar and more alarming than ever before.

The statutes of *limpieza* represent part of the response to this. Initially, pressure towards this kind of legislation came not from the Crown or from the great families, but from anxious local gentry in the municipalities whose interests were in danger of being overridden by magnates and royal agents. Many of the great families, with that disregard for taboo so characteristic of those who believe they have impregnable social power, had in fact married into households of 'tainted' blood; as the general atmosphere became harsher in late fifteenth-century Spain, this made them unexpectedly vulnerable. Spain, gathering its energies for a final offensive against the remaining outposts of Islam in the peninsula, became increasingly worried about the presence of elements threatening the purity of the Catholic kingdom; and paranoia about the sincerity of *conversos* had had much to do with the establishing of the Inquisition in Spain in 1478. The Spanish Inquisition, in sharp contrast to the Inquisition elsewhere in Catholic Europe, was an instrument of the state, administrated (from 1483) by a royally appointed committee, and charged specifically with the oversight of *conversos*. It was most active in Castile, where there was the most widespread resentment and fear directed towards the 'New Christians'. Indeed, the events in Toledo in 1485, when Teresa's grandfather had performed his public penance, had followed closely upon an alleged plot by some leading *conversos* to kill or kidnap the inquisitors and hold the city against royal troops until the Crown agreed to withdraw the Inquisition. A few short years had shown the Castilian *conversos* how effectively their position could be undermined through the exploitation of the Inquisition's sanctions by hostile fellow-townsmen. People like Juan Sánchez had much to fear. By the end of the century, the clamour for 'exclusion clauses' had grown a good deal in Castile, and claims and counter-claims about *limpieza* were an important weapon in municipal feuding.

The paradox is that the Crown, which sanctioned the statutes of purity and controlled the Inquisition, continued to ennoble *conversos* and connive at the extensive laundering of surnames and pedigrees that accompanied such transactions;[5] the court of Ferdinand and Isabella, the Catholic Monarchs, heroes of the Reconquest of the peninsula, was surprisingly tolerant of New Christians and even of unconverted Jews (less surprising if we remember that Ferdinand himself was of partly Jewish origin). This was not just cynicism or opportunism. It may have been New Christians at court, alarmed by reversions to Judaism among some of their confrères in the lax environment of governing circles, who argued for the establishing of the Inquisition. And, from the Crown's point of view, it was preferable to assimilate wealthy families of dubious background into the existing structure by ennoblement, rather than leave them as a socially rootless group, and thus far more threatening to the safety and integrity of Castilian society. It was also undoubtedly profitable to the Crown in financial terms. But what may have seemed a practical solution of the problem of social dislocation from the Crown's point of view was seen as disastrous in the Castilian towns; and pressure towards purity legislation continued to intensify in the first half of the sixteenth century.

This process was helped by the rapid decrease of New Christian influence at court. Charles V's court, with its large Flemish element, had few *conversos*; Philip II gave unequivocal royal support to extensions of the statutes of purity. By 1560, *limpieza* was a dominant concern in practically all public life. Yet the principle had now become significantly changed: what had been rooted in the determination of local corporations to preserve their traditional dignities and independence had turned into yet another instrument of royal centralism. *Limpieza*, by the second half of the sixteenth century, was a mark of the new Spain: united under a single monarch, professing a single faith, administered in ecclesiastical and temporal matters by men of pure Old Christian blood (or at least by men claiming pure Old Christian blood). The actual business of administration depended on professionals, often people of common origin or from the minor gentry; the great families retained a good deal of patronage and played a significant role in military affairs, but both Charles and Philip kept them at a distance from day-to-day government. The lower-born bureaucrat or prelate knew that, despite the wealth and display of the great nobles, he had what they often lacked: pure Christian ancestry and the trust of the king.

Alonso Sánchez's daughter thus belonged to a class more and more afflicted by what has been called 'status inconsistency': they possessed a fair amount of tangible wealth, and they could purchase the right to adorn their houses with coats of arms[6] and to be styled 'Don' and 'Doña'; they knew that many of the highest of the land shared something of their background; but they were frequently regarded with resentment, contempt and suspicion. A brush with the Inquisition could mean disgrace or financial ruin: it would destroy the already fragile bonds of credit and trust that bound them to their fellow-citizens. And, unless their pedigrees had been very thoroughly falsified, they were increasingly to find themselves cut off from the public processes of decision-making in Spain. As a group, they have a good deal in common with the kind of people who probably constituted 'the first urban Christians', to borrow the title of a well-known modern study:[7] those in the Greek cities of the Roman Empire in the first century AD who seem to have responded most eagerly to Christian preaching were precisely those whose actual social standing was out of step with their wealth and achievement: widows, entrepreneurial traders, ex-slaves, and, of course, well-to-do Jews and converts to Judaism. Such people would be among the most obvious enthusiasts for an 'alternative' society in which status depended upon some radically different principle, and in which existing divisions and stratifications were broken down.

This parallel offers some illumination for the understanding of Teresa. A *converso* might try to conceal the family's origins and succeed in the terms of the surrounding society: Don Alonso had, just, managed to do this. But it was a precarious business, and Teresa in her maturity had developed a profound scepticism about the usefulness of such attempts. Why should the title 'Don' matter so much?[8] It did not of itself entail much real power, and the struggle to retain it involved the acceptance of a whole system of pride and anxiety that Teresa saw as divisive and un-Christian. She was not the only New Christian to find the religious life precisely the kind of alternative society that the early Church had been, and for her the restlessness and social scepticism engendered by the experience of New Christian families found its outlet in this way. Research into the background of her early associates, especially the first members of the convent of St Joseph, strongly suggests that she attracted other New Christians to her enterprise; and many of her patrons and benefactors clearly shared her social origins.[9] Teófanes Egido, in his definitive study of Teresa's social context, draws attention to Teresa's account of her foundation in Toledo in 1569–70 (recorded in F 15) as a dramatic example of Teresa's defiance of local prejudice about 'impure' families:[10] the convent's endowment was provided by a wealthy merchant household, almost certainly of *converso* background, and Teresa was put under considerable pressure to look for a benefactor of pure lineage (and assured that in a place like Toledo there would be plenty of people eager to oblige: F 15.15). Only a firm and

17

unambiguous locution from God supported her initial resolve. In the hysterically charged atmosphere of Toledo, the scene of many ferocious disputes over *limpieza*, this must have been a decision of some political significance: it was an Archbishop of Toledo who, in 1556, had obtained royal endorsement for a statute which closed the cathedral chapter to *conversos*, and had drawn from King Philip the observation that *conversos* were the source of all the heresies currently afflicting Europe.[11]

We know from other sources that, although the unreformed Carmelites, male and female, observed rules of *limpieza* from 1566, Teresa herself regularly admitted New Christians throughout her life.[12] For her to have done otherwise would have been to undermine the entire rationale of the life of Carmel as she understood it. We must not underrate the riskiness of her policy and of actions like the decision at Toledo; these things could not have been incidental to her conception of her vocation. She was unmistakably giving hostages to fortune in a climate where identification with *conversos* could so easily be assimilated to heresy; and, for a woman who would be suspect on other counts from the Inquisition's point of view, her behaviour is extraordinarily courageous. But as we shall see when we come to examine her writings in more detail, it was behaviour grounded in an increasingly unified and sophisticated understanding of the nature of a society depending solely on the grace and friendship of God, in which status — in the ordinary sense — could not be an issue.

HONOUR: 'THE GREATEST LIE'

Teresa's lineage and her attitude to *limpieza* explain what is to a modern reader a rather disproportionate concern in much of her writing with 'honour'. Insofar as we have any surviving idea of honour, we associate it with self-respect, honesty and fidelity, not being ashamed of ourselves, and so on. An honourable person is one who keeps promises, observes standards, does not seek to degrade others, to look for their discreditable secrets.[13] But this means that honour is something we can have and lose, depending on our behaviour and dispositions: we find it hard to understand societies in which honour is 'objectified' as a matter of supreme public interest in such a way that an affront to one's public dignity or standing in the eyes of society becomes something worth killing for. We look with repugnance on the code of a traditional *mafioso*, and we find the notion of vendettas based on supposed affronts to honour either repulsive or comic. Teresa's society, however, was one in which this objectified view of honour prevailed; if she is almost obsessively interested in combating it, this is because there was a great deal to combat.

In what is still the fullest scholarly discussion of this issue as it appears in Teresa's Spain, Américo Castro sums up the general presupposition of Teresa's contemporaries as the belief that 'honour expresses the relation of the individual with society'.[14] The opposite of honour is *infamia*, ill-repute; but this is not simply a matter of having disagreeable things said about you. Certain *kinds* of people are innately without honour: they have no weight or worth in the social hierarchy, and are, in themselves, dispensable (though it may be a part of the duty of their superiors to look after their interests). To be associated with such people, willingly to live at their level, is in some extent to contract their worthlessness, their 'vile' or 'villein' character. Those who *are* innately honourable because of the position conferred by their ancestry must not allow this honour to be lessened by anything, word or action, that might assimilate them to the worthless. So when an honourable person does something inconsistent with the position he or she occupies, honour is compromised; and when one does not react to an attack or insult that suggests one is behaving inconsistently with one's position, that failure to defend oneself automatically constitutes a loss of honour. To quote Castro again, 'discordance between the individual and society . . . produces *infamia*';[15] and that discordance can be expressed both positively, by an act that is at odds with social expectation, and negatively, by accepting some diminution in one's public standing, some insult or offence.

There is nothing peculiarly Spanish about such a system: it is the common coin of most pre-modern societies, and, as theological textbooks never tire of pointing out, it underlies St Anselm's theory of the atonement (God must receive what is due to his honour and cannot fail to defend it, so provides the only satisfaction possible for an insult to his infinite dignity: the infinitely 'worthwhile' self-sacrifice of the divine Son). But Castro and other scholars have rightly noted the way in which these concerns are pervasive in the Spanish drama of the sixteenth and early seventeenth century (in Calderón in particular), and the object also of a good deal of satire in Spanish literature of a more popular kind: novels like *Lazarillo de Tormes* (1554), and of course the later *Don Quixote*, in which the conventions of knightly romance and the aristocratic obsession with dignity are systematically mocked.

Teresa herself gives us some vivid pictures of a society in which concern with public standing exercised a paralysing hold on many. One of the most celebrated is the vignette in F 20.2, describing a family of impeccably pure lineage, living in genteel poverty in the countryside, 'where there is a lack of Christian doctrine and of many other things that are means to the enlightenment of souls'; they will not move to the town, we are given to understand, for fear of losing their status, and they are desperately grieved that they have no sons (a son not only carries on the lineage but is also in a position to marry profitably; daughters need dowries, and so are a potential drain on financial resources). Teresa is probably implying that a poor family ought to learn to make money, instead of sacrificing material and spiritual comfort by insisting on continuing to live off diminishing rents in the countryside. There is a more disturbing story in F 10 and 11, where Teresa relates the adventures of Doña Casilda de Padillo in her efforts to discover her vocation. The youngest daughter of a highly distinguished family, Casilda had become heiress to a considerable fortune at the age of about eleven; in order to retain both fortune and name, her family had promptly betrothed her to her father's brother, after getting a papal dispensation. Teresa obviously regards this as deplorable but not exceptional; and what is shocking to the modern reader is the apparent ease with which such a form of incest was treated as a proper means for maintaining 'honour' by perpetuating an aristocratic lineage.

Theologians of the period discussed the question of honour and the legitimacy of vendettas; and there were some who considered it proper to kill in response to an act of offence, though not in response to insulting words alone.[16] However, in criticizing preoccupation with honour, Teresa had two major strands of opinion on her side. One was the firm principle established in Thomist theology and traditional asceticism that virtue was a higher good than honour;[17] the other was the humanist and Stoic view that true moral worth was an interior reality, having no necessary connection with exterior social accounts of a person's value.[18] Such ideas were a very important part of the Erasmian religious ethos — rational, moral, individualistic — that had penetrated the Spanish Church in the early years of the sixteenth century. Here again, though, Teresa's Jewish background is significant. It has been plausibly suggested that certain features of the Spanish novelistic tradition show signs of *converso* influence;[19] in addition to satirizing inflated views of honour, much of the popular fiction of the period puts forward as a positive value the virtue of candour, integrity. This is a literature markedly suspicious of insincerity, of the potential gulf between appearance and reality in human relations; and such suspicion, it is argued, fits well with the social experience of the *conversos*. We have already noted the sense of 'status inconsistency' we should expect in such circles: the reality of financial power and achievement is not allowed open recognition in the currency of public dignity. Acceptance depends upon fraud or secrecy. It would not be surprising to find here some of the roots of protest against a dishonest social order, an interest in virtue or moral achievement in its own right, and a high valuation of situations and persons that could make honesty possible, that could lift the burden of concealment. *Converso* society would be interested in value, weight, meaning *beyond* the realm of social appearance, which tells us something of why New Christians showed interest in radical religious movements that stressed interior truthfulness and purity, and the conflict between inner promptings and social networks of convention.

Teresa's observations on honour could be the subject of a book in themselves. She does not dispense with the notion altogether since it is, for her, a major part of the Carmelite calling to 'honour' Christ in a world in which he is consistently offended (W 3.6–7; C IV, 1.7, VII, 3.6); in the *Life* (21.1) she reflects on what the world would be like if monarchs sought the honour of God and neglected their own honour and safety: because kings set the tone for their societies, 'What righteousness there would be in the kingdom!' This would be a far more effective way of combating heretics than any other. As she says in *The Way of Perfection* (3.1–2), it is useless to think that anything can be achieved by force of arms. Hence the importance of creating at least some Christian communities in which God is properly served. The opening chapter of *The Way of Perfection* vividly sets out Teresa's wish to counteract the effects of the offence to God given by those she calls 'Lutherans' (in fact, the militant Calvinists of France), and her belief that this is best done, in her immediate environment, by the life of poverty and prayer. Others can argue and persuade (1.2), but she, as a woman, can only offer God friendship by a life lived in humility.

It is noteworthy that she believes offence to God can be repaired by loyal friendship. As we shall see in later chapters, she makes the ideal of friendship a pivotal one in her theological vision, which is in itself a striking emphasis in a society concerned with honour. Friendship, so people had assumed since Aristotle, was a relation between equals, and was therefore sharply restricted in scope by a system of social honour. Teresa begins from the conviction that God has freely made us friends of God, and, on that basis, she moves easily to the model of a community in which 'all must be friends' (W 4.7) irrespective of social standing. Hence the ferocity of her attacks on any sign of interest within the community in questions of status: God can only be honoured as we should honour God if we allow God's friendship to override all social divisions. Thus, although Teresa more than once repeats the conventional scholastic and Stoic view that virtue is greater than honour (F 15.15; cf. T 5, and also L 7.2, on the fallacious appearance of virtue as the ground of reputation), and thus in part endorses the notion that true honour is an interior affair, her working out of this is far from individualistic. Indeed, it would not be too much to say that in her work friendship *replaces* honour as the primary form of social connectedness.

Real honour is to do with truthful judgement, and thus, for the Christian, is strictly incompatible with the standards of a world that is passing away and which thus cannot be truly judged to have any intrinsic worth beside the eternity of God; the world's honour 'is the greatest lie and . . . all of us are involved in it' (L 21.26). Hence an unconcern about reputation and dignity is a sure sign—one of the few practically infallible signs in Teresa's eyes—of spiritual maturity. She relates the delightful anecdote of Fray Antonio de Heredia as an illustration of this (F 14.6): Teresa finds this dignified senior cleric, lately professed in the Carmelite Reform, sweeping the church porch at the new and still very primitive friary at Duruelo, and asks him 'What has become of your honour?' He replies, 'I curse the day I had any'. Contrariwise, it is a sure sign of spiritual infantilism to be sensitive on the score of reputation. Teresa describes a woman (evidently not a nun) who is a frequent communicant, experiences *devoción* in prayer (i.e., a sense of profound absorption and consolation; the word is a quasi-technical term for spiritual writers like Osuna), loves solitude and is renowned for her mild and equable temper. 'Since I saw all these virtues, it seemed to me that they were effects of a very advanced soul and of deep prayer', Teresa tells us (S 2.23–24); but closer acquaintance revealed a monumental sensitivity on any point touching *fama* and *honra*. Teresa does not judge her too harshly, assuming that the woman does not understand her own motivation since she is very ready with explanation and justification for her reactions. But her state is profoundly troubling and she is in great spiritual danger. Teresa drily observes that she is now inclined to think that some of the persecution this woman endured was her own fault, and concludes: 'she and two other souls that I have seen in this life . . . who were saints in their own opinion, caused me more fear . . . than all the sinners I have seen'.

The woman in question is a devout lay person. For Teresa, one of the foremost advantages of community life is, or ought to be, the war of attrition that it involves against preoccupation with status. She is actually talking about two rather different things, at least to twentieth-century ears. There is the social level: concern about lineage and nobility; and there is the personal level: concern about one's reputation for virtue or holiness. But in Teresa's understanding, these belong together. If you are prepared to sacrifice the status that the world gives, it must not be only to replace it with another kind of competitive and hierarchical structure. Hence the importance of *friendship*: simply to elevate virtue over honour can lead to a strongly individualist ethic, marked by just as much paralysing anxiety as the honour system. Joining a religious community is a commitment to equality, and so to reciprocal pastoral care (nurture and criticism): this is set out most fully in the first fifteen chapters of *The Way of Perfection*. It is thus also to expose oneself to the ordinary misunderstandings of common life; and to be able to live with these, not seeking constantly to defend and justify oneself, is the path to the highest virtue (W 15). Teresa admits that it is sometimes wrong *not* to explain oneself, and that she finds it very hard to sort out when this should and should not be done (15.1); but she is certain that it is incompatible with the religious life to want always to be in the right, and thus it is necessary to bear with unjust condemnation or calumny — necessary, that is, to sacrifice one's own judgement of oneself as being privileged in every circumstance. The Erasmian ideal of inner truthfulness is significantly modified by Teresa's relentless insistence on the formation of holiness in a common life in which neither one's own judgement of oneself, nor another's judgement of oneself, nor one's judgement of others, is guaranteed to be *accurate*. The very experience of inaccurate judgement reinforces the most important element in the ground of discipleship — the sense of creatureliness, ontological poverty: we are limited and deeply fallible, and nothing is simply owed to us in terms of truth and worth. We must learn that grace, vision, insight into God, world, self and others, all depend on God alone — a God who does not owe us honour yet freely gives it to us, and supremely so in the life and death of Jesus, a man without honour and dignity (W 36.5; see Chapter 3 below for a fuller account of how this theme is developed).

The common life of Carmel, therefore, is meant to undermine any sense of our worth that depends either on social standing or on an image of ourselves as truthful and virtuous, and to reconstruct a sense of worth depending on God's freedom and love. In placing the source and criterion of worth outside both human perception and human control, this common life is necessarily without hierarchy. Teresa is writing not only against the general background of honour-obsessed Spanish society, but in the context of a monastic practice deeply marked by the hierarchical patterns of society. The convent of the Incarnation at Avila was by no means an unusually lax place, but it took for granted that nuns of high social standing would have servants, and sometimes dependent relatives, living on the premises, and would continue to have disposable income.[20] (The paradox that was to cause Teresa so much difficulty later as prioress of the Incarnation convent was that a community with so much personal wealth available had so little corporate income.) Her almost comically fierce insistence on small buildings (W 2:8–10) is not simply to do with the quest for austerity in its own right, or even the avoidance of the scandal of women vowed to poverty living in relative luxury on benefactions that might have relieved the genuinely poor (2.9); it is also a practical way of preventing armies of dependants on the premises. Likewise the insistence on all sisters taking their turn at menial jobs (*Constitutions* 22) and on working to support the house financially (ibid., 9) is designed to break down reliance on lay sisters or paid servants for practical affairs, as well as to challenge the assumption that it was unseemly to work for a living.[21] Teresa did make provision for the admission of lay sisters (ibid., 21), not committed to the same disciplines of enclosure and the choir office, and so able to negotiate with the world outside the convent walls; but she clearly does not envisage the distinction between lay and choir sisters as one between menials and gentlewomen. She insists on 'complete sisterly charity' between the two groups. The fact that choir sisters were expected to do housework was certainly in intention a breaking down of the hierarchical barrier; and it is notable that Teresa's closest friend and confidant in old age was a lay sister, the formidable, intelligent, eccentric and saintly Ana de San Bartolomé, who subsequently became a choir nun and prioress.[22]

Religious houses devise their own hierarchies, and Teresa is scathing about this. The devil 'invents his own honours in monasteries' (W 36.4): those who have held high office are considered ineligible for ordinary tasks, and themselves expect certain marks of precedence and respect. For this, Teresa has no time at all: it is an entirely false humility that is produced by obsequious ceremonial etiquette, and the need for good order is not the same as a passion for complex structures of precedence (ibid.). When St John of the Cross's friend and disciple, Ana de Jesús (a woman whose relations with Teresa were not always very easy) complained to Teresa about the failure of the Prior Provincial to address her with proper formality, she earned a sharp rebuke (*Letters* II, 421, p. 939). And the complaint that she is setting impossible standards ('"We're not saints"') in demanding such indifference to etiquette prompts her to wonder whether some people ever read the story of Christ's passion (W 16.11).

Nowhere is Teresa's distance from the assumptions of her society clearer than in her attitude to 'honour'. She is not wholly consistent: she may mock and scold the practices of aristocratic society, but is quite capable of expressing pleasure that her brother has become a landed proprietor and so acquired such honour for his children (*Letters* I, 158, p. 392). But as far as her own vocation is concerned, indeed as far as the Christian calling *as such* is concerned, she allows no place for honour as understood in her milieu. Her hostility betrays a mixture of elements: the prejudices and resentments of a member of a marginalized group, with Don Alonso's humiliating experiences with his fellow-townsmen in the background; the typical *converso* refusal to separate honour from concrete achievement and the positive evaluation of paying one's own way in society; and, pervading everything, a more and more carefully worked out theology, relativizing both honour *and* achievement by its emphasis on community life in a friendship resting upon the gift of God's friendship. Centralized Spanish sovereignty, with its recent history of cutting through traditional attitudes by ennobling wealthy families without long pedigrees, may well have helped Teresa formulate her view of God ('His Majesty') likewise ennobling the innately dishonourable and impure; but we should also remember that, by the time of Teresa's maturity, the monarchy of Philip II was increasingly committed to social attitudes profoundly at odds with her overall vision. If Philip's absolutism was one factor in shaping Teresa's strong doctrine of divine sovereignty, that doctrine works for Teresa in a way that is implicitly subversive of Habsburg Spain's social order and foreign policy: Teresa, remember, is unconvinced about the rightness of using force against heresy — the cornerstone of Philip's increasingly disastrous international interventions — and longs for a king who sets God's honour above political security. And God's honour is inseparable from God's *honouring* of all humanity.

ORTHODOXY AND THE INQUISITION

To claim friendship with God might itself be seen as a politically dangerous thing to do in Teresa's Spain. Intimacy with God through mental prayer was widely and increasingly seen as the gateway to an inflated confidence in one's own individual authority in religious matters, and thus as the gateway to rebellion against the Church's hierarchy. Rebellion against the hierarchy frequently brought with it other kinds of rebellion, or at least scepticism, and threatened the single most stable unifying force in the complicated pattern of Spanish society — a shared, unchallenged loyalty to the Catholic faith. Those, such as *conversos*, who represented impure or anomalous elements in the kingdom were inevitably suspected of anomalous attitudes to the Catholic faith; and, conversely, of course, those who felt themselves alienated from the one were very likely to become alienated from the other. Mental prayer, individual communion with God, was a natural and attractive path to take for a person whose voice in society and the Church was not permitted to be heard, or heard only with suspicion and hostility: the *interior* affirmation of dignity, being spoken to freely by God and speaking freely to God, compensates for the injustice and irrationality of the external order of things. But the inquisitors, while they might not be sociological experts, were no fools, and were only too ready to recognize that an interest in the secrets of the inner life was likely to be symptomatic of deep discontents with the public order of the Catholic kingdom.

As we have observed, the Inquisition was originally established to deal with the problem of lapsed or lapsing New Christians, converts who in a relatively tolerant atmosphere were resuming the practice of a faith from which they had apostatized only under pressure. Just how real these lapses were is, in many cases, doubtful; quite often the Inquisition acted against people who were simply perpetuating Jewish cultural habits (changing clothes on Friday, washing and shaving the corpses of relatives before burial, and so on) or kept company with practising Jews. What is clear is that the lines of demarcation between Jews and Christians were thought by the inquisitors to be insufficiently clear; and they were doubtless aware also of the fact that Jewish authorities countenanced the possibility of a nominal conversion for the sake of preserving the Jewish nation itself. The sense of a highly elusive fifth column in the Church must have been very strong. And, from the Inquisition's point of view, the perception of a threat was not entirely mistaken. An intelligent *converso*, moved by practical considerations to forsake Judaism, is not likely to be a good institutional man in the Catholic Church. If he can dispense with the outward forms of Jewish faith so easily, he may sit equally lightly to the forms of Christian faith — or so an unsympathetic inquisitor might argue. The problem was not so much that of Jews continuing to practise their religion in secret (though some may have done), as of people being denied a clear identity by both their ancestral and their adopted communities and having to discover or create one for themselves.

This, at least, was what the *converso* problem had come to look like by the third decade of the sixteenth century. The Catholic Monarchs had sponsored widespread reform in the Church, largely through the work of the great Cardinal Ximénes de Cisneros, Archbishop of Toledo and Primate of Spain, who wholeheartedly supported the 'New Learning' of the day and fostered a brief golden age of Greek and Hebrew scholarship. *Converso* scholars were naturally much to the fore in all this, and were thus brought into the mainstream of European humanism. The ideals of Erasmus began to circulate in Spain: the recovery of the clear vision of primitive Christianity (and of a decent text of the Greek New Testament), the reform of superstitious abuses in the Church, a religion no longer in thrall to external observance but rational and moral. These were ideals perfectly designed to appeal to the alienated *converso*; and the seeds of the most serious hostility to the Catholic Church in sixteenth-century Spain were sown here, as Erasmian Christianity took root among a group already disposed to a certain scepticism about the workings of Catholic institutionalism.

As in Northern Europe, however, the Erasmian movement was not simply a rationalist reform. The mysticism of the mediaeval Rhineland, reacting already against a corrupt and formalistic Church, had emphasized the need not for religious activities to secure God's favour but for silence and receptivity to God; and similar trends had found their way to Spain. How much of the actual writings of people like Eckhart, Suso or Tauler was available in Spain before the sixteenth century is a good deal debated, but it is not at all unlikely that some of their Latin works reached the peninsula.[23] In the intense atmosphere of Spanish Franciscan communities around 1500, involved in reforms designed to restore the Order's primitive apostolic purity and vigour, the ideals of total spiritual nakedness and poverty before God had great appeal. Male and female Franciscans began to organize small circles of devotees practising mental prayer; and these groups represented an extraordinary variety of social classes, at least in the towns. Many of the friars and sisters involved were New Christians, as were several of their most prominent and active disciples. And from their earliest days, these groups were distinguished by allowing a major role to holy women in teaching and organization: the pivotal figure in the earliest records is the Franciscan Isabel de la Cruz, and the pattern regularly reappeared, with both nuns and laywomen exercising great influence.

All this is really to say that early sixteenth-century Spain shared very fully in the conditions which, in Northern Europe, produced the revolt of Martin Luther; and it is important to realize, with Andrés Martín, and other scholars of the period,[24] that the spiritual ferment of Spain at this time, including the Carmelite reform, is a 'reformation', not a 'counter-reformation' phenomenon. Luther and the religious radicals and reformers of Spain shared a profound hostility to scholastic theology in and of itself; a reverence for the tradition of passive abandonment to God in 'mystical' prayer (Luther much admired Tauler); a suspicion of externals, both the busy habits of piety and the attempt to secure God's favour by amassing a record of virtuous deeds; and a confidence in the possibility of hidden, interior transformation by grace. As in Northern Europe, the very different strands of Erasmian ideals — moral integrity, new learning, simplicity of doctrine — and the goals of radical contemplatives in the tradition of Tauler — passivity and surrender, poverty of inner and outer life — were interwoven in a great complex of protest movements which it is very difficult to see as a single coherent whole.

The inquisitors, however, were trained to see unities among all dissidents: the *converso* problem, Erasmian liberalism, enthusiasm for mental prayer — all these were facets of a single rebellion against Catholic order, and so must be treated similarly. A clear signal was given in 1524 when Isabel de la Cruz was arrested along with a prominent (*converso*) disciple. In the following year, the Inquisition denounced a list of 48 propositions allegedly taught by people like Isabel, mostly to do with their supposed contempt for external observance and their belief that God should be loved without thought of reward. For the rest of the century, groups accused of heresy under these charges appear in inquisitorial records up and down the country, under the generic name of *alumbrados*, 'the illuminated' (presumably a self-designation now turned into a hostile epithet). The continuing presence of *conversos* in these groups confirmed popular suspicions (King Philip's comment in 1556, that 'all the heresies in Germany, France and Spain have been sown by descendants of the Jews' simply echoes the general judgement[25]). In 1558 the Inquisition uncovered substantial groups of what sound like Erasmian rationalists in Seville and Valladolid, and executed many as 'Lutherans'. Needless to say, there was a substantial *converso* element here too. And, as the preceding pages have implied, the inquisitors were by no means wholly wrong to see family resemblances between highly diverse groups who shared the propensity to look inwards rather than outwards for their identities as human beings. What was disastrous, and also ludicrous, in all this, was the fairly typical inquisitorial assumption that a common problematic produced the same results; so that if certain *alumbrados* practised sexual irregularities, or certain Erasmians doubted the Trinity, one might reasonably expect all dissidents to do the same, and might warn against practices or opinions, inoffensive in themselves, which could be seen as 'leading' to heretical outrages.[26]

The ideal of passivity and abandonment, *dejamiento*, could and sometimes did go with some rather startling notions about the moral law: for some, it was evidently a short step from speaking about passivity and the uselessness of good works to defending a complete antinomianism, the much-maligned human will resigning all pretence of control over the passions; for others, union with God through abandonment and ecstasy meant inability to sin. The prominence of women in *alumbrado* circles constantly fostered prurient speculation in the general public, and the Inquisition — with memories of countless mediaeval parallels — was always eager to find evidence of libertinism. However, not all *alumbrados* prized abandonment in the same way. From quite early on, some of those involved in this rather chaotic renewal movement had emphasized the need for *disciplines* to make the mind receptive to God, rather than advocating pure passivity. Building on mediaeval Augustinian theology, they outlined a path of *recogimiento*, 'recollection', by

29

which the powers of the soul might be drawn away from the things of the world, stripped of their usual temporal or material objects, and so simplified or unified in a way that opened them to God at the deepest level. Several Franciscan writers developed this approach, most prominently Francisco de Osuna whose *Third Spiritual Alphabet* was first published in Toledo in 1527, and Bernardino de Laredo (*c.* 1482–1540), author of *The Ascent of Mount Sion* (first published in 1535). It clearly aimed to avoid the excesses of unqualified spiritual quietism, but, in the long run, it failed entirely to allay inquisitorial fears. To recommend the practice of *recogimiento*, particularly to women and lay people, soon became another mark of profound unreliability in inquisitorial eyes.

The problem identified by the Inquisition remained essentially the same: a problem about the 'private' religious self constructing its own pathway to God by means under its own control. As the century advanced, the Inquisition became increasingly clear about this: *any* encouragement to personal and silent prayer was dangerous; all contact with God in this life must be indirect, mediated by the public means of historical revelation as set out by ecclesiastical authority. When the distinguished (and far from 'liberal' or Erasmian) Archbishop of Toledo, Bartolomé de Carranza, was arrested by the Inquisition in 1559, one of the charges on which he was to be held without trial for an appalling seventeen years was that he encouraged mental prayer, and believed it should be taught to ordinary layfolk. The Inquisitor General of the day, Fernando Valdés, had complained of another spiritual writer (Luis de Granada — a Dominican like Carranza) that he believed in teaching mental prayer to all sorts of unsuitable people — carpenters' wives, for instance — who were thereby encouraged to think more highly of themselves than they ought.[27] The irony of such words from a man who daily thanked God, in the words of a well-known carpenter's wife, for 'exalting the humble and meek' is almost too pointed for comment. But these remarks, the savage polemic of the immensely influential theologian Melchor Cano, confrère and rival of Carranza, and for a time *éminence grise* to Philip II, make very plain the mixture of social and theological factors in inquisitorial suspicion of mental prayer.

People practising private ways of communing with God, not governed by the hierarchy, are out of their proper place — once again, anomalous and therefore dangerous, polluting. That this applies with particular intensity to women is clear from certain attitudes to the people called *beatas* in sixteenth-century Spain: lay women leading lives of prayer and devotion. They constitute quite a striking and distinctive phenomenon, still insufficiently studied.[28] Although they are often associated with groups of *alumbrados* it would be a mistake to think of them as belonging exclusively in such contexts, let alone exclusively among the more disreputable outposts of the 'abandoned'. A *beata* could be a married woman, a widow or a single woman, of practically any social background; she might live alone, in a family, in a community of other *beatas*, or in the extended family of a great house; and she was just as likely to be involved with the 'mainstream' life of a local church as with a closed group of initiates. Some wore a form of religious habit; some resisted this. Contemporary authority found it very hard to deal with them, not least because they did not fit into available categories: they were neither 'in' the world nor 'out' of it, neither strictly monastic nor genuinely lay: they spoke with authority about affairs they should have known nothing of (like mental prayer), and they required silence from male and clerical listeners. Some of them formed a charismatic focus for groups of laity and religious who would treat their words as inspired; others simply collaborated in apostolic work without any great claims for their own experience. A remarkable example of the second sort is Teresa's fellow-townswoman, Mari Díaz,[29] an illiterate peasant some twenty-five years older than Teresa whom she met in the household of Doña Guiomar de Ulloa. Mari spent the last decades of her life in a chamber attached to the main church of Avila, and played an immensely important role in the city's religious affairs. Like Teresa, she helped and was helped by the new Jesuit community in Avila; and along with Teresa's chaplain Julian, and the famous secular priest of Avila, Gaspar Daza (who was so influential in various reform movements), she was instrumental in establishing the first 'Tridentine' seminary in Avila—a diocesan college for the training of clergy. Again like Teresa, she was given much encouragement by the great Franciscan saint Peter of Alcántara, who was evidently a focal figure for a large number of women seeking to lead lives of prayer (cf. F 28.42).

Teresa herself, who (at Villanueva de la Jara in 1580) effectively took a community of *beatas* under the wing of the reformed Carmel (F 28.37ff.), was well aware of the problems arising with women living a quasi-monastic life without rule or superior (*Letters* I, 85, p. 470), but was generally warm towards the *beatas'* attempt to know God by prayer and poverty or almsgiving. Not all shared her enthusiasm: sermons were preached against *beatas* (and sometimes met with spirited heckling), and there must have been some pressure on a community like that of Villanueva to regularize its status. But the most telling condemnation of the *beatas* comes from the pen of Fray Alonso de la Fuente, the same Dominican theologian who after Teresa's death sought to have her works condemned *in toto*:[30] he argued that the *beatas* could have no place in heaven because they had no 'state of life'[31] (and therefore, we must assume, no characteristic virtues proper to their station, no demands they could meritoriously satisfy). They are, as a recent discussion puts it,[32] 'displaced persons', just like the *conversos*: just as threatening, just as vulnerable, in a world concerned about unities and keeping things in place.[33]

'As a *converso*, as a woman, as a mystic and visionary, and as a reformer, Teresa was very vulnerable': Deirdre Green admirably sums up Teresa's position in her milieu.[34] It is surprising therefore that she had as (relatively) little trouble with the Inquisition as she did. That she was aware of being at risk is clear from her writings at several points: her *Life* is barely intelligible apart from the background of its author and her position as several different kinds of suspect person. She is cautious — but not that cautious. There are moments in *The Way of Perfection* where a certain exasperation with the Inquisition, and above all with the Index of 1559, shows through — too clearly for the censor's comfort: 21.8, where she observes that at least 'they' cannot forbid the Lord's Prayer and the Hail Mary, was annotated with some alarm by the censor ('It seems she is reprimanding the Inquisitors') and duly omitted in revisions. But she would laugh off warnings about the Inquisition, and claim, rightly enough, that she was ready to take the initiative in testing her views with the inquisitors (L 33.5). Elsewhere she reassures Gracián that she is willing to die at the stake, if necessary, for she will die 'for the sake of God's goodness'. As Green points out, no inquisitor could possibly endorse the idea that a victim of the Inquisition might be a martyr, and Teresa is making a larger claim than she probably realized.[35]

However, her willingness to submit to the judgement of hierarchies and inquisitors, her own powerful subjective sense of having nothing to be ashamed of (cf. T 58.10–12 for a clear statement), did not save her from unwelcome attention. Teresa's autobiography was, predictably, lodged with the Inquisition in the 1570s and, thanks to its inefficiency, there it remained until after her death. 'Pirated' copies circulated, however, and, when the Princess of Eboli denounced Teresa and her works to the Inquisition in 1575, there was some risk of an unpleasant confrontation. The Valladolid tribunal was tracing the book back to the Bishop of Avila at about the same time that the Seville tribunal was hearing highly-coloured accusations against its author from discontented or neurotic nuns at the new Seville Carmel. Teresa was accused not only of classical *alumbrado* doctrines (despising vocal prayer, relying on her own ecstatic experience) but of what the general populace tended to think of as classical *alumbrado* behaviour with Gracián. The *Life* was mentioned in Seville as a book setting out Teresa's unacceptable teachings. Fortunately, however, the whole process had been outflanked further north. Teresa's friend, Domingo Báñez, had deposited his copy of the manuscript with the Inquisition in Madrid, where the Inquisitor was also friendly to Teresa (and had indeed been among those who encouraged her to write the *Life*), and written a favourable report, echoed by a second censor. When Seville enquired about the book, Madrid replied that it was already being investigated; Seville does not seem to have taken the other accusations very seriously, and the whole affair lapsed.[36]

This disagreeable episode had involved Teresa, and the Seville Carmel, in some direct questioning by the Inquisition—the only overt encounter between herself and the tribunal in her life, despite its pervasiveness in the background. De la Fuente's efforts in 1589 started off a chain of further investigation and some detailed criticism from a number of other Dominican theologians. Again Teresa was accused of an unhealthy interest in mental prayer and (by de la Fuente) of being influenced by Tauler in her doctrine of the soul as a manifold dwelling place for God (Tauler's works had fallen under the ban of 1559). The Inquisition took advice, filed the results, and let sleeping dogs lie—recognizing, no doubt, the difficulty in a posthumous condemnation of someone already enjoying a considerable cultus, and popular with the king and many of his court. No more accusations were made.

So Teresa was fortunate in her dealings with the Inquisition, during and after her lifetime. This good fortune depended on a number of factors: certainly she had powerful friends and protectors (though this did not save others); she professed her readiness to submit to official judgement; and accusations of alumbradist tendencies were hard to sustain in the face of a manifestly sacramental piety. Perhaps the most important factor of all was that she seems genuinely not to have doubted the legitimacy of what the Inquisition was doing, as her reported remarks to Gracián in 1575 suggest. It is anachronistic to think of Teresa as the kind of person who would object in principle to the idea of a coercive guardianship of orthodoxy; however much she disliked the notion that heresy could be overcome by force, there is no sign that she was herself repelled by the methods of the Inquisition. Her attitude to it, like her attitude to the ecclesiastical institution in general, tends to be one of acquiescence, tempered by amusement and exasperation. She does not perceive — as far as we can see — what her modern readers might: that her critique of power, honour and worldly status has implications for the Church's collusion with methods of coercion. What kept her most secure from danger with the Inquisition was the fact that she did *not* simply transcend her times in the sense of having views that belonged to later ages. We shall be returning to the question of the long-range implications of her beliefs and practice in the last chapter of this book; for now, we should simply note that Teresa's background and teaching throw into sharp relief for us the problems posed for *and* by the Inquisition in sixteenth-century Spain, and that her own perception and experience of the Inquisition's absurdity and tyranny did not in any way weaken her resolve to *belong* to a Church that worked in this mode. When we turn to reading the *Life*, we shall see in more detail how, in her mode of writing rather than in her ideas, she seeks to resolve the problems of belonging to a Church she also wants to challenge and to change.

TERESA AND JUDAISM

These reflections draw us back inexorably to the question of Teresa's Jewish identity. We have endeavoured to suggest in this chapter how her Jewishness is the key to particular themes in her writings, and indeed to some of the central problems of the Spain of her day. The intriguing question remains of how much she *knew* of her ancestry, and how she regarded it. It is perfectly clear that she was aware of her Jewish blood: her strong reaction to Gracián's well-meant attempts to find out about her pedigree,[37] her remark (F 27.12) that 'it could not be because I am from the nobility that [God] has given me such honour', a number of other rather enigmatic asides, and the whole weight of her polemic against family pride, tell in favour of her knowing that her lineage was not exactly as Don Alonso wanted his neighbours to believe. She was five years old at the time of the Cepedas's embarrassing lawsuit; something of all this bustle and anxiety may have come through to a bright child. But whether she was aware of Juan Sánchez's humiliation in Toledo in 1485 must be more doubtful.

All sorts of theories have been erected on the basis of her knowledge of her Jewish roots. Gerald Brenan believes that this knowledge 'explains how a deep sense of guilt caused by her consciousness of belonging to the race of deicides, as they were called, helped to drive her against her will along the hard path of the mystic and religious reformer'.[38] Gareth Alban Davies, following some suggestions of Bataillon, sees some of the *conversos* as inheriting a 'messianic' sensibility, thinking of themselves as an elect group (a chosen people) within the Church, charged with a special reforming mission: in particular, he suggests that Teresa's choice of religious Order owed something to her sense of racial connectedness with the Holy Land, from which the Order came, and its legendary founders the prophets Elijah and Elisha.[39] She is prone to quote Old Testament texts about 'Israel' in a way which points to a concern to hold on to the continuity between the calling of Israel and the Church's vocation today—more especially the prophetic vocation of the religious today.

Neither suggestion quite carries conviction. Whatever reason Teresa gives for her work as a foundress, she never so much as hints at a motive of *expiation*: for her, the religious life is not seen primarily (if indeed at all) as a life of penance for sin, but as fundamentally an apostolic calling. Certainly she is aware of sin and guilt to a high degree; but it would be hard to show that she was more deeply involved with this than the average sixteenth-century religious writer. Her choice of Carmel as a community was probably far less freighted with meaning than we might like it to be. It must be very doubtful whether a lay woman like the young Teresa de Ahumada would actually know very much at all about the legendary foundation of the Order—which certainly does not seem to have attracted more than its share of *conversos*; what she did know was that the Incarnation in Avila was a new and mildly fashionable house, whose observance was not too strict, and that a close friend had lately gone there as a novice. As to Teresa's Old Testament allusions: we should need to be sure that these were unusually frequent or pointed, or that they worked in a way manifestly different from the way any Christian of the period might use them. And if Teresa refers a little more than we might expect to Old Testament saints, it is worth remembering that the Carmelite liturgy retained a number of Eastern Christian features including the celebration of feast days dedicated to the holy people of the Old Testament: King David, Elijah, Isaiah, and so on. To prove a 'special' Jewish interest in Teresa would require us to examine in some detail what her liturgical diet was, and to show that her use of the Old Testament exceeds what we might reasonably expect. This task has yet to be done; but a glance at the way in which a writer like Osuna uses the Old Testament shows how little there is in Teresa that is distinctive in this respect.[40] Davies is on much surer ground in suggesting that both Teresa's rather self-conscious playing down of her understanding of Latin, and her deliberate 'vulgar' misspellings of words (indeed, much of what Davies calls 'the sometimes tiresome ingenuousness of her literary style'[41]) are prompted by caution about revealing the extent of her literacy at a time when some regarded literacy itself as the mark of belonging to a suspect class.

The supposed 'messianism' of the *converso* mind is hard to pin down, and it rests on a picture of Judaism as essentially messianic which corresponds very imperfectly to what we know of the Jews of mediaeval Spain. (There was more 'messianic' fervour in Christian circles at the time of the conquest of Granada.) But perhaps the most intriguing suggestion about continuities between Judaism and Christianity in New Christians like Teresa relates to something we do know to have been significant in the mediaeval Jewish world: the tradition of mystical speculation represented by the Zohar, compiled in Spain in the thirteenth century. Here we find a pilgrimage through the seven palaces of heaven, culminating in loving union with the King in the inmost chamber, a union sealed with a 'kiss of love' so powerful in its effects that it may completely separate soul from body. The palaces are of crystal, they may be entered by many different doors and they are sometimes represented as forming a sphere. The analogies with Teresa's *Interior Castle* are striking. We know that some Spanish Christians had made use in the Middle Ages of Zoharic or cabbalistic symbolism, and it is possible that Teresa's admirer and editor, the great poet and Hebraist Fray Luis de León, was influenced by cabbalistic themes in his exegesis. Did Teresa know anything of this tradition?

The question has been explored with care by Deirdre Green in a number of articles and in her recent book on Teresa,[42] but the answers remain inconclusive. Green is much more cautious than some other scholars about supposing direct influence from Zoharic texts, which were available to hardly any at the time (the first Latin translation appeared in Italy during Teresa's lifetime, there were no Spanish versions and only some portions available in Hebrew translation from the original Aramaic). We are working at the level of vaguely remembered oral tradition, if anything. It is true that Avila had been in earlier centuries a centre of Zoharic study, and that Toledo was once a major focus for the exoteric and esoteric learning of Judaism. The metaphor of heaven as a sevenfold crystal dwelling-place, with the King at its centre, may well have circulated outside esoteric circles and been part of a Jewish folk-piety unconsciously carried over into *converso* life by families like that of Juan Sánchez. More than this we cannot confidently say. Despite Green's learned discussion, it is hard to see any very close parallels between the out-working of the sevenfold symbolism in Jewish texts and Teresa's treatment in *The Interior Castle*. Her agenda is distinct, and, as we shall discover in Chapter 4, its goal is not simply 'mystical' union but a union in action with God's involvement in creation. The differen-tiation in Teresa between the 'mansions' is mostly in terms of dif-ferent subjective states, while the Zohar and Hekhalot traditions think rather of new mysteries to be revealed at each new level. Teresa's castle is unintelligible without the Augustinian tradition of turning inwards to find God, and her imagery is essentially a free development of this.[43] If she did, consciously or not, draw on a recollection of Zoharic imagery transmitted in her family (which is perfectly possible, even likely), we should not suppose that she was thereby necessarily making a statement about her origins, let alone her loyalties.

Teresa's Jewish blood is less important in explicating details of her language or thought than in illuminating the *whole* of her experi-ence. We do not begin to understand her as a religious, as a reformer, as a theologian, unless we see her as a 'displaced person' in the Spain of her day. She is not a committed social radical or religious individualist, and her attitude to the power structures which marginalize or oppress her is often confused and inconsistent. But (as I hope in this book to show) she cannot but do her religious reflec-tion from the specific point of view she occupies: as a woman and a Jewess, undergoing ecstatic experiences, and claiming certain kinds of authority, at a time when any one of these would have guaranteed her not being taken seriously in Church and society, except as a threat and a pollutant. Reading the *Life*, we become more and more aware of how she has to negotiate her way in an almost wholly suspicious environment. But, reading her work as a whole, we can see how the experience of impurity and dishonour itself becomes the keystone of a recovery of certain aspects of the primitive Christian story and proclamation no less radical than that of her reforming contemporaries in Northern Europe.

Notes

1 Details in A. Sicroff, *Les controverses des statuts de 'pureté de sang' en Espagne du XVe au XVIIe siècle* (Paris, 1960); pp. 88–92 describe some of the earliest moves in the religious Orders. The Dominican priory at Avila was the first house of its Order to impose a racial requirement (in 1496); the Franciscans were involved from 1525. The strong presence of *conversos* in the early days of the Society of Jesus caused many problems and a good deal of harassment (see pp. 270–90 on this).

2 J. H. Elliott, *Imperial Spain 1469–1716* (London, 1963), p. 223.

3 Ibid., pp. 106, 116.

4 The classical treatment remains Mary Douglas, *Purity and Danger. An Analysis of Concepts of Pollution and Taboo* (London, 1966).

5 On the question of surnames and the practice of *barajar los apellidos*, see Gareth Alban Davies, 'St Teresa and the Jewish Question' in Margaret A. Rees (ed.), *Teresa de Jesús and her World* (Leeds, 1981), pp. 51–2.

6 Davies, *op. cit.*, p. 51, notes that the coat of arms of Teresa's mother's family, the Ahumadas, differs substantially from the heraldic bearings of other supposed branches of the same family elsewhere, suggesting that the background of Doña Beatriz's family might not bear too much close examination.

7 Wayne A. Meeks, *The First Urban Christians. The Social World of the Apostle Paul* (New Haven, 1983).

8 When her brother Lorenzo returned from the Americas to Avila in 1575, having made his fortune there, Teresa (*Letters* I, 107, p. 232) describes how she had scolded him for insisting on the title 'Don'.

9 Teófanes Egido, 'The historical setting of St Teresa's *Life*', *Spiritual Direction* (Carmelite Studies I; Washington, 1980), pp. 122–82 [an article of the first importance], esp. pp. 163–7; see also Jean Darrabat, 'Sainte Thérèse d'Avila: son milieu et sa famille', *Bulletin de littérature ecclésiastique* 87.3 (1986), pp. 293–4.

10 Egido, *op. cit.*, pp. 165–7.

11 Elliott, *op. cit.*, p. 222.

12 Egido, *op. cit.*, p. 168. For a reference to the admission of girls of

'black' (i.e., Moorish) slave family to Teresa's Carmel, see *Letters* I 183, p. 463, and 185, p. 469.

13 An interesting recent discussion is Stanley Hauerwas, 'On Honour: by way of a comparison of Barth and Trollope' in Nigel Biggar (ed.), *Reckoning with Barth. Essays in Commemoration of the Centenary of Karl Barth's Birth* (London and Oxford, 1988), pp. 145-69.

14 Américo Castro, 'Algunas observaciones acerca del concepto del honor en los siglos XVI y XVII', *Revista de filología española* 3 (1916), pp. 1-50, 357-86; quotation from p. 34. Cf. Egido, *op. cit.*, p. 151.

15 Castro, *op. cit.*, p. 49.

16 Ibid., pp. 39-44.

17 Ibid., pp. 373-4.

18 Ibid., pp. 378-85.

19 See Regula Rohland de Langbehn, 'El problema de los conversos y la novela sentimental' in Alan Deyermond and Ian MacPherson (eds), *The Age of the Catholic Monarchs, 1474-1516. Literary Studies in Memory of Keith Whinnom* (Liverpool, 1989), pp. 134-43. On the literary treatment of 'honour' see also Sicroff, *op. cit.*, pp. 297-300.

20 The Spanish original of Egido's article—'Ambiente histórico', in Alberto Barrientos (ed.), *Introducción a la lectura de Santa Teresa* (Madrid, 1978), pp. 43-103—includes a valuable section (pp. 88-103) on the finances of Teresa's foundations overall, and her various strategies for dealing with their economic needs.

21 See Teresa, *On Making the Visitation*, 27; Kavanaugh-Rodriguez III. Egido's discussion (mentioned in the preceding note) does, however, make it clear that no convent could pay its way entirely on the profits of its work. All depended, more or less heavily, on dowries and donations.

22 Moreover, she became a spirited defender of Teresa's ideals against the attempt to introduce a *limpieza* qualification of sorts into the Carmelite houses in the Low Countries after Teresa's death: see Egido, *op. cit.*, pp. 168, and 182 note 196.

23 The basic discussion is presented in P. Groult, *Les mystiques des Pays-Bas et la littérature espagnole du seizième siècle* (Louvain, 1927); some further works are listed in Oliver Davies, *God Within: the Mystical Tradition of Northern Europe* (London, 1988), p. 202 note 6. For the whole subject of Erasmian influence in the peninsula consult M. Bataillon, *Erasme et l'Espagne* (Paris, 1937); rev. and expanded Spanish trans., *Erasmo y España* (2 vols, Mexico, 1950).

24 M. Andrés Martín, *Reforma española y reforma luterana. Afinidades y diferencias a la luz de los misticos españoles (1517-1536)* (Madrid, 1975), is an interesting, though in many respects debatable, sketch of the topic.

25 Elliott, *op. cit.*, p. 222.

26 ' "To present to the eyes of the people a single heresy, which perhaps may suggest at the same time the renunciation of sexual pleasure and the communion of bodies is good preaching technique: it shows the heretics as one jumble of diabolical contradictions which offend common sense" '; ' "The recovery of the outcast demanded reduction of the privileges of the powerful, so the excluded who became aware of their exclusion had to be branded as heretics, whatever their doctrine. . . . All heresies are the banner of a reality, an exclusion. Scratch the heresy and you will find the leper. Every battle against heresy wants only this: to keep the leper as he is".' These comments of William of Baskerville in Umberto Eco's novel *The Name of the Rose* (New York and London, 1983), pp. 200 and 203, apply as much to sixteenth-century Spain as to fourteenth-century Italy.

27 See the introduction to *The Way of Perfection* in Kavanaugh–Rodriguez I, pp. 24–5, for these and similar views; references, ibid., p. 456 notes 33–36.

28 A good introduction is given in Carmelo Lisón-Tolosana, 'The *Beatas:* feminine responses to Christianity in sixteenth-century Castile' in W. James and D. H. Johnson (eds), *Vernacular Christianity. Essays in the Social Anthropology of Religion* (JASO Occasional Papers 7; Oxford, 1988), pp. 51–9.

29 See Jodi Bilinkoff, 'St Teresa of Avila and the Avila of St Teresa' in *Centenary of St Teresa* (Carmelite Studies III; Washington, 1984), pp. 53–68, for an introduction to this figure (pp. 61–4), as well as a good deal more in the way of valuable source material from unpublished records.

30 Full details in Enrique Llamas Martínez, *Santa Teresa de Jesús y la Inquisición española* (Madrid, 1972), summarized in Deirdre Green, *Gold in the Crucible. Teresa of Avila and the Western Mystical Tradition* (Shaftesbury, 1989), pp. 137–9.

31 Lisón-Tolosana, *op. cit.*, p. 58.

32 Ibid., p. 59.

33 On religious practice as the attempt to keep things in their proper place in the cosmos, see the work of Jonathan Z. Smith: most recently *To Take Place. Toward Theory in Ritual* (Chicago, 1987).

34 Green, *op. cit.*, p. 145.

35 Ibid., pp. 145–6. I think this is the correct interpretation of a rather ambiguous text which is given in its Spanish original in Efrén de la Madre de Dios and Otger Steggink, *Tiempo y vida de Santa Teresa* (Madrid, 1968), p. 584: Teresa is reported as saying that she was not afraid of the Inquisition because she was ready to die many deaths for the sake of God's goodness.

36 Stephen Clissold, *St Teresa of Avila* (London, 1979), pp. 188–90, is an excellent summary. See also Michael Williams, 'St Teresa, Doctor of the Church (orthodoxy and public opinion)', pp. 89–103 in Rees, *op. cit.*, esp. pp. 97–100.

37 Egido, *op. cit.*, p. 154.

38 Gerald Brenan, *St John of the Cross. His Life and Poetry* (Cambridge, 1973), p. 95.

39 Davies, *op. cit.*, pp. 59–62.

40 Of course, Osuna too might have been a *converso*; there is no evidence one way or the other; but the point is that nothing in Osuna's use of Scripture is the least surprising in a mediaeval devotional writer. Both Davies and Green are rather too eager to see signs of unusual interest in the Old Testament where the texts in question were the common coin of liturgy and also of popular drama and didactic literature in late mediaeval Spain; see Margherita Morreale, 'Vernacular Scriptures in Spain' in G. W. H. Lampe (ed.), *The Cambridge History of the Bible* II (Cambridge, 1969), pp. 465–91, esp pp. 486–90.

41 Davies, *op. cit.*, p. 67.

42 Green, *op. cit.*; a longer and fuller, but in some ways less critical discussion can be found in Catherine Swietlicki, *Spanish Christian Cabala: the Works of Luis de León, Santa Teresa de Jesús, and San Juan de la Cruz* (Columbia, 1986). A plausible case in respect of Luis can be made, but Swietlicki is over-optimistic about Teresa, as Green recognizes.

43 Green's interesting book suffers from its very sparse reference to the tradition of exegesis and spirituality in which Teresa was actually nurtured, and so, I think, concludes that the *Castle* is more eccentric than it actually is in structure and vocabulary. The result is that the originality of *thought* in Teresa's work is rather obscured.

2

Finding a pattern
Teresa's autobiography

LOYALTY AND CONFLICT

Teresa's *Life* caused her a great deal of trouble, both in its composition and in its consequences. She had already, in the years following her new beginning in the life of prayer, composed some notes on her experiences for the benefit of her directors:[1] largely, it seems (L 33.5), because the proposal for a new foundation (the house that was to become St Joseph's) had aroused hostile gossip about Teresa's circle. There was a real risk of Teresa's being delated to the Inquisition; and although she did not take this particularly seriously she thought it advisable to be as candid as possible as soon as possible. She consulted Fray Pedro Ibáñez, and wrote two quite lengthy accounts for him of the state of her soul, in terms both of her experiences and of her hopes and dispositions. The project of writing a fuller record of her life was suggested from more than one quarter in 1561–62: the *Life* itself is addressed to Fray García de Toledo, as was another substantial note or 'testimony' not long after the completion of her first draft of the autobiography; but we also hear of a discussion with the Inquisitor of Toledo, Francisco de Soto y Salazar (T 58.6),[2] who, while reassuring her that he saw no grounds for official action, suggested that she send a description of her experiences and her methods of prayer to John of Avila. Teresa finished her first draft in June 1562, having worked on it during her stay in Toledo with Doña Luisa, and sent the text to Fray García for his comments. As several passages in the present text make plain, he asked for further details, especially on the sensitive subject of visions and other communications from God, and on her fears and temptations; he also queried certain turns of phrase (Teresa endured a good deal from clerical ghost-writers during and after her life), and proposed an additional section on the foundation of St Joseph's. Teresa rather uncharacteristically took her time in making the revisions and the completed text was probably not in García's hands before 1565; it is not clear exactly when it finally reached 'Maestro Avila', though we know that it was forwarded by Doña Luisa from Toledo.

Early reactions were favourable: Maestro Avila wrote (late in 1568) in encouraging terms, and the *letrados* who read the revised manuscript (García, Báñez and Ibáñez certainly, and probably some other of her Dominican mentors — perhaps Baltasar Alvarez as well) agreed that it should be copied, though there was no question of its being distributed to a wider audience.[3] Teresa herself tells us that *The Way of Perfection* was written at the suggestion of her directors so as to make available to her sisters the insights of the *Life*. Only in 1574 did the work come directly under inquisitorial suspicion, thanks to the vindictive malice of the Princess of Eboli. The manuscript (and, we must assume, any copies circulating among Teresa's friends in the Dominican Order or the Society of Jesus) disappeared in the wasteland of the Inquisition's files until after Teresa's death, and was recovered only through the initiative of Ana de Jesús. Although Teresa was assured that there was nothing unacceptable in it (Báñez, fortunately, had been one of the Inquisition's censors), the saurian slowness of inquisitorial bureaucracy prevented any action being taken to restore the manuscript to her.

This means, of course, that Teresa did not have the *Life* before her in composing her later works, nor did she have the opportunity of further revision. Its account of progress in the life of prayer and its terminology represent one specific moment in Teresa's development — her first attempt at a coherent overview of what had happened and was still happening to her. What largely dictates her priorities is a concern directly related to the theological and pastoral problems posed by the *alumbrados* and touched on briefly in Chapter 1 of this book. Inquisitorial anxiety was normally concentrated upon anything suggesting that the soul could make itself passive to God in such a way that the divine activity worked on and in the soul without any kind of mediation (historical, institutional and doctrinal). Teresa was in a most delicate position here: the authentication of her sense of a divine commission to renew the life of the Order required her to insist upon the reality of divine action in her experience; there had to be a level of Christian prayer at which

> the conscious occupation
> Of the praying mind, or the sound of the voice praying[4]

no longer determined what was going on, where the soul's capacities were activated simply by God. Yet this had to be articulated in full awareness of the risks of diabolical deceit that threatened those who claimed that there was no contribution from their own creatureliness in God's action in and through them.

Balancing these considerations is a major part of Teresa's task in all her writings, but perhaps most specially in the *Life*, written as it is in the wake of years of inner and outer conflict over such matters. From chapter 23 of the *Life* onwards she describes the prolonged misery caused her by the recurrent suspicion of confessors and others, determined to prove to her that her visions and communications must have been from the devil. 'Contradiction on the part of good men', she writes in L 30.6, was identified for her by Peter of Alcántara as one of the most heartbreaking trials of all in the life of discipleship. Her self-trust was seriously undermined: we see her warning others that she may be unwittingly deceiving them (L 30.13), a memory that argues a very deeply disturbed and tormented state of mind. The *Life*, therefore, is anything but an anecdotal compilation of rare and interesting experiences; Teresa has a perfectly clear apologetic purpose. She has to show that she cannot be an *alumbrada* enthusiast because she wants only what God wants, and, more specifically, what God wants through the mediation of the teaching Church. If her chosen, willed style of spirituality expresses faithfulness to the Church, then what comes to her 'at an angle' to her will and choice, overriding but not contradicting, should be in fact entirely continuous with this active spirituality. The difficulty lies in *showing* the continuity underlying the profound experiences of interruption and dislocation Teresa lives through. The *Life* uses a particular set of techniques to do this, but it is not until the composition of the *Castle* that Teresa finds a full theological integration for the conflicts of her autobiography as a believer.

To understand the *Life*, then, we need to read it as the story of a twofold victory. On the one hand it is about the triumph of discipline, about the shaping of a Christian discernment by reading, friendship and conversation, sacramental practice, the candid and unsparing exposure of what might have been an exciting 'private' world of experiences to the common speech and culture of the Church; the triumph of discipline over plain idleness, over the obsessive concern for status and reputation in Teresa's society, over the construction by the *self* of an identity as 'holy' or 'special'. On the other hand, it is a story of *God*'s triumph even over the disciplined spirituality of a loyal Catholic—the triumph that makes it possible and legitimate for a loyal Catholic to be also a prophet and critic. Thus the main interweaving themes in the *Life* are Teresa's willingness at every point to submit her experience to the judgement of others (though not necessarily to submit in the sense of *accepting* their judgement) and her inability to resist the disturbing impulsions coming to her in prayer. The *Life* is, centrally and basically, about struggle and conflict—Teresa's struggle for acceptance and legitimacy, and God's struggle to be present to Teresa. Teresa did not doubt that obedience to the Church and obedience to God were one and the same: she seeks in her writing to display that sameness in a narrative of discontinuities. To this extent, it reproduces something of the technique of Augustine's *Confessions* (no accident that this work features at a critical moment in the *Life*) in its endeavour to point to the unity of God's purpose and act behind the muddled contingencies of a human biography. But Teresa is out to do something more: to show obliquely that her reforming programme is consonant with the welfare, peace and continuity of the Catholic Church by showing how, in her own life, obedience to the Church in a life of discipline is itself the foundation for response to the disturbing and 'untraditional' calling of God.

The additions that she made to the *Life* between 1563 and 1565 are largely a matter of elaborating this theme. It was at the point that she composed the long 'digression' on the four methods of irrigation as a metaphor for the stages of the soul's journey (11–22), and, at García's prompting, the chapters (32–40) on the foundation of St Joseph's and its aftermath—chapters that most vividly depict her own crises of self-confidence in the face of the contradiction of good men. Fray García seems to have grasped what Teresa was trying to say (even if neither she nor he would have articulated it in the terms proposed in the preceding paragraph), and to have helped materially in clarifying the theological focus and the tactical direction of the text. The bafflement of the ecclesiastical censors, manifestly uneasy with Teresa's idiom, and with the whole idea of a nun presuming to commend and anatomize mental prayer, yet unable to fault her orthodox intentions, is a testimony to her success.

CONVERSION

Teresa's account of her youth in the *Life* (including her reflections on her early years as a nun) begins to set the scene for the later chapters on her struggles with her confessors and advisers in that it shows a keen awareness of the difficulties of recognizing true motivation, especially in a context where rigid convention prescribes what it means to be loyal or virtuous. Teresa is intrigued by the possibilities of doing right for the wrong reason; of distorted ideas of virtue working against the grace of God; and, above all, of the gulf between reputation and reality. In other words, her youthful experience has shown her that it is hard to be truthful. In spelling this out so fully, she turns the flank of possible attack. Is she self-deceived, as so many believe? Well, perhaps (she implies); but at least she knows what self-deception looks like. She cannot be accused of a bland reliance on her own perceptions or an unawareness of the devil's skills. Thus she recalls her first real loss of virtue in connection with her reading of romances as a teenager (2.1ff.): she becomes vain and fastidious, longing to be thought well of by the world (in particular the fashionable world to which she is introduced by her cousins). Her natural (and virtuous) fortitude becomes the motive force in sustaining her passion for social 'honour' (3), and the fear of offending God that ought to motivate virtue is replaced by the dread of scandal. She is saved from moral disaster — and social disgrace — by a mixture of temperamental caution or prudery and the intervention of her father (6). What preoccupies Teresa is not so much the memory of risky amorous episodes as such — the text in any case makes it quite clear that she was *not* involved in a seduction or affair[5] — as the alliance between certain strengths of temperament and character and a weakness or vacuity in her goals and hopes. Fear of scandal is a potent motivation in preserving sexual virtue, but, since it has no inner or personal force, it can give no moral shape to a life: the question will always be, 'What can I get away with?' If the fundamental moral question, 'To whom or to what am I being true?' is posed, the appeal to public honour is a very weak answer; honour does not of itself require truth or integrity of me, since reputation can, to a fair degree, be preserved without truthfulness.

So at the very beginning of her narrative Teresa shows her familiarity with the problem of appearance and reality. She knows that she and others may seem to be what they are not, and that motivation is a tangled web. And we meet, for the first time in the *Life*, the God who acts *against* Teresa's will to bring her to her senses—in this case by means of Don Alonso's suspicions and intervention: 'God delivered me in such a way that it seems clear he strove, against my will, to keep me from being completely lost' (2.6). Teresa's picture of herself is of a strong will, perfectly capable of deluding itself, which is nonetheless vulnerable to, subject to, the overruling purpose of God: she wants to disarm the critic by insisting that, by the grace of God, her capacity for falsehood is not limitless. Here it is a simple case of a headstrong teenage eroticism being disciplined from outside. As the story unfolds, this discipline will become internal.

Part of the process by which this happens is the attractiveness of holy lives. Teresa lays great stress in chapter 3 of the *Life* upon the importance to her of the 'good companionship' of a friendly nun at her convent school and of her devout uncle, Don Pedro. She learns to recognize an interiorly motivated goodness, and thus the emptiness of her previous ways. But the overall effect of this is ambiguous: she learns to fear hell, and decides that she is called to the cloister because it is 'the safest state' (3.5). Precisely because her motivation is 'servile fear', she is shaken by doubts and apprehensions; only when she is actually in the convent, sweeping floors, does God give her a sense of personal 'rightness' and joy (4.2). The happiness given awakes that generosity without which there is no serious prayer; and the reading of Osuna's *Alphabet* propels Teresa towards 'recollection' (4.7). Here she comes up against a difficulty in presentation: recollection is becoming suspect, as distracting people from the spirituality proper to their station,[6] and Teresa is writing in the immediate aftermath of the Inquisition's edict of 1559 banning a large number of vernacular works on prayer. One of Osuna's major works had been withdrawn, and although the *Alphabet* was not directly condemned, it was not to be reprinted until 1638.[7] Teresa is careful to say that reading Osuna made her go more frequently to confession. But, more interestingly, she takes up one aspect of Osuna's scheme and works it very thoroughly into her own apologetic concerns. Osuna had described three stages of prayer:[8] vocal prayer, of which the Our Father is the model; reflective and meditative prayer ('holy and devout thoughts, whether of the passion of the Lord, or of the Church, or of the Last Judgement, or of any other thing'[9]); and 'mental or spiritual' prayer. The transition between the second and the third levels is what he describes as the onset of *devoción*, 'devotion'. Although this may seem to come more easily with vocal prayer than with 'holy thoughts', it is important to persevere with meditation until these thoughts produce equal fervour. At this point, both words and thoughts give way to 'more comprehensive' aspirations of love, simple and direct expressions of response to the felt love of God. Teresa, however, writes here (4.7–9) exclusively of her *failure* at the second level. She struggles to sustain the holy thoughts commended by Osuna and finds only 'solitude and dryness'; she cannot picture to herself even the humanity of Jesus (cf. 9.6). But this failure, with all the labour and frustration it entails, is in fact a *shorter* way to 'contemplation' than success in Osuna's terms. The person who is able to meditate, says Teresa (4.8), is in a position to defend herself against temptation and distraction; the non-discursive mind, in contrast, is profoundly vulnerable to these. Thus the non-discursive person, the failed meditator, is more immediately aware of the need for 'purity of conscience', the need to grow into the kind of inner integrity that alone will minimize distraction. She is thrown on the resources of others: Teresa describes how she could not begin to pray without a book to help her concentrate, and how the words of a book could sometimes still her mind rapidly. She comments, rather mischievously (4.9), that she is grateful for *not* having found anyone to teach her about meditation. Convinced as she is that she has no aptitude, she believes that the mixture of aridity and distraction with reliance on spiritual reading did her more good than learning the techniques of reflection. It is not the long practice of 'holy thoughts' that leads her into recollection, but the awareness of an inner fragmentation drawn together only by words and ideas given her from outside.

The shift in emphasis is clear and very significant. Once again, Teresa points the reader to her malleability before God. She has no resources in herself to generate a private mysticism, no ideas of her own; she tacitly accepts the usual charge that women do not have the capacity for sustained mental labour only to claim that this incapacity, far from keeping her bound to the 'safe' territory of vocal prayer, is a central factor in impelling her towards true recollection.

As she will more than once repeat in the *Life*, she is not striving to lift herself Godward by her own efforts: effort of the approved kind issues only in a bitter knowledge of weakness. Yet it is that very experience of inner muddle and the need to be fed by others that exposes her more swiftly and radically to God than any 'technique' can do. To the eye of an unsympathetic censor, she presents a skilful and ironical argument. Is she endorsing the suspect Osuna? No, for she draws from Osuna only a deepened obedience to the Church; and she recognizes her inability to practise the interior prayer judged so unsuitable by the Inquisitors for non-clerics. Is she setting herself up as a teacher of prayer? No, for she admits that she cannot follow, let alone recommend, Osuna's path, or any other scheme of progress. In good Pauline fashion, her credentials are her weaknesses. Her authority must be established through the relating of her failures.

She is not being coy here; the chapters that follow are quite genuinely about weakness, failure and untruthfulness, as Teresa sees it. She is still preoccupied about her dignity, she tells us (5.1), sensitive to criticism and eager for admiration. And when she turns to a description of her experience at Becedas, where she is undergoing a 'cure' for the unspecified illness that afflicted her at this time, she is again able to display the interweaving of mixed human motivation and divine overruling that has now established itself as a controlling theme. The story is quite well known: the parish priest at Becedas, already keeping a concubine, forms a strong attachment to Teresa, which she reciprocates; as a result of their friendship, Teresa persuades him to give her the amulet by which, he and his servants believe, his concubine maintains her hold on his passion. As a result, he is able to break away from the relationship, and — not long after — to make an edifying death (5.3–6). Teresa admits very bluntly her moral confusion at this time: she was genuinely anxious for the priest's welfare, but is also quite aware in retrospect of the sexual undercurrents in the relationship between them. She was flattered and grateful to be the object of his love; and although they never overstepped the bounds of 'decency' the mature Teresa knows that a man and a woman discussing God and sin together in an emotionally charged atmosphere will be deceiving themselves if they think this is a straightforwardly spiritual or pastoral encounter. He gives Teresa the amulet to 'please' her: she recognizes the ambiguity of this, and hints at her own feelings of jealousy or possessiveness. But out of it all comes the harvest of his good death. The incident is not elaborated further, but simply left as another witness to the young Teresa's continuing inner fragmentation.

This becomes the theme of chapters 6 to 8. After her near-fatal illness Teresa finds her religious fervour increased: she becomes an exemplary member of her community, painfully sensitive to her sinfulness, eager to talk about God and to have time for solitary prayer, surrounding herself with *objets de piété* (though she hastens to add, at 6.6, that she never cared for the more extravagant extra-liturgical devotions popular with women of her time and class). At the same time, she is in fact leading a thoroughly distracted life: no one does much to keep an eye on her activities, and she is left free to indulge in the kind of social life thought appropriate for a clever and attractive nun in her sort of community: gossip, the hosting of something like a *salon*, mild flirtation. Teresa grants that not all of this need be particularly harmful to a mature Christian (7.3), but sees it as a major problem for any community seeking to *form* souls. For her, the symptoms of something being fundamentally wrong are the pervasive but rather unfocused sense of sinfulness that constantly prompts her to tears, and the real fear of anything beyond vocal prayer which holds her back from the intimacy with God that her early efforts and failures had induced (6.4, 7.1, 8.5–7). She half-persuades herself that she is holding back from mental prayer out of humility (7.1, 11; 8.5), but is conscious of the falsity of this when she tries to explain to her father that she no longer practises the disciplines she is recommending to him and others (7.11–13): 'I was allowing myself to get lost and striving to save others' (7.13).

Modern readers have sometimes found these chapters baffling. It is by no means clear what sort of prayer Teresa does and does not practise; and it is hard to see why she judges herself so very harshly in the period being described (a period of about eighteen years, on her own reckoning at 4.9, 5.3, and 8.3). We should obviously allow again for sheer tactics: it is in the interest of her present freedom and authority to stress the discontinuity with her earlier years as a nun. But her 'tactics' in the *Life* are inseparably bound up with what she truly believes: that God has consistently overruled her selfish will. Beyond this lies the deep personal awareness of the possibility of deception: what dismays her in this period is the relative ease with which she sustained a reputation as a good, even saintly, nun, and the way in which she was able to find edifying excuses for her own conscience. At that time, she implies she was a good nun outwardly and a spiritual shambles within; now, as she writes, she is regarded by many as a bad nun. Perhaps those who so regard her will be warned against just those hasty judgements she had made or encouraged others to make of her in the past. And her repeated reference to the lack in this period of sensible spiritual direction is a further warning, to clergy and their penitents: it is perfectly possible for a spiritually and intellectually lazy confessor to do far-reaching damage by colluding with the idleness or fearfulness of a penitent. Teresa wants herself and her pastors to be responsible to something more than the cosy self-images nurtured by excessive concern for public reputation and ease of relationship. Her complaint is that, at a time when she was badly disoriented, combining a vigorous conventional piety with fundamental unhappiness and self-doubt (shown in her weeping fits and her dread of intimacy, 'friendship' (7.1) in prayer), no one *challenged* her.

She tells us that she continued to struggle with some kind of private prayer during these years, except for one patch of rather more than twelve months when she gave up entirely (7.11, 8.3). What was her prayer like? We know from 4.7–10 that she constantly used a book to focus her mind; but it seems that she also continued, for the whole eighteen years, to try to use her mind in the approved fashion — 'thinking of how I have offended God, and of the many things I owe him, and of what leads to hell and what to glory, and of the great trials and sufferings the Lord endured for me' (8.7). The effort involved made the prospect of prayer alarming; she speaks of the depression she regularly felt on going into chapel to pray, and describes how on many occasions, she waited impatiently for the clock to signal her release. Yet she perseveres: finding that what God gives in prayer is quite disproportionate to her felt enthusiasm. God responds, not to the state of her emotions, but to the desire and direction shown in her life overall: to her knowledge of her neediness and fragmentation, not to any eagerness to acquire spiritual experiences (8.8). In contrast to what had happened in her teenage years, God's discipline is now exercised in accord with her own deepest decisions. The discipline she sets herself of meditation even when it is not attractive or congenial is a declaration of *some* willingness to open herself to God, however much she fears the result and in some ways tries to hold it off. And with such an acknowledgement of her dread of God's active irruption into her superficially orderly religiosity she again attempts to turn aside the charge of generating mystical communications out of her own preferences or fantasies. She wants both to be left alone with a religious life she can (more or less) 'manage', *and* is painfully aware that 'managing' herself is both ultimately impossible and not what she really wants.

She wants to surrender to God and does not know how. Chapter 9 of the *Life* describes how the surrender begins, as a result of super- ficially accidental moments (as we might expect from the whole drift of the text thus far). Teresa has already mentioned two preternatural experiences (7.6–8), quite early in her monastic life, which she had taken as warning against an unsuitable friendship;[10] there are few details, and no suggestion of any strictly 'converting' results. These visions simply have an unpleasant and frightening effect: Teresa can still recall the experience of 'seeing' the face of Christ staring disap- provingly at her. But the image that begins to stir her, many years after, is an *ecce homo* of a standard late mediaeval type – a 'man of sorrows' displaying his wounds. Teresa's first reaction is no less standardly mediaeval: a sense of ingratitude and culpable indif- ference. However, the feeling more lastingly aroused in her is, as she describes it, less simply conventional: she gets into the habit of turn- ing her mind to the figure of Jesus in his moments of *isolation*, above all in Gethsemane (9.4). She does this from a conviction that Christ in his vulnerability cannot refuse her presence, her 'consolation', however unworthy she may be, so great is his need: 'He had to accept me'.

This is striking, not only because the wounded Christ speaks to her in a way the judging Christ, years earlier, had not, but more significantly because the theme of being accepted and being *needed* has been so pervasive, at several different levels, in the book. The whole project of writing has to do with her acceptability to ecclesias- tical authority; but we have already seen how she identifies many of her early problems as arising out of the urge to be loved and admired. When she remarks of her experience at Becedas that she took it for granted that she should be 'grateful and loyal' (5.4) to anyone who showed her affection, it is hardly fanciful to detect the voice of someone who finds it extremely hard to believe herself to be love- able. She knows she is, humanly speaking, 'desirable': attractive both sexually and in other ways. But this intensifies the underlying problem. To be desirable is to be involved in the impossible double bind of a society and Church obsessively interested in female purity: what is desired or needed in women is precisely that which makes them dangerous or contaminating, so that to be 'desirable' is *not* to be loveable in religious terms. At Becedas, Teresa is grateful for a love that survives her clear declaration of faithfulness to her vow of chastity; yet, looking back, she sees how much she needed to persuade herself that this friendship was innocent, out of the danger zone, so as to be able to believe herself loved for something more than 'carnal' attractiveness: when in fact the relationship was full of the ambiguities she sought to escape. But now, in meditating on the needy Christ, she is able to see herself as needed and welcomed simply as a human companion, as someone whose mere presence might be a grace or comfort in the suffering of another. The themes that are to flower so richly in her later work come fleetingly in sight here: *friendship* with Christ, faithfulness to the 'honour' of God, not of oneself, and the possibility of human community created by these two dispositions.

Teresa goes on to record (9.7–8) her reading of Augustine's *Confessions* at about the same period. It was a work that might well be expected to speak to her experience: 'As I began to read the *Confessions*, it seemed to me that I saw myself in them'. But she notes particularly Augustine's account (in book 8 of the work) of his own final conversion, prompted by the child's voice from the neighbouring garden reciting, 'Take and read': 'it was I the Lord called', says Teresa. As with her experience before the man of sorrows image, she senses herself to be *wanted* directly by God. And the tenth chapter of the *Life* develops precisely this. Apart from any question of merit, God gives grace—compunction and repentance, but also the new and unexpected touches of intimacy that Teresa is now receiving; and when such gifts are given, it is false humility to deny or ignore them. We must acknowledge that, for all our natural poverty, we are enriched by God and are given favours in order to share them (10.4–5): and she concludes, 'how can anyone benefit and share his gifts lavishly if he doesn't understand that he is rich?' (ibid., 6). Only when we are fully aware of what God is doing in us can we find courage and authority to speak for God; and only when we see ourselves as loved by God can 'we desire to be despised and belittled by everyone' (ibid.). The pledge of God's love, in other words, is the only thing that can enable and authorize the life upon which Teresa has embarked—a life of witness to God through protest and reform, in total disregard of conventional 'acceptability'.

So, as this first section of the *Life* draws to an end, Teresa draws various threads together. Throughout her early life (and these chapters, remember, cover her first 39 years) she has allowed herself to be hampered and controlled by anxiety about acceptability. Her worries about this have, from her teens onward, pushed her into relationships of which she is ashamed, and into a confused and fragmented religious life, dominated by the longing to be acceptable to both the conventionally worldly and the conventionally pious. *Conversion*, for her, has meant simply the discovery of being desired in her entirety, as she is; being 'needed' by Christ. She has found an integrating reality for her life, and thus a spring of motivation not dependent upon her social and ecclesiastical context and its imme-diate pressures; and so she is able to conclude chapter 10 with a strong statement of detachment from what she has written. By all means let these opening chapters be published: they are simply the history of a sinner, and may help to dispel any illusions about her sanctity (10.7). But what is to follow is more controversial, since she is going to venture some theological reflections on her unusual experiences: Fray García can do what he likes with this except publish it under her name. It is a triumphant conclusion to her first section. God has won through in her life by sheer gift, and her riches are not her own; it is her own emotional confusion and insecurity that have both held God at a distance *and* enabled her to recognize the love of God as achieving for her what no human relationship can – a comprehensive setting free from the constraint of needing to be approved. 'Teresa's need for love came to be transposed onto spiritual levels', writes one recent student of her works.[11] This is manifestly true, but has less to do with her own expression of love for God, important as this is, than with the sense of being needed for a distinctive personal task that is not wholly defined by what was normally thought proper for a female religious of her day. Her con-version is the acquiring of a particular awareness that *she* has a gift to offer God and God's people, which she alone can give: it is the receiving of that authority that enables her to write the book at all.

'MYSTICAL THEOLOGY'

Chapters 11 to 22 form the major addition made by Teresa to the body of her text at García's insistence, and are the nearest thing in the whole book to a programmatically ordered vision of the life of prayer. She is not developing a 'theory' of mystical experience, but attempting to do justice to the sense of a frontier crossed which she has been describing in the chapters immediately preceding. As early as 4.7, she has noted graces given her when she first began to read Osuna: sometimes God bestows *quietud*, 'quiet', sometimes even 'union', though she has at this stage no conception of what is happening. 9.9 and 10.1 record how similar experiences came once more, unsought, as she began to picture Christ in his suffering, and sometimes when she was reading. The experiences she identifies are of 'suspension', displacement, and a measure of confusion: there is the awareness of love and longing for God, an absence of any impressions in the memory, and an experience in the understanding that might be described as an overloading of the circuits. Too much is coming in to the understanding to be 'processed' in the ordinary way, and so there is a feeling of bafflement and stupidity. Teresa distinguishes this very carefully from the sense of warm devotion that can be generated by a good meditation (9.2); she has been familiar with this, and sees it is a co-operation between effort and grace; whereas the sense of 'suspension' is not at all something that can be induced. Of the latter she says, 'I believe they call the experience "mystical theology"' (9.1), and she picks up the phrase again at 11.5. Presumably she had found the expression in Osuna:[12] the second chapter of his sixth treatise in the *Alphabet* distinguishes between 'speculative' theology and 'hidden' (*escondida*) or 'mystical' (*mística*) theology, the first relating to the understanding and the second to the will. The first is accessible to anyone in principle (including devils and heretics); the second only to those whom God is sanctifying, and therefore of higher dignity. The word 'theology' here is apt to mislead: Osuna follows Pseudo-Denys and his mediaeval interpreters in according to *theologia* its early sense, common in the Greek Fathers, of 'knowledge of God'. Theology is not the name of an area of study but of a kind of knowing and learning: speculative theology is a knowing about God by reasoning and argument, true as far as it goes, so long as it is faithful to revelation, but depending on human excellence, human skill ('the learning tools of any science', says Osuna[13]); while mystical theology is a knowing formed in the soul by God's own action. In an important sense, it can be taught only by God, and its presence has no necessary relation to what we ordinarily think of as theological skills. It is important to note, though, that 'mystical theology' is a real *knowing*: it is not that the will (in the modern sense), let alone 'feeling', is given its head and understanding laid aside, but that the understanding (as indeed Teresa says) acquires its knowledge simply by being receptive rather than active or discursive.

What Teresa now proposes to do is to try and elucidate the transition from the state in which you do things for God to the state where

God does things in you. The result is in fact—yet again—more radical than Osuna's doctrine, and also in some ways less open to the Inquisition's objections. As we have seen already, Teresa tacitly dismantles the orderly progression Osuna envisages so as to leave the initiative wholly with God (St John of the Cross, interestingly—and characteristically—stands somewhere between Osuna and Teresa on this question). Teresa's main modification is really a matter of taking completely seriously the distinction between what the human subject can do and what God does. For Osuna, it seems that there can and should be a *decision* to go forward into *recogimiento*, 'recollection': we are to empty mind and heart of everything created, to become like Mary, 'who, when everything was emptied, offered her extraordinarily pure heart, cleansed of all distracting operations, so that when the Holy Spirit descended on her, the virtue of God engendered divine darkness in her heart and there in the shadows the Son of God was conceived'.[14] This lovely image, with its echoes of the Rhineland mystics, presupposes that when I *make* myself empty, God will fill the vacuum and come to birth in my soul. Thus, while recollection involves God's action in the soul when its own powers are still and receptive, being still and receptive is something we can decide upon.

Teresa is sceptical. What we can *do* in prayer is read and think. This will not necessarily be enjoyable or particularly fruitful in producing pious feelings, but it has to be done. When she speaks of recollection, as in 11.9, she often uses the word more literally and prosaically than Osuna to mean simply the effort of disciplining the senses and the imagination; certainly it has connotations of what contemporary writers now like to call 'centring', but it cannot be said that Teresa really envisages, in the *Life*, an actual discipline of emptiness or receptivity. All we know, as we begin serious prayer, is that the garden needs watering, and, boring as this may be, as we fetch endless buckets from the well with aching arms, it is essential, and, what is more, it is a sharing in the pain of Christ (11.10). We may have very little emotional reward, but we shall be learning 'justice and fortitude of soul and . . . humility' (11.13). All being well, we shall eventually become habituated to an intermittent sense of emotional engagement, moments of joy or sorrow helping us towards firmer resolutions, greater ease and candour in petitioning God, sharing our emotions with God more freely, and so on. The sense of 'devotion' described by Osuna as leading from his second to his third level of prayer is not completely absent in Teresa by any means, but she is more interested in the overall confirmation of the soul's desire to be useful to God (12.1–3). We are to some extent sustained in our purpose by occasional visitations of intense feeling—the rare occasions on which (so Teresa believes) our efforts and God's grace manage together to produce a result not entirely spiritual but not entirely unspiritual either. What *is* missing is the security and permanence of 'devotion' promised by Osuna to those who persevere in meditation. For Osuna, the onset of regular devotion prompts us more and more to silence and emptiness; for Teresa, the mixture of boring effort and intermittent consolation simply trails on until *God* interrupts it.

'Taking it upon oneself to stop and suspend thought is what I mean should not be done', she declares firmly (12.5). We are right to be suspicious of any impulse to what we think is a 'higher' kind of prayer, because we (women in particular, she dutifully adds) are chronically subject to illusion (12.7). There may well be no permanent harm done, if the soul is genuinely desirous of coming closer to God, but the effort can only confuse our sense of the distinction between what we do and what God does. Teresa's chief concern in the *Life* is again apparent: the systematic rebuttal of any suggestion that she is so eager for extraordinary divine favours that she might have been able to generate them from her own resources. However, she is also venturing some plain pastoral advice. When we *try* to stop thinking, we fall between two stools and become cold and stupid; we are neither turning our minds to God nor letting our minds be formed by God. When God stops us thinking, the intellect is stupefied not by having too little but by having too much presented to it (12.5). There can be, then, no *policy* of emptying the mind: as elsewhere, in the whole of Teresa's early experience, God must act by cutting across what we do.

There is a theological point here which comes to the fore some years later in her famous *Vejamen*—the semi-serious comments she made on the interpretations offered by various friends and advisers when she shared with them words she had heard in prayer.[15] She had asked her brother for his views on the words, 'Seek yourself in me'; and the earnest Don Lorenzo had canvassed the opinions of the weightiest spiritual men in Avila, and forwarded them to Teresa. She, however, decided to treat these solemn judgements in the spirit of the traditional doctoral disputation in the universities, when one scholar was expressly detailed to make fun of the theses advanced by the candidates (the practice still survives in a few European universities): she simply mocks her friends, quite mercilessly. But the serious side of this is visible particularly in her riposte to John of the Cross: 'Seeking God would be very costly if we could not do so until we were dead to the world'. John's comments, she says, are all very well for those who want to follow the Ignatian exercises, disciplining their minds and hearts; but she is thinking of something more fundamental. Women in the gospel — the Magdalene, the Samaritan woman of John 4, the Syrophoenician woman who wants her daughter exorcized — find Christ quite independently of any disciplines of self-emptying; they are met where they are and as they are. With rather unexpected sharpness, Teresa concludes: 'God deliver me from people so spiritual that they want to turn everything into perfect contemplation, no matter what'. And, turning to her unfortunate brother's response, she pours scorn on his recommendation that people practise the prayer of quiet: 'as if this were in their power'!

Teresa does not offer an interpretation of her own, beyond pointing out that the dictum can hardly refer to those already touched by God, given the 'supernatural' gift of receptivity, and united to God by God's own act: these have already found God (and so, presumably, themselves). Her response to John hints at her own view: God does not turn away those who look for God, whatever the mixture of their motives or the imperfection of their lives. Seekers like these will only find their identity and integration — as Teresa herself did — by meeting God's acceptance. As she says in her comments on Julián de Avila's interpretation, union is a gift whose sole precondition is love. Not, obviously, just a pure selfless love, but the kind of dumb and confused longing to be wanted that had somehow sustained Teresa through so many years in the convent, and that had characterized the 'unspiritual' women of the gospel stories. Teresa's view of grace is both more and less radical than that presupposed by Osuna, John and others: it is more radical in insisting that nothing whatsoever on our side can constrain God to grant his favour; less radical in concluding that we do not have to work at wholly cancelling out our natural dispositions before we can begin to encounter God. Theologians like Osuna and John, it might be said by an unsympathetic reader, suspect everything in human nature except the will (reinforced, of course, by grace), in that they assume it is possible to carry through a drastic emptying of mind and affections by effort. Teresa wants us to trust nothing, not even the will to empty oneself: the emptying is only done when God is already present, absorbing, transforming or overcoming all other desires.

This is hardly fair to John of the Cross, it must be said: his poetry at least makes it quite clear that the formidable programme of policies of self-denial in *The Ascent of Mount Carmel* is itself generated only by the gratuitous and elusive touch of God's love prior to all striving. But Teresa has a point. Just as much as any modern Protestant critic of 'mysticism', a Karl Barth or Anders Nygren, she is unhappy with any language that suggests God can be lured into giving favours by the straining Godwards of human eros. Just as much as Barth, she sees human nature as more or less comprehensively sinful in its empirical state, but, for that very reason, comprehensively useable and transformable by God: it does not, as Teresa's narrative has already shown, have to purge itself of impurities before it can become the vehicle of God's action.

The trouble is that we are left with a very sharply-drawn antithesis between a human effort that is known to be necessary but arid — the watering of the garden — and a divine activity that somehow forces its way through. Teresa does not think much of what might be called an 'acquired passivity', an active discipline of mental stillness: though in practice this may well be what her meditative reading and her picturing of the suffering Christ amounted to (see, perhaps, 13.11). She is just as wary as the inquisitors of the human urge to fill the void of understanding with comforting projections; and while she has ample fortitude for dealing with the labour and frustration of meditating (8.7, 11.11 etc.), she is afraid of the 'chill' and disorientation of simply abandoning meditation or active reflection. Of course, John of the Cross and others are clear that no one should do this until they feel they simply cannot sustain it further (*The Dark Night of the Soul* I, 9–10, especially 10.4–5): the dryness and stupidity experienced when meditation fails is, for John, a sign that God *has begun* to act more deeply in the spirit and must be allowed to go on doing this. The effort and stress of meditation may get in the way. This is close to Osuna, but more nuanced. Teresa, on the other hand, wants us to go on despite any amount of boredom or strain, until we find ourselves irresistibly taken up by God. These differences, no doubt, are partly temperamental: Ruth Burrows comments that Teresa 'does not seem to have been of a contemplative temperament . . . she was not naturally passive',[16] and this must be allowed to be a fair assessment. She needs to be sure that either she or God is manifestly doing something. It may well be (and there are other passages in her writings which bear this out) that for some kinds of people the pressure towards mental stillness or receptivity actually induces *more* anxiety than is involved in the efforts of meditation; whereas St John and his followers, like Fr Baker, have other problems in mind: the anxiety of the person tortured by the effort to think on the one hand, and the dangerous complacency of the proficient conceptualizer on the other. A good director might have helped Teresa to find the least stressful kind of mental activity appropriate; he would have encouraged her to read and to look at pictures, as she likes to do, and discouraged her from formal exercises.[17]

But, as she tells us, no one was much help until the time when she was in any case moving beyond this phase and receiving strong and irresistible communications. She remains grateful for this lack of help, as we have noted, because it keeps her dependent on books, and so on the accepted wisdom of others. The great insight coming through all this — when all the reservations or qualifications have been entered — is the absolute gratuity of God's grace, given beyond expectation or deserving. We need not wait to welcome God until we are perfect. This, however, also means that it is proper for us to *want* to be saints, to want to be taken further than our efforts can take us. So, although we must on no account try to induce different, 'higher' forms of prayer, we can try to practise detachment from comfort and success and praise, and to train ourselves in asceticism (13.4ff.). Here again we must beware of false humility, and of the devil's attempts to keep us protective of our health and welfare. But we must also beware of the temptation to interfere with the spirituality of others (13.8–10): our zeal for holiness is primarily *our* responsibility, and ill-advised attempts to teach others when our own lives are in confusion will be unhelpful. Here Teresa wanders into a digression on the importance of consulting learned theologians, *letrados*, even when they are not necessarily experienced in prayer. In a director experience and discernment are essential and theological learning a bonus; but the theologian must be on hand to correct the ignorance of both priest and penitent (13.16). Teresa sketches her ideal director, judicious, spiritual and learned, and admits that she has no inclination to submit to the unsupported opinion of a theological illiterate (13.19). As elsewhere, she distances herself from the suggestion that she might be relying only on her own judgement, demanding, in effect, that the director be *accountable*, as she is, to something other than whims and impressions; once again, the would-be critic is given no handhold, even when a quite provocative statement about obedience is being made.

She returns in chapter 14 to her main discussion of the movement from human to divine action in prayer, and continues to elaborate her metaphor of watering the garden. God has begun to take hold of the soul and act directly: so the laborious business of carrying buckets from the well gives way to a primitive irrigation scheme, a water-wheel and ditches. What this image seeks to capture is what Teresa (at 14.4) calls the slower pace of the intellect in a prayer where it is responding, not initiating. The will is held in a kind of relaxed, loving absorption: that is to say, I am conscious of wanting only what is given me, the presence of God's love, and so of wanting only what God wants. Memory and understanding drift around rather, sometimes focusing on God, sometimes looking desperately for stimulus elsewhere. But these ramblings do not affect the basic consciousness of loving and being loved, and the will should not try to discipline the other faculties (14.3, 15.6): they will eventually fall into line of their own accord (15.1). We will inevitably feel a touch of anxiety about losing this general calm and quiet (Teresa uses again the word that has appeared earlier, in 4.7, *quietud*): the soul 'dares not move or stir . . . nor would it even want to breathe sometimes' (15.1). But this is pointless, since such an experience will last just as long as God wants it to, no more. *This* and this only is the point at which reflective activity must be abandoned; or, more accurately, since it has been displaced by God's seizure of the will, the intellect must not try to start up again, 'running about . . . looking for many words and reflections so as to give thanks for this gift and piling up one's sins and faults in order to see that the gift is unmerited' (15.6).

What Teresa is warning against is a particular kind of self-consciousness (in the rather derogatory, colloquial sense of the term): we should like to *know* that we are responding appropriately to God's gifts, and so the mind attempts to organize and examine its response ('to compose speeches and search for ideas', says Teresa at 15.7). This is a particular temptation for the learned, and Teresa boldly claims that she has good advice 'for the learned men who ordered me to write' (ibid.). The intellect should be content to be 'near the light'; to be conscious of this is to be a stranger to oneself (ibid.), that is, *not* to be in control of one's responses. Meanwhile the will makes simple aspirations and acts of gratitude, and that is all that is necessary. A few words and thoughts, even a few vocal prayers are quite in order, but 'if the quiet is great, it is difficult to speak without a good deal of effort' (15.9).

61

There has been a certain amount of scholarly uncertainty about whether Teresa is here describing a properly 'mystical' state, and whether it corresponds precisely to the 'prayer of quiet' as described in the *Castle*. Teresa's use of *quietud* is vague, and Trueman Dicken very reasonably concludes that she has not yet, in the *Life*, developed a coherent and accurate idea of quiet as strictly mystical passivity. Dicken takes the phenomenon of 'not daring to move' as characterizing properly passive recollection, the state immediately preceding the prayer of quiet in the later and narrower sense of the *Castle*; since in the *Life* it is used of the 'second water', this cannot strictly be the prayer of quiet.[18] And since the metaphor for the second water still presupposes human agency (the water-wheel must be constructed and set in motion), we must think of this phase as spanning both active and passive recollection, in technical terminology: both the soul's affective strivings, its self-generated feelings of devotion or tenderness, and the grace of God drawing and holding our love independently of meditation and conscious aspiration.

However, this rather distorts Teresa's own emphasis. What is distinctive for her about the second water is precisely that it marks the transition to God's work as opposed to ours. The 'not daring to move' phenomenon, as we have seen, arises from the soul's failure to grasp that its state depends on God's act, not its own stillness. Although this state may be accompanied or punctuated by simple conscious acts of love and thanksgiving, it seems to be, in Teresa's eyes, *essentially* passive. The intermittent aspirations of the will and the undirected workings of memory and understanding happen against the steady background of God's gift of a sense of presence. At least some of the difficulty arises from Teresa's reluctance to see any intermediate stage between active meditation, leading to 'active recollection', Osuna's sense of 'devotion', and God's gift to the will of joy in the divine presence. She was, as Dicken argues exhaustively, very unclear about the place and nature of 'passive recollection' when she wrote the *Life*. The second water represents a dramatic diminution of the awareness of effort in prayer and thus has much in common with what I earlier called the 'acquired passivity' commended by others — a form of prayer in which there is a specific attempt to still or empty the mind, rather than struggle to form ideas. Because Teresa is so loth to allow that there is a place for this, the diminution of effort is for her the effect of a direct grasping by God. Thus, as we have seen, there is no decision to drop meditation *before* the experience of this direct grasping, only a decision not to restart it when it has been overtaken by God's gift. For others, like St John, the transition from active meditation to expectant receptivity happens as we respond to the working of God gradually 'blocking' efforts to meditate; as this happens, we learn to silence the mind's striving (even if we cannot wholly stop its activity). For Teresa, there is no intermediate stage of willed receptivity; and so she strongly underlines God's part in this transition, not trusting the soul to be sufficiently self-aware to judge when meditation must stop: hence the telescoping of all the early stages of prayer beyond meditation, and the rather confusing stress on passivity and *quietud* in the second water.

To sum up: all Teresa wants to do here is to identify a state of prayer in which we sense ourselves 'anchored' in the presence of God, quite independently of or disproportionately to our efforts, a sense powerful enough to make sustained reflection impossible. In the loosest sense, our wills are 'united' with God's in such an experience, but we cannot yet say that God is the exclusive and abiding object of the whole mind. The question of whether or not this is 'mystical' is unhelpful, since Teresa does not use the term in the strict sense of later Catholic analyses; she obviously sees it, however, as the beginning of that mystical theology which is the direct communication of truth from God to us. And although it is true that the image of the water-wheel still assumes human labour of some sort, Teresa uses it (14.1) to characterize a state in which action alternates with rest. The mechanism has been set up: give it a turn and the water will flow. In fact, it is *not* a very apt image for the condition in question as there is no real and regular alternation of divine and human action, no cranking of the wheel by effort which allows grace to flow. If the image works at all, it is simply by providing something intermediate between unmitigated labour and comprehensive passivity, the sense of a cessation from *effort* without a complete cessation of *activity* (since memory and understanding are still liable to wander off doing things). It is not the only occasion when Teresa's metaphysical structures creak under their load.

Difficulties of interpretation do not cease when we come to her third stage, in which the garden is watered by a stream channelled through it. Teresa calls this phase 'the sleep of the faculties' (16.1), an expression that has been the despair of several commentators. Although something similar appears in Bernardino de Laredo,[19] it is hard to see anything much in common between the two users. Laredo seems to think of his *sueño de las potencias* as a *prelude* to the state of passive recollection—a silencing (by the will) of the mind's concern with creatures. Teresa, on the other hand, treats the 'sleep' as a state of quite extreme 'interference' with the ordinary exercise of the mind's powers: 'the faculties neither fail entirely to function nor understand how they function' (16.1). There is a marked intensification of the sense of delight, so much so that the soul does not know whether to laugh or cry (ibid.). Words may pour out, songs or poems may form themselves (16.3, where Teresa compares this to what she imagines David must have felt when playing his harp and praising God); profound restlessness and dissatisfaction are experienced, the longing to suffer for God and to die, to be free of the agonizing sense of the contradiction between God's glory and the everyday world of imperfection and sin and attending to the body's need (16.4). Clearly, this is a stage at which initiative is taken completely out of our hands.

However, Teresa also makes it plain that she does not think our human subjectivity is *wholly* absorbed here: we know what is going on, we can be astonished to see ourselves in such a state. The 'faculties', as she says (16.1), are working, but in a way we cannot make sense of. This is why (16.1, 6) we may seem to ourselves to be mad: we are dramatically out of control. Perhaps this is why Teresa calls this state a 'sleep', though this is not a very obvious image for a condition of some tension and hyperactivity; when we are asleep, the mind is working, but in a way we cannot control or grasp. If we compare what she says here with some of Augustine Baker's descriptions (in his *Confession*) of experiences in his own phase of transition to a new form of prayer, we can find a good many echoes,[20] notably the sense of losing control over what one wants to say. Teresa and Baker are certainly describing something very like 'speaking in tongues'; and this suggests that the violent irruption into 'ordinary' behaviour represented by such a phenomenon gets something of its violence from the fact that it tends to happen to those for whom a *discipline* of passivity has not been customary (Baker had had problems about meditation very similar to Teresa's). Dicken rightly compares this state to a shock inflicted on a physical nerve centre.[21]

What has often confused interpreters (here as elsewhere in the *Life*) is that Teresa makes little or no distinction between the third water as a stage in the spirit's growth and the kind of experiences that she believes to be typical of it. She will say (17.4) that there may be a union here of the vocations of Mary and Martha—a favourite theme of hers, though she attaches it to a variety of states and stages. The soul is content, even eager, to engage in practical works ('charity and business affairs') where before, in the second water, it was afraid to stir for fear of upsetting the delicate equipoise of its prayer; but it is aware that its real focus is elsewhere. 'It's as though we were speaking to someone at our side and from the other side another person were speaking to us; we wouldn't be fully attentive to either the one or the other.' This may not make for the most efficient conduct of charity or business, the reader may feel; but Teresa's interest seems to be in the fact that one can be almost subliminally aware of the divine pressure or the divine grasp with a consciousness that is also dealing with other data at the same time. The divine pressure is always 'in the corner of the eye', as we might say, and constantly on the point of spreading more widely into our awareness with all the disorienting consequences already mentioned.

In other words, the experience of 'madness', exhilaration, intense frustration and restlessness, not knowing whether to laugh or cry, is typical of the third water, but does not exhaustively define it. There is no contradiction in describing a phase in which the disorienting consciousness of God is always around and liable to take over, and yet one in which that consciousness not only coexists with but in some sense sharpens up our awareness of practical duties. What has changed between the second and third stages, for Teresa, is really the degree of our confidence in being held by God. In the second water, we felt we had to guard the 'quiet' given by our own stillness, not yet fully realizing how little it depended on us. In the third water, there can no longer be any doubt that God is at work and in control; we see effects in our lives so utterly disproportionate to merit or effort that we cannot suppose we are responsible. We can only be humbly grateful (17.2–3). Thus, in Teresa's own phrase, God gives 'leeway' (17.3) to the consciousness—freedom to recognize what is going on and to act in a whole variety of ways, by clarifying the fundamental *controlling* presence of the divine act.

Teresa wants to say (ibid.) that there is a 'union of the whole soul' with God in this phase but knows that this cannot be quite right. It is the will that is primarily united. When the other faculties fully register this, they are in some sort overcome by the fact and, fleetingly, have God for their object, with the consequences described in chapter 16—perceptibly 'abnormal' states of feeling and consciousness. In fact, she attempts to distinguish three levels of union here. The most elementary is the Martha-and-Mary condition in which the will is more or less continuously attracted to and held by God, while memory and intelligence do their necessary business. The most complete is the consuming 'madness' of comprehensive awareness of God. But, in 17.5–7, Teresa identifies an intermediate stage: the will is held by God, the understanding is occupied with God (though in a dazed and unsystematic way), but the memory continues to throw up distracting images to try and recover the company of the understanding. Precisely because the understanding refuses to co-operate, these images remain disconnected, fleeting, and, 'like little moths at night', extremely annoying, though incapable of doing serious damage. There is nothing much to be done about this, alas, since only God can finally capture the memory and unite it to the divine life. It is, incidentally, important to realize that memory and 'imagination' are bound together; this helps a little when we come later to examine her distinctions between the intellectual and the imaginative in visionary experiences.

Throughout chapters 11 to 17, Teresa has been struggling to identify a pattern in her experience: more particularly, her experience *after* the breakthrough described in chapters 9 and 10. However, looking back, she sees similar phenomena at an earlier stage (4.7) before the spiritual loss of nerve she sees as having clouded most of her first twenty-odd years as a nun. The results are vivid and suggestive, but not completely successful—chiefly because the brilliant image of the four methods of irrigation does not correlate all that easily with the distinctions she wants to make between different levels and kinds of experience in prayer. The second and third waters are a continuum rather than two clearly distinct stages, and their subdivisions take some untangling. She rightly sees the whole process as one in which God's initiative gradually takes over from ours—gradually, though also in 'leaps' of intensification. Because she is disposed to see God's initiative as *essentially* something interrupting our habitual activity, her analysis of the stages of growth— over and above the very serviceable fourfold outline provided by the irrigation metaphor—depends rather too heavily for comfort or clarity on her own impression of being interrupted, overtaken or held by God's agency. And these difficulties are nowhere more evident than when she attempts (18–22) to deal with the 'fourth water': the highest state, as she believes, of receptivity to God.

UNION AND ECSTASY

Up to the fourth and final level, Teresa says (18.1), the created subject is still *doing* something, even if it is only registering with wonder the gifts that are being given; in the final stage, we enter upon a prayer in which self-awareness itself is suspended, at least to the extent that, in prayer, it becomes quite impossible to verbalize what is going on, to be in any way distanced from what is happening. This is what she will here call 'union': a fairly natural projection from the way she has been using the term throughout as a gauge of the increasing degree and scope of absorption felt by the mind (or 'soul' or 'spirit'—Teresa declares firmly at 18.2 that she cannot see what the difference really is). This comprehensive union is a kind of 'swoon' (18.10), involving a degree of physical numbness or anaesthesia; initially it is a brief occurrence, though it may eventually be as long as half an hour. Predictably it is intellect and memory that weaken first and return to something like their usual workings (18.12): over a period of some hours, there may be an oscillation between complete and incomplete absorption, however, since intellect and memory remain dazed and disoriented and are relatively easily drawn back into 'union'. Strictly speaking, of course (as Teresa recognizes in 18.14), the faculties are still *there*, still working, but are not objects to themselves as they normally are: in contrast to their usual state, they are intensely conscious and not at all conscious *of* that intensity.[22] And it seems from 18.15 that they are conscious above all of the omnipresence of God: that is, the objects that present themselves to the ordinary processes of the mind are grasped simply as signs of God, not held on to as things in their own right.[23]

From this state flow emotional consolation (there may be unconscious shedding of tears, a phenomenon widely paralleled in the literature of spirituality, and always contrasted, as here, with tears of sorrow for sin) and moral resolution (19.1-2); and no less importantly, the urge to communicate the experience of such uncovenanted generosity. Since the soul's needs are so fully met, it has no fear of giving away (19.3). But this does not mean that the soul is beyond vulnerability. Teresa knows that after her early advances in prayer and her occasional experiences of absorption, she continued to lead a life of self-pleasing (19.13-14). 'Union' does not mean perfection; virtues and discernment have still to be worked out, and there is a continuing need for direction and discussion (19.15). Teresa yet again walks the familiar knife-edge of insisting upon both her openness to the Church's challenge and critique and her confidence in the presence of God's agency as the mainspring of her eagerness to pass on her experience. She refuses to 'canonize' the experience of absorption as the solitary goal of the life of faith.

However, she is abidingly fascinated by the dramatic and unusual in her experience; and the twentieth chapter of the book is a phenomenology of 'mystical' effects that has drawn rather disproportionate attention since its composition. Beyond 'union' lies 'ecstasy' or 'rapture': not simply the suspension of the faculties in stillness, but a sense of *physical* involvement in the inner process that Teresa describes as a sensation of being irresistibly lifted from the ground (20.3–7) — being weightless and deprived of the power to move of one's own accord (20.18). She clearly believed she was physically levitating and needed to be held down (20.5), but most of what she says is compatible with strong, vertiginous physical feelings generated by shock, by unusual or sudden changes of posture, and other factors, feelings reported by those whose ordinary physical rhythms have been unconsciously affected by profound absorption. That we are dealing with unusual and striking effects of 'spirit' on 'body' cannot be doubted (I shall allow the dualistic language to stand for the time being), but I do not think this passage or comparable passages have any clear evidence to offer about the phenomenon of levitation.

Teresa continues with a most interesting account of the sensations supervening after such experiences. The ending of 'rapture' brings with it a sense of total desolation and abandonment, a lassitude and misery that affects the body as much as the soul (20.9). Teresa is quite clear that this is no less given by God, because she knows it is not self-generated. Here God is communicating the divine life paradoxically, she suggests, by showing what emptiness there is apart from God. It is a crucifixion 'between heaven and earth' (20.11): the soul cannot give its attention to anything but God, yet God is not 'there' for it. This state, which produced in Teresa acute physical tension and exhaustion (20.12), becomes more and more common as rapture becomes less usual; and it brings with it a longing for death (20.9), both in order to see God at last and in order to be relieved of constant agonizing discomfort. At the same time, the soul (or at least the 'superior part' of it) is fully aware of this as a grace (20.15), as a sharing in the cross (20.15), a way of purification (20.16).

This state is 'more than rapture' (ibid.), and it is now, at the time of writing, Teresa's most usual experience of prayer, so it seems. It obviously has something in common with the passive night of the spirit as described by John of the Cross, though it would be wrong to make a hasty and total identification. John's night follows not a period of regular ecstatic experience but the steady self-attrition of the 'active night', the disciplined refusal of specific objects by the mind and will. More importantly, for John the passive night is part of the transition from the illuminative to the unitive level in prayer: it marks the movement from a condition in which we are being gradually educated to understand the greatness of God to that in which we are habitually at home with God. Only when God has become wholly and terrifyingly a stranger to us, can we 'know' God otherwise than as a projection of our wants; only when we so know God can we be at one with God in truth. This dialectic is not something that comes naturally to Teresa; and she seems largely to identify union with the transition which *precedes* this painful and desolate prayer, the movement into a phase of regular and dramatic suspension of all mental faculties. In fact, this vivid account of spiritual desolation is one of the most important grounds for concluding that Teresa's idea of 'union' in the *Life* remains unclear. Quite apart from the remarkable fact that she can speak of rapture or ecstasy as higher and better than union (20.1), it is evident that the word is being used not of the final goal of the entire life of prayer but of a specific sense of comprehensive absorption of the mind. While Teresa is free to use what terminology suits her, of course, this particular convention is confusing. It does, however, bring into focus the pervasive problem of the *Life*: it is brilliant and clear as individual phenomenology; strained and muddled as a structural map of Christian growth. It is no accident that the ultimate stage of prayer here described is the tormenting tension of chapter 20. We have not, despite the tidiness of the fourfold irrigation metaphor, reached a full overview.

Teresa is aware of the incompleteness of what she has so far articulated. Apart from the insistence that growth in the virtues is still going on, there are some very significant observations in chapter 22 that develop the remarks in chapters 20 and 21 about this desolate prayer as a sharing in the cross. Chapter 22 very firmly contradicts what Teresa had read or been told by various authorities about the need to abandon explicit reflection on the humanity of Jesus as an 'advanced' level in prayer. She would have found in Laredo's *Ascent of Mount Sion* the injunction to pass from the 'truth' of Christ's humanity to the 'goodness' of his divinity, retaining only a 'tacit' memory of the humanity, with an active turning of the mind towards it.[24] Osuna insists that the *body's* task is to follow Christ in his humanity, while the soul 'takes wing' to his divinity;[25] though the latter is impossible without the former, we are left in no doubt of the superiority of 'following' the divine Word. And in the prologue to the *Alphabet*, Osuna has already recommended the abandonment of meditation on the sacred humanity to those who want to be 'perfect'.[26] For the imperfect, the humanity may indeed be a necessary ladder for climbing to God, but, like all other created objects, it will stand in the way of real growth if we continue to be attached to it. Teresa resists. She can, she says (22.1), see the point of putting aside the distraction of sin, or of corporeal objects that simply gratify our most unreconstructed desires. But she refuses to allow that the humanity of Jesus is just a physical object like others (ibid., and 22.8). Of course in 'union' there are no specific objects for the mind; but what the mind must *not* do is struggle not to think of Jesus. On the contrary, insofar as the mind can do anything at all, it should try to keep Jesus — especially the crucified Jesus — before itself. Not to do this argues a lack of humility, 'wanting to be Mary before having worked with Martha' (22.9), and imperils progress (22.5). We are held back because we need the *companionship* of Jesus: we can make no progress in our trials unless we see the suffering Jesus in solidarity with us in our pain (22.6–7).

'We are not angels but we have a body' (22.10). Tacitly correcting Osuna's notion that the soul should properly be joining in angelic worship,[27] Teresa insists that, if we are to make any sense of the contradictions in our experience, the struggle to maintain awareness of God in the middle of pain, dryness and busyness, we must turn to Christ in his human weakness. What he accepts, we can accept. It is ridiculous to want to be what we are not: toads cannot fly, she observes drily, however much they might want to (22.13) — perhaps a barb aimed at Osuna's liberal use in the *Alphabet* (17.5) of the language of the soul 'flying' (which is 'much easier and carries us further in a shorter time'). Osuna and others may talk of a short way to God by abandoning meditation on the man Jesus, but, while Teresa allows (22.2, 11) that there may be a 'short cut' for some by this route, she sees no obvious path except constant thinking about Jesus that will truly secure humility.

On this matter, Teresa never changed her mind; we shall see later on how these remarks in the *Life* become the foundation of a wider and deeper incarnational theology of prayer in her mature works. But for the time being two comments should be made on the place of these observations here in the *Life*. First, they are one more example of that sustained hostility to *technique* that Teresa has already shown—technique, that is to say, aimed at a deliberate elevation of one's level of prayer. The policy of not thinking about Jesus, like the policy in general of emptying the mind, is trying to do what God alone can do: suspend our mental activity. Thus her enthusiasm for the sacred humanity as expressed here reinforces her overall argument—that she has not sought extraordinary experiences but had them thrust upon her—and the fact that she experiences visions of Christ in turn reinforces her confidence that she is right not to abandon interest in the sacred humanity (22.4) and thus supports the general correctness of her spiritual policy (or deliberate non-policy). A sceptic might detect a touch of circularity here, but that would be unjust: the main point is that the divine irruption, here as earlier, leads to a deeper acceptance of, not discontent with, the constraints of the present: that is, to humility and ecclesial obedience. The second point is that we should not exaggerate the gulf between Teresa and her tradition or her mentors. It is true that she does disagree; but she is *not* recommending that the mind simply go on meditating discursively, reasoning about Jesus. The traditional caveats about the humanity of Jesus are often directed more at this than at what Teresa defends, which is the regular use of some simple visual representation of Jesus (22.4; cf. W 26 and, for a fuller discussion, C VI, 7, which clarifies the distinction between keeping Christ before one's eyes, and meditating formally on his life). Here as elsewhere, Teresa in effect defines a kind of 'lay' piety, non-cerebral and non-technical, as a kind of middle way between the intellectual activity of meditation and pure contemplative passivity. As we shall see in the next chapter, this is very much the tenor of the whole of *The Way of Perfection*.

Her Christocentric concern thus leaves the way open for a fuller integration of the pattern she has begun to sketch; she knows, at some level, that the end of the story cannot be either rapture or desolation alone. And her earlier reconversion in response to an image of the suffering Christ that called out her compassion bears fruit in what was to be a lifelong sense of companionship between Christ and the suffering Christian. Tantalizingly, this is as far as she goes in the *Life*. Chapter 22 marks the end of her 'theoretical' section, and she returns to the detail of her life in the critical period leading up to the foundation of St Joseph's. Most of the detail of this need not concern us here. But we should certainly note the way in which the earlier sections of the *Life* have prepared the ground for the last seventeen chapters. Teresa has stressed her frailty and fallibility on the one hand, and the irresistibility of her experience on the other; she has also underlined (22.9), in a Christological context, the need for 'human support' — the fellowship and criticism and nurture needed by the embodied soul for its growth. She now relates at length how she sought this support, and how both her frailty and the authority of her experience became manifest to her friends and directors. If chapters 1 to 10 describe God's victory over Teresa's weakness, 23 to 40 set out God's victory *through* Teresa's weakness over the scepticism and hostility of the religious establishment, and how this victory in turn overcomes Teresa's own doubts and scruples.

A certain amount of space is given in these chapters to attempts at analysing the nature of the 'favours' granted by God to Teresa, in particular the 'locutions' (verbal communications) and visions that were a regular feature of Teresa's experience up to her death, continuing even when 'rapture' ceased. She is trying to explain herself to people who are only too well aware of the rich possibilities of self-deception in the spiritual life, and so treads cautiously, herself drawing attention to the danger of illusion. On the subject of locutions, she begins (25.1) by stating firmly that she is not thinking of words heard by the ears, but sentences presented, clearly and completely, to the mind in such a way that we cannot block out awareness of them as we can with ordinary sounds. There can be no question of such things being composed by the intellect; these communications are not in any way under our control, and occur at times when the intellect is otherwise dazed and liable to woolgathering (25.3–5). Too much is said, too rapidly and clearly, to be attributable to the calculations of a disoriented mind, and although we may grasp instantly the sense of what is being said, its import can baffle the understanding for days on end (25.9). Most importantly of all, however, is the knowledge that God's words in some sense effect what they are about: '[the words] the Lord speaks are both words and works' (25.3). They make the soul receptive to whatever divine purpose is being communicated; they are always — as we might say — 'performatives'. It is relatively easy to see when someone is deluded or deluding others, as they will claim these communications as comparable to ordinary physical hearing,[28] and treat them as easily and unambiguously understood (25.9). Authentic communications

bring peace and assurance; diabolical counterfeits produce unsettlement: which is one reason why locutions challenging doctrine or contradicting scripture are easily recognized as false (25.3, 6, 10–13).

As in earlier passages, Teresa makes a rather sharp disjunction
between divine activity and planned or conscious human activity,
with nothing much in between. The phenomenon she describes has
much in common with 'prophecy' as understood in modern charismatic contexts, and perhaps with the experience of clear and complex verbal units being 'heard' in dreams or drug-induced states.
Looking at such things, it is hard not to see them as recompositions
of available mental material, even when there is no active composi-
tional work or intention to do such work involved. Teresa's locutions, as she records them especially in her *Spiritual Testimonies*, are
generally words of reassurance (often using scriptural phraseology),
encouragement to undertake some project, or, more rarely, rather
generalized predictions of the future. One case (T 36, from 1575) is
particularly interesting: Teresa receives divine sanction, in both
vision and locution, for her sense of special spiritual intimacy with
Gracián and is encouraged to make a personal vow of obedience to
him. It seems plain that much of all this is indeed Teresa's own
'work', though not in any sense she would have recognized. But to
say this[29] is not to write off these experiences, or to say Teresa was
deceived. She was confident of her mission; and the experience of
locutions generally follows the period in which this confidence was
being forged in the sense pervading her whole experience of being
accepted and authorized by God. These communications are at their
most regular in the years when she is most active in the Reform and
in the struggles surrounding it. It makes perfect sense to say that
her awareness of her own authority in these events was a matter of
grace, the gift of a profound serenity in the love of God, while at
the same time seeing her locutions as an unconscious crystallizing
and projecting of this security. Early experiences of locutions produced some conflict and alarm (24.5), because she was becoming
aware that her God-given confidence was beginning to produce
stresses in relation to her confessors: at this point she needed to give
clear form to the 'givenness' of her security, yet knew at some level
that this would also sharpen these stresses. Locutions were thus both
necessary and frightening for her. But as her overall experience is
vindicated in the ways described in the *Life*, locutions can come
more freely and fearlessly. In short, it is possible to grant both that
these experiences are the fruit of a life lived in grace and that they

are in some degree the creation of her own need, and therefore vulnerable and fallible (T 36 most poignantly expresses Teresa's need, as poignantly as her correspondence with Gracián).

We shall be returning to the question of visions, and Teresa's careful distinctions between varieties of vision, when we look in more detail at *The Interior Castle*. I have paused here to consider what she has to say about locutions because this discussion appropriately draws together some of the main strands in our examination of the *Life*. Teresa's purpose, through the whole of this remarkable book, is to vindicate her sense of authority — her freedom both to reconstruct the corporate life of her Order and to discuss and instruct in matters of prayer. Both for herself and for her sympathetic but critical readers, theologically trained and wary of all claims to individual spiritual authority, she needs to show that her history is one in which her own effort and aspiration are profoundly weak and confused, so that her present strength and purposefulness cannot be ascribed to wilful spiritual ambition. This has the distorting effect of driving a very firm wedge between divine and created action, so that what God does must regularly be represented as overriding or interrupting what human beings do; and what is not humanly controlled must be acknowledged (after due discernment of its compatibility with doctrine and scripture) as coming from God. Such assumptions make it hard for Teresa to disentangle her attempt to describe a pattern of divine working, applicable in some sense to all souls, from her struggles to describe and organize her own unusual experiences.

Yet so much here pulls in a different direction. She insists upon the companionship of Christ, in joy and desolation, as the central fact in the growth of the soul in virtue, quite over and above the dramas of rapture or vision; she seems to associate at least one sort of ecstatic experience with the sense of God present in all things; and she recognizes that the experience she calls 'union' is an induction into a longer process of human growth. In her later writings her task will be to work all these insights into a pattern larger than the structure offered in the *Life*. And her ability to carry through this task is bound up with two factors in particular. The first is simply her own growing maturity, her ability to rethink and criticize her ideas without anxiety; this was nurtured by her small army of loyal and supportive but candid confessors and friends, as well as by her well-founded sense of success in the enterprise of reform she had undertaken. The second is to do with the audience for which she writes: *The Way of*

Perfection and *The Interior Castle* are written not primarily for confessors or inquisitors but for her sisters in religion. She feels free to be more dogmatic on some matters or less discreet. Above all, she has nothing to defend here except her vision of the Carmelite and Christian life as it might be. The *Life* has done its job, and, in its aftermath, she is able to take a longer and more detached look at her experience — which itself deepens and changes over the years. To understand that the *Life* is indeed a story of God's victory in Teresa, we must read the work in the perspective of the freer and more searching writings that followed the fruits of victory.

Notes

1   *Spiritual Testimonies*, 1 and 3.

2   A former Canon of Avila and acquaintance of Teresa's. This conversation may have occurred in 1561, but most scholars follow a chronology more in accord with the phrasing of T 58, and place it after the completion of Teresa's first draft: that is, in 1563 or 1564. Yet Teresa writes as though Salazar were the first to propose an 'autobiography', and the possibility of an earlier meeting should not be ruled out.

3   Teresa recognizes this at the end of *The Way of Perfection* (42.6), where she advises anyone interested in reading the *Life* to approach Báñez.

4   T. S. Eliot, *Little Gidding*, 46–7.

5   Victoria Lincoln's apparent interpretation of this episode and of the events at Becedas (*Teresa, a Woman. A Biography of Teresa of Avila*; Albany, NY, 1984) seems to fly in the face of what Teresa actually says, and to underrate the seriousness of such an affair in the climate of Teresa's age and culture.

6   See above, pp. 29–31.

7   Dates of publications in Mary Giles's introduction to her translation of Osuna's *Third Spiritual Alphabet* (London and Ramsey, NJ, 1981), p. 8. Giles does not mention the explanation for the remarkable hiatus in publishing, and ignores entirely the Inquisition's attitude to Osuna's other works — though she is right to say that Osuna *in his lifetime* had no problems with the tribunal.

8   These are described in the thirteenth treatise of the *Alphabet* (pp. 337–59 in Giles's translation). Relatively few discussions make it clear how Teresa modifies Osuna for her own purposes, or even flatly contradicts him; for a good brief account of this, see Tomás Alvarez and Jesús Castellano, *Teresa de Jesús enséñanos a orar* (Burgos, 1982), pp. 138–41. Further discussion in J. Baudry, 'Thérèse d'Avila contre la recherche du "vide mental"', *Carmel* 3 (1978), pp. 205–18.

9   *Alphabet* 13.3, p. 346.

10 Apparently before the onset of her first serious illness in 1538.

11 Deirdre Green, *Gold in the Crucible* (Shaftesbury, 1989), p. 11.

12 It is also used by Laredo in the third book of his *Ascent of Mount Sion*.

13 *Alphabet* 6.2, p. 162.

14 Ibid., 4.5, p. 133; cf. 13.4, p. 354, on recollection before sleep 'so that the interior and exterior senses are motionless': the soul must 'sleep' in this way before the body does.

15 The incident took place in 1576; text in Kavanaugh–Rodriguez III, pp. 359–62.

16 Ruth Burrows, *Guidelines for Mystical Prayer* (London, 1976), p. 98.

17 E. W. Trueman Dicken, *The Crucible of Love. A Study of the Mysticism of St Teresa of Jesus and St John of the Cross* (London, 1963), pp. 164–8 — on Teresa's difficulties with inexperienced and insensitive directors, and the general problems of recognizing this stage in spiritual growth correctly.

18 Ibid., pp. 203–14, esp. pp. 206–7.

19 *Ascent* III.19; see M. Andrés Martín, *Los Recogidos. Nueva visión de la mística española, 1500–1700* (Madrid, 1975), pp. 215–18, on Laredo's views. The second edition of the *Ascent* (1538) seems to accentuate the passive element in recollection itself so that the preliminary phase of 'sleep' appears more clearly as some sort of action. Cf. also Osuna's 'sleep of the soul' (above, note 14).

20 *The Confessions of Venerable Father Augustine Baker OSB*, ed. Justin McCann (London, 1922), pp. 94–7, 101–2 ('uttering and venting forth his foresaid senseless aspirations'). Baker is clear that what he is talking about is an 'active' exercise (p. 101), despite its involuntary nature.

21 *Op. cit.*, pp. 186, 212.

22 'This is it, I think, this is it, right now, the present, this empty gas station, here, this western wind, this tang of coffee on the tongue, and I am patting the puppy, I am watching the mountain. And the second I verbalize this awareness in my brain, I cease to see the mountain or feel the puppy. . . . It is ironic that the one thing all religions recognize as separating us from our creator — our very self-consciousness — is also the one thing that divides us from our fellow creatures': Annie Dillard, *Pilgrim at Tinker Creek* (London, 1974), pp. 78–9.

23 For a discussion of this theme as it appears in St Augustine see Rowan Williams, 'Language, reality and desire in Augustine's *De Doctrina*', *Journal of Literature and Theology* 3 (1989), pp. 138–50.

24 Andrés Martín, *Los Recogidos*, pp. 231–2.

25 *Alphabet* 17.5, pp. 464–6.

26 Ibid., p. 42.

27 Ibid., p. 464: 'Following his divinity is a sublime matter, known to few and carried out by fewer still. It is proper to angelic people who seek for God wherever they go and keep in his presence as though angels. . . . The one who follows the divinity must be the brother of angels, in office as in life.'

28 However, note the experience recorded in L 39.3: 'I heard it with my bodily ears and without understanding a word'.

29 Burrows, *op. cit.*, p. 98: 'so obviously from her own subconscious'.

3

'When books are taken away'
The Way of Perfection

A LIVING BOOK: COMMUNITY LIFE AS TEXT

'When they forbade the reading of many books in the vernacular, I felt that prohibition very much because reading some of them was an enjoyment for me. I could no longer do so since only the Latin editions were allowed. The Lord said to me: "Don't be sad, for I shall give you a living book"' (L 26.5). The Index of 1559 had not, in fact, banned all that many Spanish treatises, but its effect was certainly to put vernacular writing on spirituality under a cloud.[1] Teresa's own *Life* was still enjoying very restricted circulation a year or so after its completion, and, although word of it had spread among her nuns and many were eager to see the text, Báñez categorically forbade her to show it around (Teresa tactfully refers to this prohibition in the prologue to the *Way* and hints at it elsewhere, as in 25.4). However, Báñez obviously felt sufficient confidence in Teresa's judgement on the basis of the *Life* for him to encourage her to offer some teaching about prayer to the new community at St Joseph's in response to the natural demand of the sisters for spiritual reading in the vernacular — a demand somewhat frustrated by the existing climate of disapproval of lay, non-Latinate interest in prayer.

The *Way* is perhaps Teresa's most consciously mischievous book. Its first, uncensored version has more candid expressions than any other of her works of her sharp and often ironic perception of the ecclesiastical institution she lived in. Like the *Life*, it is written in full

78

awareness of the background presence of the Inquisition; but unlike the earlier work, it is conspicuously unapologetic. It is almost as if Teresa, gossiping freely with her sisters, dares the censor to doubt her fundamental orthodoxy. She prefaces the whole book with a statement of unconditional submission and loyalty to 'the Holy Roman Church', inviting the *letrados* who will read it to correct it as they please; and there is certainly no doubt that she meant every word of this. But by writing as she does — with acid comments on clerical and monastic pomposity, blunt rebuttals of misogynistic prejudice, and even thinly-veiled mockery of the Inquisition — she is in effect inviting her censors to recognize that wholehearted obedience to the teaching Church, at least in intention, is not incompatible with a certain scepticism about the conventions and policies of the Church as an empirical institution. It is the same basic point that is being made in the *Life*, but here Teresa's critical perceptions are put forward with little or no attempt at concealment (it is not at all surprising that, by the time the work was first published, she had been told to leave out some of her more pithy and controversial observations). As for the problem of a woman's right to teach about prayer, Teresa deflects any possible criticism in her prologue: the problems she will be tackling are so trivial and elementary, so mundane and widespread, that the learned will have far better things to do than discuss them. But she and her sisters are weak women, susceptible to such small-scale attacks by the devil. Teresa has no qualification but her own history of weakness and temptation, and her loving concern that others should not fall into the same traps. Thus she is in no sense competing with any other authority. In this way she disclaims any intention of writing about the higher reaches of prayer; yet she goes on immediately to say that the *Way* is intended as a digest of at least some of the teaching of the *Life* — which both sisters and censors knew to be rather more than a discussion of mundane or trivial matters. If we recognize here a certain degree of deliberate and almost provocative irony, we shall have an important key to the tone of the whole work. It is a conversation between Teresa and her sisters carried on before a rather suspicious audience; we should expect to find a certain degree of faintly conspiratorial wit, the amused sideways glance to see if the audience is paying attention. Even more than in the *Life* (e.g., 33.5), Teresa insists that she has nothing to fear from any examination of her orthodoxy; but here, in the *Way*, she is writing with the licence of her confessor, with the knowledge that the *Life* has met with at least some qualified approval, and thus with a quite striking detachment and lack of anxiety.

The 'living book' promised to Teresa is, we must assume, the presence of Christ in prayer, giving instruction to the soul. What Teresa sets out to do in *The Way of Perfection* is to make available such a 'living book' to her sisters, by setting out how prayer is itself a learning process. However, the first eighteen chapters (out of 42) deal basically with the rationale of the Carmelite life as a whole; only then do we proceed to general instruction about prayer and the great exposition of the Our Father which occupies most of chapters 28 to 42. She begins (as we have noted in the first chapter of this book) by reminding the sisters of the job they are doing for the whole Church: at a time when the honour of Christ is under attack from heretics it is essential that Christ have good friends (1.2). It is not secular force that can turn back the tide of heresy, but earnest prayer and the life of poverty and devotion (3.1–2). Thus the entire vocation of the sisters is seen in terms of the needs of Church and world (Teresa has sharp words at 1.5 for those laypeople who try to use contemplatives and their intercessions to satisfy their own selfish or material wants: intercession must be set free from trivia); and the prayer for the sake of which the sisters have undertaken their withdrawal and renunciation is impossible without the virtues of Christian community life. If the sisters' calling is to prayer for a 'world in flames' (1.5), their learning of prayer must also be a learning of mutual love, detachment and humility, mortification. Anyone possessed of these virtues will be doing her job even if she does not reach the heights of contemplation; and no one can be a real 'contemplative' without them (4.3).

Thus learning from Christ's 'living book' entails a particular form of shared life: the 'book' is to be found in the conventions of the reformed Carmel. In this sense, learning from Christ is bound up with learning from each other. Teresa's insistence on the necessity for small numbers in her reformed houses here finds a kind of theological foundation: the community must be of a size that does not preclude friendship between all its members. In chapter 4 of the *Way* she attacks disproportionate, 'excessive' love within the community (4.6) — the 'particular friendships' of monastic lore — but the severity of the attack is wholly without reference to any danger from erotic elements in a relationship: it is exclusively to do with the risk of faction. 'Excessive' devotion to one other sister (she thinks women more prone to the failing than men) means being preoccupied with *one* other person's supposed feelings and interests, and committing yourself to defend her against others; and all this is deeply inimical to the harmony of a small group. Of course we find some people more attractive or congenial than others, but our task is to avoid letting such inclinations dictate to us in such a way that we actually become slaves to the whim or temperament of someone else, rather than obedient to God (4.7–8). The greatest dangers arise when sentimental friendship is mixed in with family loyalties (4.7; cf. 9, on family ties), and when the superior is given to favouritism.[2]

In the new Carmel 'all must be friends, all must be loved, all must be held dear, all must be helped' (4.7). Yet Teresa seems to imply that in a different kind of community, with larger numbers, even sentimental friendships are better than none at all (ibid.) — a startling testimony to her conviction of the importance of sheer human support. She returns to the subject in chapter 7, apparently aware that her advice may sound a little contradictory. It is essential 'to take time for recreations' with the community, whatever your scruples: it can be a sign of 'perfect love'.[3] In St Joseph's, of course, there should never be any question of any other kind of love, so there should be no problem (7.7). The message seems to be that, even in a convent where the recreation period is primarily an opportunity for gossip, for the forming and breaking of schoolgirlish attachments, it is important to participate. It is also, after all, an opportunity to offer help and affection to those who need it, whatever the risks, so long as there is discretion in everything that affects religious obedience. Teresa's convoluted syntax and generally awkward expression in these passages underline the fact that she is trying to prescribe for situations she knows to be full of complexities. All sisters should know the basic distinction between merely spiritual love, and that mixture of 'sensual' or natural attraction with spiritual love which is where we are bound to start (4.12; see also the earlier version of this which she abandoned, printed in the notes to the Kavanaugh–Rodriguez translation, pp. 459–61). If we are so anxious to avoid imperfect friendship that we deny our natural need for human support, we shall never learn pure love: genuine spiritual friendship builds on partly sensual foundations, but learns at last to see the loved friend in the light of what God wants for him or her. If this happens, we shall no longer be anxious about what *we* think the friend ought to be, what *we* regard as their welfare, but shall be ready to let them be free before God:[4] and Teresa gives eloquent testimony to her indebtedness to all those who loved her in such a way (7.1-4). If a friendship is not capable of developing like this, it should be cut off (7.4; and cf. chapter 20). In short, Teresa is not attempting to present the religious life as devoid of emotional risk, or legislating for relationships that are made safe by being formalized; she wants her sisters to be capable of adult discernment in their friendships, so that it is more important that they be able to learn how to love someone non-possessively than never to have felt or admitted the pull of ordinary human attraction. Teresa is concerned for the sisters to know the pitfalls of friendship rather than to avoid it altogether.

Chapter 6 has provided a detailed account of what perfect love might be. Teresa's exposition is manifestly in debt to the whole Augustinian tradition of interpreting the proper dynamic of love, learning to love the things of this world in the light of God and for the sake of God — or rather to love God and to take pleasure in the world (rather than, strictly, to love it) for God's sake (6.4). Such love of God frees us from the human longing to be loved by others at all costs, to be consoled or reassured; but the result of this can be that others feel their love is not being properly returned (6.5-7). Those who do not understand such love feel excluded: the holy person's love of God may be thought to rule out 'real' love for human beings (6.7). Teresa handles with skill what was obviously a practical problem in the communities she knew. The mature Christian by loving God is able to accept and rejoice in the concrete and material world, her body and the bodies of others (6.4), but will not treat these as ends in themselves. She will know that she cannot command the love of others as of right, and so will assume that when she is loved, it is God that is being loved in her, *and* God that is loving her in the love of others. Thus she will not feel that someone else's love lays her under obligation to return it in the same coin; and, in fact, *not* being loved as we want to be loved is the greatest benefit we could have in these circumstances. 'All things considered, I sometimes think what great blindness would be involved in this loving to be loved — except when it is a longing to be loved by these folk I'm talking about, who can help us get hold of perfect good things.' (This translation is rather different from the Kavanaugh–Rodriguez version of 6.5, which is misleading at this point; Peers's version has the point clear.)

The mature lover of God knows she does not need what 'ordinary', cosy and semi-sensual love has to offer. She is familiar with the pangs of anxiety that belong to worldly friendship (the wanting to know that I am as important to my friend as she to me), but she has learned how vacuous it is simply to be bound in mutual admiration. We long to be loved in return, but 'however much we have been loved, what do we really get of what we longed for?' (6.7, again retranslated). No other person's love, at the usual human level, will give us the inexhaustible and unconditional focus upon our good that God alone gives.[5] We should want only to be loved for the sake of our spiritual benefit. Does this sound chilly? it would be a great mistake to think so, says Teresa. Those who love us for our spiritual benefit love us more truly and with more energy. Teresa originally wrote, 'with more passion', then had cold feet about this ambiguous word, and substituted 'even without passion'; but 7.1, with its reference to the 'impassioned' character of spiritual love, makes it quite plain what she *wants* to say. Spiritual love is an urgent longing to recreate the loved friend as God wants her to be, and so to secure the friendship for ever. If we are overcome with attraction for someone, yet know that she cares nothing for God, we must know also that the friendship will die with our own deaths. Thus, to care for someone as they are before God is to love them with an 'eternal' love, to love them in the only way not vulnerable to human mortality, and consequently in the only way that can make sense of the impetus to love unconditionally and sacrificially (6.7–9, 7.1–4). This is why we should *want* to be loved spiritually: it is not being loved impersonally, but in a way that is absorbingly concerned with our transformation into the person we might be before God, and a way that admits of no abandonment and betrayal, no anxious haggling, no foreordained conditions.

Perfect love is simply the imitation of the love of Christ (6.9); but, although Teresa can say this, and suggest that perfect love is concerned about giving, not receiving (6.7), it would be wrong to read her as claiming that the perfect lover is a self-sufficient, quasi-divine subject, loving out of the abundance of an inner fullness. Teresa's perfect lover is someone aware, first and foremost, of being causelessly loved by God: like it or not, the lover is primarily and inescapably a receiver of love. And Teresa hints at a further insight which will recur later in her life. God loves the lover and is loved in the lover: the lover will always assume that God is doing the loving in and through her and other lovers, and thus that God must be loving God in our loving relationships, since nothing in us as creatures has a claim to the kind of love God offers. There is in the background an inchoate sense of being caught up in a trinitarian pattern—the love of God for God — which would give an extra dimension to the idea of perfect love as Christlike. We are free to give love, not because we need no love, but because (as in Christ's relation to God the Father) we are already recipients of an eternal love, and any need we might have is met in advance. So our own human relations of love, based on our hunger for affirmation, should develop in such a way that we discover that our profoundest need has been already, eternally, met. Hence our urgent, even desperate, 'need' to be loved by those who love God. 'A good means to having God is to speak with his friends' (7.4). It is pious nonsense to say that, if we know the love of God for us, we no longer need human relations of the creative kind Teresa is trying to describe; on the contrary, to pass beyond the hungry and selfish needs of 'normal' love we *need* to be in love with God's friends, who will give us not what we think we want, a greedy love that mirrors our own, but what we most deeply need in order to be human as God would have us be.

The 'living book' is in effect identical with the life of a healthy community and the lives of Christianly mature persons in it. It is also the life and words of a good spiritual director. Teresa discusses at considerable and candid length the relations between her sisters and their confessors, once again acknowledging possible risks, but encouraging proper intimacy and friendship. The sister must exercise discernment: confessors may be silly or sinful and if you discover one to be such, find someone else, as tactfully as you can (4.13). A bad confessor indulges your failings, even encourages them, and if there is inflexibility in the community about changing confessors, many will find themselves acutely miserable, because the confessor is at odds with their conscience (4.16). The superior should not allow a situation to develop where sisters are afraid to be honest, 'a situation in which if the prioress gets along well with the confessor no one dares to speak either to him about her or to her about him' (5.1). Teresa pleads for liberty to discuss matters of conscience with as many qualified people as possible, and deplores the *amour propre* that exalts the superior's right to impose a single confessor or forbids contacts with members of other Orders (5.1-2). In support of this plea, Teresa points out the sheer diversity of the needs of souls ('one confessor perhaps will not know them all', 5.5), and appeals to the authority of those theologians and prelates who have authorized for St Joseph's the freedom she wants. We can be assured that God will see to it that there will be someone who will love us properly, desiring the best for our souls (ibid.).

Proper love in community involves deep sympathy with the real needs of others (7.5-6), and we must *not* be nervous of the 'natural tenderness' stirred by this, so long as it does not become the kind of sentimental partisanship that destroys corporate life. This is why it is important not to sympathize with self-pity or self-justification. Teresa's chapters on detachment and humility lay a good deal of emphasis on bearing unfair accusations patiently, and she insists that it is no sign of friendship to encourage the self-righteous resentment of someone who (rightly *or* wrongly) believes herself to be suffering unjustly. Our greatest practical service to each other in community is, for Teresa, the mutual destruction of that sense of 'honour' which the very existence of the reformed Carmel is meant to challenge; and so the refusal of sympathy over slights and even slanders is of considerable importance. We are to be consistently helped to find our honour in the friendship of God. (Chapters 12 to 15 deal particularly with all this, and with the problems of monastic hypochondria.[6])

We have seen that Teresa is alert to the different patterns and different requirements of people's spiritual growth. Chapters 16 to 18 spell this out further in a discussion of the different 'perfections' of contemplation and action that begins to recapitulate some of the themes of the *Life*, but with a new concreteness. Pervading all her comments is the fundamental conviction of the *Life* that it is not up to us whether or not we become 'contemplatives' – that is, as Teresa uses the word here, caught up in regular experiences of passivity in prayer: 'this is not a matter of your choosing but of the Lord's' (17.7). God does not necessarily want everyone to be a passive contemplative, certainly not all at the same stage or the same time (someone has to do the practical jobs, as Martha did – an unusually conventional use of the Martha–Mary text for Teresa, 17.5-6): 'if contemplating, practising mental and vocal prayer, taking care of the sick, helping with household chores, and working even at the lowliest tasks are all ways of serving the Guest who comes to be with us and eat and recreate, what difference does it make whether we serve in the one way or the other?' (17.6). The humble sister who plods on patiently with ordinary mental prayer, or just saying words, is not inferior to the one to whom special graces are given (17.3).

Yet for all this admirable counsel, Teresa is reluctant to let go of the idea that 'contemplative' experience is what God must *really* want to give, and there are passages where she seems to come close to saying that not to have experiences like hers is a sign of not being perfectly devoted to God (16.9, 17.3-5, 18.7); certainly the joys of the contemplative will be given to all in heaven (17.7). Contemplation may not be everyone's cup of tea immediately, but the joys of this state can be hoped for by all ultimately. However, we have to bear in mind the quite complex background of Teresa's observations. She is convinced that, in the long run, there can be no distinctions between the degrees of God's grace bestowed upon human souls — there is, as we saw in the first chapter, a definite theological egalitarianism at the heart of her entire vision. So, if God gives exceptional graces, ecstasy and so forth, to some, he must will to give them ultimately to all. But there are three factors making for caution in discussing this. The first is the governing concern of the *Life*: that passive contemplation cannot and must not be actively sought or invited; the second is the related anxiety arising from inquisitorial hostility to the suggestion that passive contemplation might be for all; the third is simply Teresa's pastoral awareness that a sane religious discipline ought not to put pressure on people to generate specific sorts of experience, least of all the dramatic and attractive phenomena Teresa associates with passivity to God. With this last point in view, she adds in chapter 18 a description of the trials attending the contemplative — though characteristically remarking that to be given trials is a testimony to the soul's strength (18.4).

We must desire the best and fullest of God's gifts; but as Teresa turns to discuss the beginnings of prayer in general terms, she recognizes that the desire for God can take pathological forms. God's gift is pure — the refreshing and cleansing water of grace that is the central metaphor of the *Life* (19.2-8); but its effect upon us may be ambiguous. We are imperfectly equipped to tolerate the access of delight that God's love brings: the strain may literally kill us (19.8), if God does not give us the resources to bear it. But we may also find ourselves hungry for pain or even death. God's grace is a shock to the system, and we may feel we are losing our grip on our lives; but this experience may encourage us to try to reproduce and intensify the shock, the pain, the risk of death by techniques of our own, above all by a disproportionate asceticism and abuse of the body. So Teresa warns (19.10) of the dangers of spiritual extremism: if we find we want to die, we must be careful to turn our minds quite deliberately to other things and reflect on how such experience can be opened up to others if we go on living in the desire to serve God. Time for prayer needs to be limited; if the nervous or physical system is under strain, it is time to break off (19.13; compare what is said in *Foundations* 6, about the effects of self-indulgent spiritual reverie combined with inadequate attention to bodily needs).

Teresa has not made her task easy in the *Way*. She is constantly trying to find a point of balance between errors of which she is only too keenly aware. Friendship, but not collusive and partisan affections; contemplation for all, but affirmation for those without the gift; readiness for suffering, and a robust disregard for anxiety about one's health, but severe discouragement of the deliberate neglect of the body or seeking physical pain. The point is that if the Carmelite life is to do its work, it will be inherently perilous in a good many ways. The interest of the *Way* lies precisely in Teresa's candour about the various dangers involved. The Catholic Church must relearn the realities of friendship with God if it is to respond adequately to what Teresa sees as the organized blasphemy of heretics. Friendship with God means the corporate learning of virtue and prayer in a context where the self-regard and obsession with status that stand in the way of virtue and prayer are systematically opposed. The structure of the life of Carmel must be such as to keep all this unfailingly clear, so that lives may be nurtured that speak of true friendship for God; and since friendship with God requires poverty and mutual love, a serious awareness of the human diversity of vocations, willingness to expose oneself to the full force of God's presence and will, and willingness to communicate the effect of this so as to win more friends for God, Teresa needs to keep a great many pieces in play as she attempts to describe her ideal. The stakes are consciously high: it is very clear by the time she moves into her treatment of prayer that she is *not* restricting herself to mundane problems rather than the dangerous issues of prayer; and what the first eighteen or so chapters of the *Way* show us is that in fact the radical exposure to God's will involved in praying seriously is not separable from the structure of the life in which such exposure is made possible. The *Way* is, as Teresa more than once says herself (e.g., 19.1), a disjointed work, but it is not simply a manual for convent behaviour stitched on to a treatise on prayer. If the sisters for whom she writes want a vernacular text on how to draw close to God, they have one to hand in the disciplined relationships of their own houses, in friendship with each other and with right-minded clergy; and it is against this background alone that they will be able to make sense of the disciplines of common prayer as a complementary text of instruction.

THE COMMUNITY AT PRAYER: TERESA ON THE
OUR FATHER

The Carmelite life is an education in prayer; but Teresa is writing for women who are used to being told that they cannot aspire to anything much more than formal verbal prayers without danger and presumption. They need considerable encouragement to be able to resist the warnings regularly heard, which Teresa catalogues (in 21.2) with wit and economy: '"it's not for women, for they will be susceptible to illusions"; "it's better they stick to their sewing"; "they don't need these delicacies"; "the Our Father and the Hail Mary are sufficient"'. Teresa's strategy is, as she has already said (19.1), to address herself to those who are alarmed by the thought of formal meditation of an intellectual kind, to take the most basic and prosaic elements of familiar piety and to show what they may become when used by someone whose imagination and desire are not confined by the satisfying of external criteria alone. It is simply a matter of praying in such a way that the whole self is involved. Teresa advises on what should be said to an unsympathetic questioner (21.10): you should explain that you have a rule of unceasing prayer, and, 'If they tell you that the prayer should be vocal, ask, for the sake of more precision, if in vocal prayer the mind and heart must be attentive to what you say. If they answer "yes" — for they cannot answer otherwise — you will see how they admit that you are forced to practise mental prayer and even experience contemplation if God should give it to you by such a means.'

Teresa sets out to demystify mental prayer. It is not a speciality, let alone an optional extra, for Christians (22.1–2), but simply prayer that is fully conscious of what it is, prayer that recognizes the extraordinary character of what is going on — God becoming accessible to sinful creatures. God listens to us out of a divine 'humility',[7] insofar as we come to God ourselves in humility (22.4), in awareness of the fact that we have no claim, no 'honour' that would compel God's attention. God looks on the *person*, while worldly regard concentrates on income and status (ibid.). This is remarkable, cause for wonder, and to remember this *is* mental prayer: 'don't let the name frighten you' (25.3). Thus, saying the ordinary prayers of all Christians with some degree of imaginative clarity is all that is immediately required from the sisters. They will, of course, be reciting the Church's offices, but Teresa has little to say about this: her 'lay', vernacular and egalitarian interest leads her to stress simply what

Christians as such are bound to say in prayer, 'so that people won't be able to say of us that we speak and don't understand what we are talking about' (24.2).

How then do we begin to say these prayers 'mindfully'? We need solitude, says Teresa (24.4, 5), remembering Jesus' precept and example; we must examine our conscience and express our repentance, making the sign of the cross; and then we must think of Jesus as present with us (26.1). As Teresa develops what this means, we have a vivid insight into what 'meditation' on the humanity of Jesus meant for her: it is a coming to know ourselves *through* Christ. The awareness of Christ is what makes us aware of what is done in prayer. In the world, the wife has to observe and conform to her husband's moods ('See what subjection you have been freed from, sisters!'—26.4); but the spouse of Christ has a husband under her authority, following *her* moods. Christ risen and glorified may be summoned by our joy: Christ in loneliness and torment is there for us in our own suffering. This is some way removed from conventional injunctions to reflect on the humanity of Christ; and what makes it particularly interesting is the assumption that our own awareness of our state of mind dictates what we look for in Christ. However, Teresa is not simply recommending the use of episodes from the gospel as projections or dramatizations of our condition: we summon up the appropriate image of Christ so as to set our feelings in a new context. When we are joyful, we turn to the risen Christ to see what abundance of joy he desires to *give* us; our joy becomes gratitude when related to the overflowing of life that is the joy of Christ. In our sorrow we turn to Christ in pain, and, finding him deserted and alone, we strive to console him as he consoles us.[8] When we find that he turns away from his own suffering both to help us and to help us help him, we shall be ashamed of our self-pity and be strengthened in our resolve to bear suffering with and for Christ (26.4–6). In other words, Christ as companion both affirms and challenges our emotions. There is a significant interplay between identification with Christ and confrontation with Christ.

Teresa's Christ is never simply a symbol of the self. In him we find our humanity fully present, so that we do not have to strip off our human particularity to pray: remember that Teresa is not an advocate of trying to 'still' the mind *before* prayer can begin. But if we begin our prayer by recognizing and accepting our emotional state, by accepting the contingent facts of our changeable mental and affective life, and then locating this in relation to the human contingency of Jesus' experience, our turbulent and variable condition is not suppressed but reordered. We are being encouraged to 'sense' ourselves through the medium of the story of Jesus, and thus to discover a distance from our emotion that is not simply a denial of it. By so relating what we feel to the humanity of Jesus, we relate it to a fundamental action of loving gift; we have to see how feelings like our own can be caught up in a movement of love without being annihilated, and so to open up our affective life to the possibility that through it, as through Christ, God can communicate love.

This is how Teresa deals with the quite complex question of the solidarity of the believer with Christ, a theme which is naturally much in her mind as she discusses the petitions of the Lord's Prayer. Being 'in Christ' is, for her, primarily about the interchange between humanity and God brought about by the Incarnation—a theme central to the thought and imagination of early Christian writers but rather overlaid by some aspects of mediaeval devotion to the suffering, human Jesus.[9] Teresa is not interested in the generating of specific sorts of pious feeling but in how we become the instruments of God's self-communication; for her the fact of Christ's humanity is a fact about the transfiguring of our humanity. The beginning of the Lord's Prayer immediately impresses precisely this upon us: Jesus authorizes us to pray *alongside* himself, saying '*Our* Father'. By thus pronouncing himself our brother he claims for us from the Father that love which the Father has towards him. Teresa indulges in some dramatic play here on the notion of honour: it is natural, inevitable, that Christ as one of us should seek our good; but does he not remember what is due to his family pride? He humiliates himself by coming to earth, but surely he is not going to embarrass his Father by demanding equal treatment for his newfound poor relations (27.3)? Yet Jesus shows us abundantly that he wants only what the Father wants: wildly improbable as it may seem, this 'humiliation' is what God desires.[10] So Christ's unity with us means that Christ will act in our interest; but Christ's unity with God the Father means that this acting in our interest is the Father's will (27.4). Our interest, in practical terms, becomes identical with God's—or, in the terminology used by the contemporary theologian Schillebeeckx, God makes our 'cause' as human beings God's cause in the history of Jesus.[11]

Thus the very words 'Our Father' are the direct articulation of God's gift: by saying them in consciousness of what they mean, we make the gift our own. Here then is a cardinal instance of the necessary unity between vocal and mental prayer. If we say 'Our Father' without some grasp of the magnitude of what is said, we are not merely uttering a truth we do not fully appreciate, we are—at the very least—in danger of uttering a lie. Saying 'Our Father' means, if it means anything, becoming aware of the consequences for our human self-perception of Christ's identification with us, and being ready to realize that self-perception in the concrete reality of our life. This is why Teresa immediately goes on to another diatribe on the subject of honour. If God is our father, we have no ground for making distinctions of lineage, and should boast of no parent but God. So it was in the apostolic community, when the fisherman Peter took precedence over the royal Bartholomew (27.6: Bartholomew's royal lineage is a familiar mediaeval legend). In a way very characteristic of this work, the style of community life is closely bound up with the undergirding theology through the practice of prayer.

This is further reinforced as Teresa turns to consider the words, 'Who art in heaven'. To recognize our intimacy with God in Christ is to know that 'heaven' is not a distance place; heaven has been brought to us because God has come to us. And if God is immediately accessible in this way, we have no reason for any false humility about 'approaching the divine presence'. We must 'speak with him as with a father, or a brother, or a lord, or as with a spouse' (28.3); and this easy familiarity is seen by Teresa as the best means to 'recollection'—here defined simply as collecting the mind's faculties so as to be consciously present to and with the God who is within us. We do not need to make elaborate pictures in our mind of the events of the passion: when we are 'centred' in ourselves through converse with God, through the conscious appropriation of Christ's gifts, we can simply associate ourselves with Christ's self-offering to the Father, and in this way 'meditate' on the passion. As usual, Teresa is speaking to those without any aptitude for conventional meditational exercises: recollection comes as a result of something very like chatting to God—while being conscious all the time of what this rests upon, the gift of Christ. Her concern is that we should develop the habit of conscious companionship with Christ. If we know who it is we are talking to, we shall be arriving at the point to which meditation of a more formal kind is meant to lead (29.5), the kind of communion with Christ that enables God to give us greater and greater fullness of grace. Once again, there is an appeal to the incarnational pattern, though Teresa's phraseology was not congenial to the censors, and the reference was excised. God wants to come-to-be in the smallness of my soul, 'And so he wanted to enclose himself in the womb of his most blessed mother' (28.11). God's absolute freedom is shown in the capacity to be present in limit and constraint, and we then have to learn, bit by bit, how *large* our souls can be if they contain God. God inhabits the soul and, as God makes this presence in us clear to us, also pushes out the frontiers of our 'inner life' to receive more and more of the divine gift: we have to learn, for our part, how to leave space for this freedom to work in us (28.12).

Here the main image of *The Interior Castle* is anticipated (in 28.6 and 9 we already have mention of the 'castle' or 'palace' within). The discovery of the self in and through 'conversation' with Christ is a discovery of the kinship with God bestowed by grace; and this is a discovery of an ever-expanding space of human growth in love and understanding. The turn inwards to find God in the soul—the Augustinian vision explicitly invoked at 28.2—is not a reduction or constriction of the self, but, as for Augustine himself, an expansion and liberation. It is a fatal error to think that we have to leave ourselves and journey to somewhere distant in order to find God. That will only intensify our fragmentedness. We need only to remember God's accessibility, and to try to keep speaking to God: however badly we do this, 'he will understand us as if through sign language' (29.6), and we shall gradually settle and centre ourselves. As in the *Life* the self acquires its sense of worth, of being needed, from reflecting on Christ, so here the self finds its unity, its coherence, in speaking the sort of words proper to a child of God in the constant 'company' of God.

The regular awareness of God's presence, God as one who may constantly be spoken to without anxiety or specialized and intense preparation, is an awareness of being in heaven (being where God is). Thus the prayer, 'Thy kingdom come', is a petition for this sense of the presence of the kingdom of heaven to become habitual so that God's name may be fitly glorified: 'hallowed be thy name' immediately requires the prayer for the coming of the kingdom (30.1–4). It is worth noting that Teresa identifies the kingdom with a state in which we rejoice in the activity of a *shared* praise and a universal holiness (30.5): the stability of our prayer owes much to the sense of its being a common prayer. Something of this may be experienced on earth in the prayer of quiet (30.6; note the implication that this prayer has a corporate dimension, involving some awareness of being borne along by or with the holiness and contemplative perfection of others). Teresa insists (30.7) that there can be a natural transition from recollected conversation with God to the beginnings of contemplation in the strict sense: there may be sisters who dislike the whole notion of contemplation, but if they are conscious of praying vocally with attention, and of that prayer being taken up into Christ's, they are, says Teresa, contemplatives whether they like it or not. It is noteworthy that here and in the chapter on the prayer of quiet that follows, she is less disposed than in the *Life* to describe the prayer of quiet as an irruption into the active life of vocal and imaginative devotion. Natural and supernatural, human activity and divine, shade off into each other as the soul is gradually given a fuller consciousness of God's presence holding and drawing. Here is the expression 'they don't dare stir', just as in the *Life*'s account of the second water, and the description of difficulty in framing words — it may take an hour to get through the Lord's Prayer just once (31.3); here too the reference to Mary and Martha working together in this condition (31.5). And Teresa repeats her caution about trying to hold on to this state by struggling to keep still and quiet, as if the sense of stability and peace depended on us (31.6). It is, in other words, just as much a passive state as in the *Life*, but simply described as something that almost imperceptibly takes over as we develop the habit of Christ-centred and reflective vocal prayer.

'The soul is like an infant that still nurses when at its mother's breast, and the mother without her babe's effort to suckle puts the milk into its mouth in order to give it delight' (31.9).[12] As in the *Life*, the process of nourishment by God goes on in a way more akin to natural processes than to the effort of intellectual discovery. The loving and receptive will shares a house with the noisy and hyperactive intellect, as if in a not very harmonious marriage (31.8), but must on no account waste time and energy trying to control the intellect; it must simply go on with the low-key activities that are possible and appropriate in the condition of *quietud* (compare pp. 59ff. above). Vocal prayer of the kind outlined by Teresa, the slow and thoughtful recitation of familiar words is seen by her as essentially an act of the will, *not* the intellect; and in this condition, where 'quiet' supervenes upon the recitation of prayers, the will is — rather contrary to appearances — the strong, dominant element in us, not the intellect. Because the will is being steadily fed, it is gaining strength, and this strength will eventually, without deliberate effort, attract the rest of the fractious interior family of the human soul. We are a long way from what we usually understand by 'will' in our own age. Teresa is not talking about the capacity to make and effect decisions, nor even about the active energy of the ego; 'will'—as again, in the whole Augustinian tradition—is the faculty by which we *take up an attitude* to what is around us, dispose ourselves for this or that kind of relation. Thus it has a reflective (what we might think of as an 'intellectual') component insofar as it involves perceiving and intelligently assessing our situation. But, in contrast to intellect in its pure state, the words that the will may find to say will necessarily articulate a relationship in which our desires and policies, our wanting and hoping are bound up. This is what 'attitude' and 'disposition' mean, and words like this often serve far better than 'will' in telling us what Teresa has in mind.

This is why the will is in fact, if not in appearance, so strong in the state of *quietud*. The discursive and organizing mind may run around in boredom, euphoria or panic, while words are spoken and attitudes reinforced from further down in the psyche, where some kind of direction of desire, some basic inclination, has already begun to be fixed. The 'intellect' does not and cannot create such an inclination and may be puzzled and frustrated by it: what the intellect finds to say can certainly not be guaranteed to articulate what is most central in the self. And this helps to explain why Teresa insists that the appropriate words for the state of quiet are the simplest ones—words not chosen or planned, but *given*, like the words of common, everyday Christian devotions, the Our Father and Hail Mary.

Her discussion of *quietud* here is really a filling out of the idea of heaven within us, the kingdom of God established in the soul. Thus the opening petitions of the Lord's Prayer form a close unity: God in Christ gives us intimacy and kinship with the life of the Trinity (so that, as in 27.7, we, like Christ, are bound to the Father by the Holy Spirit), and so we are, in a very straightforward sense, the place where God is—heaven; finding God more fully is finding that heaven of loving presence within us; and the prayer of quiet is simply our entry, by God's gift, into the reality of God's action, God's love and self-giving, which we have both acknowledged and actualized in saying 'Our Father'. As our fundamental wanting of God becomes stronger and simpler, it becomes readier to be held and nourished by what it seeks and 'inclines' to. The next petition builds upon all this, leading us to reflect on how the giving of God *to* us is given *in* or *through* us, 'once the earth has become heaven' (32.2).

We know from the life of Christ something of what this involves. To be united with God in such a way that our earth is heaven is to be exposed to suffering. God's love for us is too great for us to be given anything less than is given to Jesus, and to Jesus is given the grace of *giving* grace by his human agony. For the Father's will to be done means for the world to be set free from sin, and this is achieved only by the cross. Thus the measure of our identification with God's love for the world is our readiness to suffer, to take the cross (32.6–7). But, as we have seen earlier in the *Way*, we are not to seek out suffering as a technique: the acceptance of the risk involved in vocation is really the fruit, not the cause of God's relation with us in *quietud*; and, although we have in Jesus the assurance that suffering for God's sake is rewarded, this reward can only be seen as the intensifying of a gift already given, not something we earn by piling up planned, deliberate self-mortification. God's will is not that we should suffer, never mind how; so it is no use offering God the kind of suffering we can manage and control (Teresa will have more to say about this in the third mansion of *The Interior Castle*). God's will is that we become agents of love, and this is sufficiently difficult and risky for us to be sure that it will involve suffering, the kind of suffering we *cannot* control. It is no use choosing crosses that look congenial, because the point of the true bearing of the cross is the displacing of self-oriented desires by openness to God.

Chapter 33 begins with precisely this point, that God's will is for the concrete good of human beings, and is painful because we are slow to let go of our mental and material comfort. The will of God is that the rich should sacrifice their luxury when others are starving; that the carping and gossiping person should understand the obligation to love the neighbour; that the independent and self-indulgent monk or friar or nun should remember that he or she is vowed to poverty, and that religious vows are not awkward school rules to be evaded or kept with no more than minimum standards, but the definition of an integrity of life that should challenge the whole Church (33.1). So – unsurprisingly – doing God's will, with all the difficulty involved, is firmly placed in the context of just and loving community life, the context of the whole of *The Way of Perfection*.

This wider context is what Teresa goes on to discuss from a rather different angle in what follows. We could not begin to do God's will without the faithful presence of Christ before the mind's eye, Christ praying with us to the Father, Christ sharing our human experience; but this presence is not just a matter of what our individual devotion can discover. Jesus knows our weakness and our need; he desires, with God's own desire, to go on being with us as he was with us in the incarnate life, in humility and vulnerability. This is the divine desire we encounter in the sacrament of the Eucharist: the sacrament itself becomes for Teresa the primary and most immediate sign of God's unconcern with honour and self-protection, the sign of the divine longing to be unconditionally at hand for us. 'He allows himself to be crushed to pieces every day' (33.4), and is exposed to the blasphemy and insults of heretics (those semi-mythical 'Lutherans' who so preoccupy Teresa in this work). Christ in the Eucharist is our daily slave; here above all we discover what the sovereign will of God is.

Teresa devotes two more chapters to the Eucharist, the longest sustained meditation on the subject in any of her writings. She has no doubt at all that the petition 'Give us this day our daily bread' referred only to the sacrament: 'Would [Christ] get us involved in something so base as asking to eat?' (34.2; the censors were evidently not happy about this). But her certainty has to do, more than anything else, with the conviction that – since the Eucharist is so preeminently the sign of God's desire to be with us, God's humility and faithfulness in being unconditionally accessible to us – we should expect to find it at the heart of a prayer that is so pervaded by the acknowledgement of this divine availability from its first words onwards. She is not by any means dismissing the importance of real bread for the hungry, but stressing that to ask God for this at this central moment in the Lord's Prayer sounds as if it is casting doubt on God's ability to provide for our material wants (34.4–5).

She speaks of Christ's presence in the sacrament as the enactment *now* of the events narrated in the gospels (34.8). At Communion, we are *not* to picture these events to ourselves as we might otherwise do, nor should we in our prayers after Communion use a visible image of Christ: such images are helpful when we lack the sense of Christ's presence. But after Communion we have the tangible assurance of that presence, in the event that has just been transacted (34.8–11; on pictures of Jesus, cf. 26.9 for a recommendation that we habitually carry an image of Jesus to remind us of his accessibility and to encourage us to talk to him). Teresa gives us a moving glimpse of her own eucharistic devotion in 34.6–7, a passage which throws some light on her comments in the *Vejamen* on John of the Cross's spiritual counsels (above, pp. 57–8). Christ's availability to all, and especially to the sinner, is what she perceives in the Eucharist; even when she has no devotional feeling about this, she remains wholly confident that she is in Christ's company no less than was Mary Magdalene in the Pharisee's house (Luke 7:36–48; Teresa naturally takes for granted the traditional identification of the unnamed woman in this passage with the Magdalene). So, as she says in the *Vejamen*, Christ does not wait for us to arrive at integral contemplation before making himself available: and the public and exposed nature of the eucharistic presence is here implicitly presented as a corrective to any idea that Christ's presence depends on our effort or virtue. There may be other occasions when devotion comes more obviously and easily, but thanksgiving after Communion must remain the very centre of our spirituality (35.2), focusing all the themes of the gospel.

We know that Teresa herself found post-Communion meditation the heart of her prayer. Even when in later life she was experiencing fewer 'raptures', she records in the *Spiritual Testimonies* a considerable number of occasions when communications and intellectual visions occur in the time after Communion (ten such references from 1570 onwards). One of the most remarkable of these (52, probably to be dated in 1575) takes the eucharistic theology of the *Way* a step further. In Communion, the Father receives the Son's sacrifice *in* the soul: that is, presumably, the Father is present already in the soul but the Son must come to him there. More precisely, the Trinity is present in the soul; but the graces God wills to give us are 'released' by the coming of the Son *in his humanity* into the soul. When this happens the joy of the eternal trinitarian life is realized on earth. This encapsulates the chief theme of her earlier thoughts on the Eucharist: what is enacted here is the completion of the divine will. God is present as creator and sustainer at the centre of the soul, but is present as a transforming act of love only as the humility of the incarnate Christ draws the whole world into its proper harmony with heaven. The image of God's humble love returning to God through our souls and bodies in Communion is a striking summary of Teresa's whole Christology as well as of her thinking on the sacrament.

One further reference to the Eucharist in Teresa's writings may be mentioned here, coming as it does from a period not long after the composition of the *Way*. The *Meditations on the Song of Songs*, the first draft of which was probably finished by 1567, have a tantalizingly brief discussion of the words, 'Let him kiss me with the kiss of his mouth', in the first chapter of the Canticle—words that had already prompted long and full reflections from earlier commentators, especially St Bernard.[13] It sounds a presumptuous request, says Teresa; yet we approach the sacrament with, in effect, just such a request on our lips (1.11). The bride in the Canticle could be asking for Communion in a kind of prophetic desire, or asking for the incarnation itself — the ultimate state of 'friendship' between God and humanity, just as the kiss of the mouth testifies to the highest human friendship (1.10). She is certainly, at any rate, asking for what we are given — Jesus Christ. If we are shocked by this, we have not yet understood what we are doing at the Eucharist; we are taking Communion for granted, failing to see the *majesty* of Christ there because the *humility* of Christ fails to make sense to us (an echo of St Augustine, perhaps, in *Confessions* VII. 18: 'I was not humble enough to conceive of the humble Jesus Christ as my God'). If we really knew what we were daring to do at Communion, we should understand — she says later on — that taking Communion only once in our lives would make us rich enough: 'How much richer from approaching so many times as we do' (5.13).

In the light of this extraordinary wealth of eucharistic meditation, it is easier to see why Teresa, throughout the *Way*, returns to the scandal of 'Lutheran' desecration of the sacrament. She has not the faintest idea of Lutheran theology, but knows only that eucharistic cultus is under attack and that the Mass as she knows it is being taken away. For her this can only be an assault on the Gospel itself, the good news of God's humility and vulnerability for our sake. For the historian of theology, the paradox is that her Christocentric piety, her profound understanding of the cross, and above all her sense of the grace of God acting without regard to our merit or achievement all echo Luther himself so closely.[14] What is distinctive, though, is precisely this linking of a theology of the cross and of the sovereignty of grace to the eucharistic presence. And what must be remembered in reading anything Teresa writes about the Eucharist is that it is for her the one concrete and contemporary sign of the reality on which everything depends — the desire of God to be *with* creation, at all costs — and is thus the centre and touchstone of all that is said about Christian life and prayer.

So, as Teresa turns to the remaining petitions of the Lord's Prayer, she is (as she makes plain in 36.1) assuming the Eucharist as the rationale and the nourishment of what those petitions look to. We pray to be forgiven as we forgive — or rather, as Teresa rightly observes, as we have *already* forgiven: 'he doesn't say "as we will forgive"' (36.2). At first sight, it seems that we are being promised forgiveness in return for a very small thing: What have I to forgive, since the world owes me nothing in the first place (ibid.)? But the realization of this is far from common; religious communities are still deplorably full of people with a powerful sense of what is owed to them in terms of respect. Communities that ought to exhibit that essential equality in honour, that mutual friendship which God's friendship creates are as much in thrall as any other group to anxieties about precedence and dignity (36.3-4). But we have seen how Christ regards his 'dignity': he gives away all honour in the humiliation of the cross, and so *gains* honour for the whole human race (36.5).

The more we think that the forgiving of others is a great achievement, a testimony to our generosity, the more we misunderstand what is at issue here (36.6). What we must learn is not so much the art of graciously overlooking slights to our dignity as that positive realization of love in community that will help us simply not to notice what is due to us in terms of special individual rights. 'When truly the Lord has given his kingdom here below, the soul no longer desires honour in this world' (36.8). So being able to forgive slights and injuries is a byproduct of that life of the kingdom of heaven which Carmel attempts to manifest. Becoming accustomed to the life of the kingdom *is* difficult, and it is perhaps because of this that Christ promises forgiveness to the forgiving, not to those who excel in outward observance: what matters in Carmel, what assures the sisters of mercy, is not observance or sacrifice or devotion but simply being a community of friendship (36.7). We are left with the suggestive paradox that forgiving is no great matter, as an event in itself—but becoming a forgiving person, through the disciplines of community, is.

This is a sovereign test of the authenticity of contemplation, says Teresa. Passive graces given in prayer may be given to those who are in many ways imperfect or immature, but they will always produce at the very least a willingness to bear 'dishonour'; they will be eager to let others know of their own unworthiness, and may be rather tactless with others on matters of status, since they will find it hard to believe that anyone could really take this sort of thing seriously. And even if other virtues waver, this one will not and cannot (36.9-13). Presumably, as the *Life* suggests, real passive graces will always be out of proportion to what we know we can achieve or have achieved, and so will always leave us with a sense of humility and thus with a disinclination to stand on our dignity.

This petition and the petition that God's will be done can be seen as summing up all the others, says Teresa (37.3), just as the Our Father itself sums up the whole process of prayer, and can be taken at different levels by people of differing degrees of maturity (here Teresa *does* allow that it may be right to pray for literal daily bread, 37.2). And the two great petitions bespeak a certain confidence, proper to the prayer as a whole, and particularly marked in those praying with sincerity. That is why the Lord's Prayer ends with a petition designed to counteract the dangers of this confidence: we need to be reminded 'that we have enemies' (37.5), that it is still possible to be deceived. In other words, the stability of our spiritual maturity cannot be left to depend only on our inner *sense* of assurance. We continue, as long as we are 'exiles' on earth, to be vulnerable to the devil, who is able to counterfeit so many of the effects of passive contemplation. So the conclusion of the Our Father — 'Lead us not into temptation, but deliver us from evil' — testifies to the loving forethought of Christ, guarding us against the perils we might so easily ignore.

The temptations described in the concluding chapters of the *Way* are almost entirely connected with the erosion of humility and the risks of seeing oneself in a privileged position over against others. The devil may produce exciting spiritual experiences that are very plausible counterfeits of God's grace; and although some may have the sense to use these to advantage, becoming increasingly aware of their unworthiness to receive extraordinary gifts, others may be less discerning (38.3-4). Even more dangerous is the belief that we have great virtue. Virtues are God's gift: the active possession of a virtue like detachment or courage will vary according to God's will, since God may want to reinforce humility in us. There are times when, for instance, 'it seems to me that I don't care at all about things or gossip said of me; and when I'm put to the test this is at times true — indeed I am pleased about what they say. Then there come days in which one word alone distresses me' (38.6). Any sensible person should know that virtue is not something of whose permanent possession we have any right to be sure. Poverty of spirit is the ability not to concern ourselves with our supposed virtues or attainments (38.7-8) — and it includes not being unduly confident that we are poor in spirit (38.9)!

Teresa's concern is that the moral life should be lived without the deep corruptions of self-consciousness: the devil's work is to make us *interested* in our spiritual state in an obsessive way, whether this takes the form of self-satisfaction or of false humility, paralysing anxiety about one's condition (39.1-2). Real humility produces not anxiety or wretched self-distrust but calm reliance on God when we have discovered how little we can rely on ourselves. 'Let your prayer always begin and end with self-knowledge', she writes (39.4) — self-knowledge nurtured by contact with a wise spiritual director. Proper self-awareness is, for Teresa, the opposite of self-consciousness, not fascination with oneself but familiarity with oneself, candour about strengths and weaknesses, alertness to dangers.

It is right and necessary to have a fear of offending God as well as a warm assurance of God's love (40-41), but this should by no means find expression in tension and scruple. We must resolve not to offend God; and, by another of Teresa's paradoxes, this resolve increases confidence in God and scepticism about our own resources (41.4). What is more, such confidence in God makes it possible to mix without anxiety with those who do not share monastic or similar commitments, knowing that you will be able to transmit to them some increased sense of discipline or devotion: 'go about with a holy freedom, conversing with those who are good even though they may be somewhat worldly' (41.4); 'be affable and understanding in such a way that everyone you talk to will love your conversation and desire your manner of living and acting, and not be frightened and intimidated by virtue. This is very important for religious; the holier they are the more sociable they are with their sisters' (41.7). In a way, this advice is comparable to what Teresa says about the possession of *quietud*: if we are anxious, 'not daring to move' lest we lose the state we are enjoying, we have misunderstood what is going on, ascribing it to our own resources. So here, all we can do is maintain the will not to offend God: in early stages (41.4) we *do* need to exercise discretion and avoid idle and secular conversation, but the goal is the freedom not to have to do this. Discipline is not something to be steadily intensified, but rather what makes discretion and integrity second nature.

The person who enjoys this freedom is very vulnerable to misrepresentation; Teresa takes occasion to warn against the censoriousness of the consciously righteous. Even those who are still training themselves by constraint need to avoid the tight and condemnatory attitudes that will deter others from any discipline at all, and must take great care not to judge hastily those who are being led by different and less strict paths (41.5-6). The advice represents venerable monastic tradition: not to judge one's neighbour is one of the chief points of monastic virtue in the eyes of the fourth- and fifth-century Desert Fathers of Egypt.[15] But we may also suspect here a touch of personal feeling: we know Teresa was thought by many to be a bad nun, and, at the time of the foundation of St Joseph's, she mixed freely and regularly with clergy and laypeople outside her community. She has spent a substantial period of time as a guest in the house of a *grande dame*. It is a telltale sign that she defends mixing with the world on the grounds of having no confidence in one's own virtue or achievement: it is the characteristic strategy of the *Life* in rebutting criticism, turning attention to the sovereignty and sufficiency of God's grace. These passages are probably among the most deliberately apologetic in the second part of the *Way*.

THE LIKENESS OF CHRIST

At the end of the last chapter, we saw how Teresa's faithfulness to the practice of reflecting on the human Jesus gave her a way of thinking about the *whole* story of Christian spiritual growth, over and above her concern with exceptional or preternatural episodes. *The Way of Perfection* fills this out with a wealth of detail. Although the work is badly planned (on her own admission) it is far more closely unified than some readers have recognized. In essence, it is an exploration of how Christ, the incarnate Christ, is to be communicated to the world in the lives of Christians in general and Carmelites in particular, at a time when God seems to have few friends, and when the authorities of the Church do not seem over-eager to help people grow in the friendship of God. Teresa presses on this nerve, repeating several times that at least the Our Father 'cannot be taken away', whatever else may be banned (42.5, recalling 21.3 and 8, and implicitly 24.2). Christ is portrayed as our primary teacher—in giving us the Lord's Prayer (24 *passim*) and the Eucharist (33–35); and thus he teaches by identifying his prayer with ours and by continuing the work of the incarnation in an unceasing movement into the heart of the world. Already here the full structure of Teresa's mature thought is rapidly taking shape. It is still marked by that world-weariness or world-sickness that results from intense psychic disturbances of the kind described in the *Life*. The very last chapter of the *Way* (42.1) interprets 'deliver us from evil' as Jesus' longing to be delivered from the burden of earthly life. We for our part cannot ask to be delivered from the inevitable pains of mortal existence (42.2), but we can, like Jesus, pray for death to remedy them — as nothing else will (ibid.). However, this is a rather unrepresentative passage: the theological pressure is more and more towards the notably different emphasis of the *Castle* and of some passages in the *Foundations* as well.

How are we to become friends of God? Teresa never defines friendship in general terms, for all her constant interest in the subject, but we can piece together from this work in particular what she thought essential to it. Friendship is not a relation in which one partner makes unilateral claims on the other from a position of superiority: so much is obvious from Teresa's picture of Carmel as a community of friends (and in this respect she is echoing, albeit no doubt unconsciously, Aristotle and St Thomas[16]). It is wanting the fulfilment of another human being's potential according to the law of God. Precisely because friendship has 'exclusive aspects', and is not simply a general benevolence, the religious community of Carmel must not be too large to permit of real affective relations between all its members; and while it is inevitable and right that we should find ourselves particularly involved with or dependent on some rather than others, we must not understand friendship in this intense mode as requiring uncritical partisanship and bitchiness towards less intimate acquaintances. All this hangs together, and, as we have seen, makes complete sense of Teresa's almost obsessive polemic about the damage done by 'honour'. But how is it to be applied to our relations with God? We may honour God rightly, but how can God give us the equal honour necessary to friendship?

The fundamental answer is that we are adopted — through the Holy Spirit — into the relation of God to God, Father to Son: the Father treats us as deserving of the loving respect that is due to the Son. But the method of adoption is something which radicalizes the idea of friendship itself still further. To make us friends of God, God wholly abandons dignity and status: it is not that God simply brings us up to an acceptable standard and then deigns to treat us as friends. In the incarnation, the Son renounces all claim to 'special' status and comes to be identified with suffering men and women, and this renunciation expresses the desire of the whole of the trinitarian godhead to be present to the human world without reserve or condition. Friendship with God begins with God's refusal even to introduce the question of status, with God's longing for companionship, or rather, longing to share the companionship of mutual self-gift that constitutes the divine life. God initiates this friendship by resolving to have no interest at heart but ours, and we appropriately respond by resolving to have no interest but God's.

God's 'interest', though, is never other than self-sharing, diffusing the divine love in creation; so if we are to have God's interest at heart, our friendship with God lies in making ourselves wholly available to the work of redeeming love, to God's 'mission' in the world. We know what such availability means, and what it costs, in the life and death of Christ; but if we are truly to be the recipients of the transforming friendship Christ offers, we must grow into that likeness. And our common life, no less than our individual lives, must enact and give voice to the divine initiative in the creation of friendship with God; which is why the religious community must have no place either for moralistic judgement of others or for standing on the dignity of birth or achievement. The 'text' of community life narrates, ultimately, the saving humility of God.

Despite the superficially rambling style of the *Way*, this is a remarkably coherent theological structure, much in advance of anything in the *Life*. Here the absolute priority of the divine initiative is not simply something adduced to make sense of the irruption of extraordinary phenomena into the life of prayer, but is filled out in terms of God's will for men and women to be both friends of God and agents of the divine friendship. The Christological 'cues' of the *Life* are taken up, and a powerfully Christocentric and incarnational framework provided for the whole of the spiritual life. The crucial experience recorded in the *Life* of Teresa's discovery that she was wanted, even needed, by the suffering Christ opens out in two directions — towards a more developed doctrine of God's will for salvation, and the divine humility entailed by this; and towards a stronger sense of Christ's absolute identification with human pain, mental and physical. Her pages on the Eucharist in the *Way* provide a kind of keystone for all this, presenting the Eucharist as, above all, the sacrament of God's unconditional commitment to the world.

Into this structure of theological insights, a number of passages on the practicalities of 'contemplation' (in Teresa's sense of passive graces) are inserted, largely recapitulating the *Life* — with some tactical and prudential qualifications, as we have seen. This is the most obvious bit of unfinished business in the *Way*. Teresa still treats rapture or ecstasy as the climax of the way of prayer, and associates the summits of 'contemplation' with the kind of interruptive experiences so fully detailed in the *Life*; and she puts at the end of her exposition of the Lord's Prayer a clear commendation of praying for death, and ascribes such a sentiment to Christ. This sits rather awkwardly with her stress on Christ's absolute commitment to the world , and on the Christian's active participation in the 'mission' of God's desire in the world. As in the *Life*, the intense emotional and psychic upheavals of passive contemplative experience shadow the horizon, and produce the kind of spiritual exhaustion that explains the longing and prayer for death. There is a further step to be taken.

In the ten years that followed the writing of the *Way* Teresa added little on paper to what she had already said — though that little is interesting enough. The *Meditations on the Song of Songs* represent a very bold step indeed, the assumption of authority to teach her sisters about Scripture:[17] there are echoes, as noted already, of the theology of the *Way*; an interesting defence (1.8) of a certain carefully delimited liberty in the imaginative reading of the Bible (nothing wrong in picturing to ourselves aspects of the events recorded and dimensions of meaning not explicit in the text, so long as nothing contradicts the Church's public teaching), and of the right of women to undertake this (ibid.); a vivid image for our adoptive kinship with Christ (the children of a marriage between the king and a peasant have royal blood, 3.9); and an affirmation that we must not be ashamed of the weakness of the 'flesh' since Christ endured it too (3.10): but nothing substantially new. The general account of prayer follows her earlier treatments. But two things may be noted as showing some movement forward. When she speaks of the prayer of quiet and the sleep of the faculties (4) she finds herself making a terminological distinction between 'intellect' and 'soul', the latter representing the entire self or the depth of the self, and she will take this up again in the *Castle*. More significantly, there is an account of union (7) underlining very strongly the apostolic effects of this state. The soul in (ecstatic) union would happily die; but 'sometimes His Majesty gives it light to see that living is good for it', and the soul is happy to leave its delight for the sake of works of service to God and the neighbour (7.3). The conjunction of Martha and Mary, which up to now has been treated at an *earlier* stage, the sleep of the faculties, is here clearly shifted to the final levels of union.

She is moving towards the synthesis of the *Castle*. In the next chapter we shall be exploring that synthesis, and some of the factors, internal and external, that may have pushed her in the directions hinted at in the *Meditations*. The fully incarnational pattern of spirituality, which seems more and more to be required by her experience and her theological reflection alike, is finally emerging into the light of day.

Notes

1 Details of works condemned in 1559 can be found in Andrés Martín, *Los Recogidos* (Madrid, 1975), ch. 16.

2 It is ironic that the Carmel of Lisieux at the time of St Thérèse illustrates so eloquently some of the problems Teresa sought to avoid, including arbitrary favouritism (and arbitrary hostility) on the part of superiors, and the tensions caused by strong family loyalties in a small house.

3 *Constitutions* 26 and 28. But note also Teresa's strong discouragement in an earlyish letter (*Letters* I, 4, p. 39, from 1568) of nuns discussing too freely their spiritual problems.

4 Compare the classic treatment of this question by Augustine in *Confessions* IV.7–9.

5 A theme superbly explored in Sebastian Moore, *The Inner Loneliness* (London, 1982).

6 On which, see also 10.5–7; Teresa shares with her tradition some difficulty in articulating consistently the idea that bodies *are* to be loved (*contra* 10.5) – at least in the sense that sustained indifference to bodily needs is spiritually damaging. Her major anxiety at this point is over nuns who use concern for their health in a purely self-protective way.

7 This was changed to *benignidad* in the Toledo manuscript, which incorporates the revisions originally thought necessary before the work could be published. Teresa's original wording survives in the Escorial ms of her first draft. The Kavanaugh–Rodriguez translation has a brief account of the complicated history of the various redactions of *The Way of Perfection*.

8 Cf. above, p. 52.

9 Osuna's *Alphabet* 17.1–4 deals with the transforming effects of Christ's solidarity with human suffering and the need for reflection on Jesus as human exemplar, but quite sharply separates this from consideration of Christ's divinity, which is the object of the soul's highest contemplation. The dimension of the Christian's share in Christ's eternal *and* temporal relation to the Father, Teresa's characteristic delight in sharing 'kinship' with Christ, is almost entirely absent.

10 Cf., once again, the theme in the *Life* of being urgently *wanted* by God.

11 See, e.g., E. Schillebeeckx, *Jesus. An Experiment in Christology* (London, 1979), p. 269.

12 John of the Cross, by contrast, regards the transition to passivity as an advance from breast-feeding to taking solid food; see, e.g., *The Ascent*

THE WAY OF PERFECTION

of Mount Carmel 2.17 (esp. 8, where he uses Paul's remarks on milk and solid food in 1 Cor 3:1–2), and *The Living Flame of Love* 3.40 (recension A), 3.37 (recension B). I owe this point to Dr Sarah Coakley of Lancaster University.

13 Sermons 1 to 8 of Bernard's homilies on the Song of Songs deal with this text; there is no evidence that Teresa knew Bernard's sermons, though she may have come across some references to the mystical interpretation of 'Let him kiss me with the kiss of his mouth' in her reading or through sermons. *Pace* Green (*Gold in the Crucible*, pp. 114–18) there is nothing here to suggest a Jewish or cabbalistic undercurrent of any kind. Teresa, in commenting on the Song of Songs, is certainly doing something rather revolutionary for a nun of her period; but *what* she is doing and how she does it are profoundly traditional in terms of the history of spirituality.

14 On Teresa and Luther, see Jürgen Moltmann, 'Teresa of Avila and Martin Luther: the turn to the mysticism of the cross', *Studies in Religion/Sciences Religieuses* 13 (1984), pp. 265–78.

15 For examples, see *The Sayings of the Desert Fathers. The Alphabetical Collection*, trans. Benedicta Ward SLG (London, 1975), pp. 15, 79, 81, 119, etc.

16 For Aquinas's view of friendship see esp. *Summa Theologiae* Ia IIae, 23 and 27; IIa IIae, 114. There is a good general discussion in Gilbert C. Meilaender, *Friendship. A Study in Theological Ethics* (Notre Dame, 1981).

17 The date of this work's composition is obscure, but it probably had its first draft in 1566/7 and its second in the early 1570s.

4

God at the centre
The Interior Castle

THE PROBLEM OF FALSE SPIRITUALITY

The ten years or so separating the writing of the *Life* and *The Way of Perfection* from the composition of the *Castle* saw the development of the Carmelite Reform from a tiny community in Avila to an influential network of houses (twelve by 1577), and from a local and more or less personal problem for the ecclesiastical authorities to a major headache for the Order, the Inquisition and the papal nuncio; it had extended itself to the male branch of the Order (from 1568, when John of the Cross and Antonio de Heredia made their vows to the Reform), and had attracted enthusiastic support from a number of influential aristocrats and the friendly interest of King Philip himself. There had been disturbing, even disastrous episodes: the early days of the male Reform were dominated by the eccentric, if not hysterical, figures associated with the priory at Pastrana and the adventures of the widowed Princess of Eboli caused some of Teresa's worst problems. As we have seen, it was this woman, quite as silly as she was wealthy and influential, who pursued her personal vendetta against Teresa by denouncing the *Life* to the Inquisition in 1574.[1]

By 1577, when she began to write the *Castle*, Teresa had ample experience of the pathologies of the religious life. When, in 1573/4, she had written *The Book of her Foundations*, recording her experiences in the first six years of the Reform, she had devoted five chapters early on in the work (4–8) to the problems faced by superiors. 'In observing what has been happening spiritually during these years in these monasteries, I have seen the need for what I want to say', she declares (4.2). She is confident (more confident than she was in the *Way*) that practically everyone in her Carmels reaches 'perfect contemplation', and a fair number experience raptures and revelations (4.8). This, however, is a mixed blessing: the delight that is felt when God begins to be sensed by the soul can make us reluctant to turn to the works of obedience and love; it is as much a distraction from these priorities as is the pleasure of thinking about God. 'The soul's progress does not lie in thinking much but in loving much' (5.2); but that love is not the inner sensation of delight in God, but the concrete task of good community life—obedience and service. This is what gives joy—and service—to Christ: Teresa quotes Matthew 25:40, 'What you did for one of these little ones you did for me', and appeals to the model of Christ's own obedience (5.3). We are reluctant to leave the enjoyment of God, she suggests, because self-indulgence is almost inevitably mixed up with it; but 'it would be a distressing thing if God were clearly telling us to go after something that matters to him and we would not want to do so but want to remain looking at him because that is more pleasing to us' (5.5).

The goal must be to find delight in the will of God—not, that is, in the sensed presence of God but in doing gladly what God (and especially God in Jesus Christ) does. Religious obedience is an attempt to simplify this by accepting an external arbitrator in our decision making—an effortful surrender, but one which gives us the kind of sovereignty over our wills which frees us from depending on transitory states of feeling (5.12). If, by the exercise of the monastic life, we are equipped to respond obediently to the call away from solitude to charity, we shall be on the way to the only 'union' with God that finally matters—union with the will and act of God. 'This is the union that I desire and would want for all of you, and not some absorptions, however delightful they may be, that have been given the name "union"' (5.13). We are a good way here from the language and thought of the *Life*. And the Christological theme so fully developed in the *Way* is deployed eloquently in defence of obedience: Christ 'came from the bosom of his Father out of obedience to become our slave' (5.17).

The practical import of this is that the religious superior must be consistently suspicious of interiority pursued for its own sake, whether by prolonged periods of supposedly prayerful absorption, or by a kind of obsessive devotion to frequent Communion (seen as an individual privilege, rather than in the apostolic perspective of the *Way*). Chapter 6 of the *Foundations* deals at length with the problem of what might be called pseudo-meditation. Genuine rapture is irresistible and brief, says Teresa; but there is a state somewhere between the prayer of quiet properly so called and rapture, which is fraught with great danger and ambiguity (6.1). It is like 'spiritual sleep', in the sense that the faculties are not working normally: the imagination (which for Teresa, remember, is connected with memory) is focused 'without distraction', but in a kind of hypnotic stillness. As Teresa says, this is not restricted to prayer: mindless absorption in something is a common enough phenomenon—sheer absent-mindedness, being unable to tear attention away from some object or thought, even if we are not *actively* attending to it, falling into a mental fog of one kind or another, all these are familiar enough (6.2–44). To confuse this with rapture is quite a serious error; and presumably, though Teresa does not say so explicitly, we should have to distinguish it from the 'sleep of the faculties'. In the latter, the mind's operations are chaotic and unfocused, in a rather dreamlike way, and the soul's fundamental relation with God is an almost imperceptible cleansing of the will, which enjoys a kind of stability not yet evident in or to the normal consciousness (above, pp. 63–6). But in the 'sleep' of this ersatz meditation the faculties are not disoriented in the same way: instead of wandering, the mind, or its imaginative faculty, is all too fixed. The overall sensation is not at all unpleasant: a vague, hypnotic 'gazing' at some remembered image or phrase, or even just an absorption in one's own mental stupor. It may be caused by undernourishment, Teresa suggests (6.5), or simply not having enough to do. However much its object may be of impeccable theological propriety in this state, it is the soul's duty to break off its absorption (6.7): the long-term effects are psychically and physically, as well as spiritually, damaging (6.3, 7, 14–23).

It is not easy for the modern reader to be clear as to what exactly Teresa is talking about, though the general tenor of the chapter is plain. It sounds as if there are two slightly different phenomena in question—though the symptoms will be much the same. You may find yourself dwelling on a phrase or picture without thought, in a way that does not actually *involve* you at any significant level; or you may find, especially if you are physically and mentally overtired, that you have nothing in particular in mind at all, only a sense of pleasurable inactivity from which it becomes increasingly hard to rouse yourself. What (I think) Teresa sees these states as having in common, apart from being rather difficult to break out of and having enervating effects, is that the will is not engaging with anything outside itself. What it consents to or loves is simply the state of inactive absorption itself; whereas, in the true prayer of quiet, and in rapture, the will is drawn to God in a way it cannot generate of itself. It is precisely this dumb and compulsive *wanting* of something outside the self that makes the later stages in Teresian prayer so superficially uncomfortable and frustrating; there is a wellnigh unbearable feeling of confusion and unfinishedness, even when, objectively, we enjoy 'quiet': that is, the cessation of our efforts to reach God as God touches our desire directly.

This pseudo-meditation is, consequently, quite at odds with the whole pattern of Christian life as Teresa has sketched it in *The Way of Perfection*. By turning will and love *inwards*, it cuts them off from that single transfiguring movement of *divine* 'wanting' which flows from the Father through the life and death of the incarnate Son, and, by the grace of the Spirit in prayer and sacrament, into us. The acid test of 'spirituality' (that un-Teresian word) is, now more plainly than ever, identification with the humility of Christ in leaving heaven for the love of us. So the prioress, faced with the problem of a sister given to this self-indulgent absorption, can do no better than to give her something to do for someone else, distract her by work in the community. Teresa admits, with her usual honesty, that she knows the problem from the inside: she had an unbalanced attitude to receiving Communion, she confesses (6.17; cf. T 31, from as late as 1572, on her fondness for being given a large host at Mass), which she only slowly came to realize was largely selfish. Since a devout soul will habitually feel warmth and tenderness at the altar, it is not surprising if some want frequent Communion for the sake of the pleasant sensations engendered. This is obviously a specially serious corruption, given Teresa's conviction that the Eucharist is what identifies us with the 'outward' movement, the other-directedness of God; and in such circumstances it is better to forbid someone access to the sacrament — a very drastic measure, but fully intelligible in Teresa's terms.[2] What the sacrament has to give us can only be received in its entirety by someone who has learned obedience, and Teresa attributes some of her own mature sense of the Eucharist's importance to having been disciplined in this way (6.20). If the response to discipline of this sort is anger and resentment, we may be sure that we have 'a love of God (I do not mean that it is really love but that in our opinion it is) that so stirs up the passions that one ends up offending the Lord' (6.21).

Not surprisingly, Teresa moves on in chapter 7 to discuss 'melancholy', a term which, as her recent translators observe, 'includes a whole series of emotional and mental disorders'.[3] Teresa is aware of some confusion in what she writes (and perhaps in what she feels) about this; but the gist of the chapter is that 'melancholy' is all too easy to use as an excuse for failures in communal charity. The superior must treat the chronic depressive (this is most nearly the term we should use) as sick, and should make sure that her diet and surroundings are not making things worse; she should also be prepared to show affection to the sufferer. But it is essential that the 'melancholic' should be held answerable for her actions, given real responsibilities and punished for failures (7.8–9). Left to itself, to be indulged at will, 'melancholy' breeds madness; disciplined, called to account, it remains a torment, but is held firmly in proportion and perspective. Christ does not lack compassion for the person so afflicted, and neither should the community (7.10).

In the last of her chapters directly devoted here to the problems of true and false spirituality, Teresa turns to visions and revelations. She declares at once that she is not going to discuss the 'signs for discernment' between visions from God and visions from the devil (8.1): her concern is simply with the problems that will be encountered by the sister who admits to visionary experience. Confessors are liable to panic over it, and may give advice that has painful effects, productive of much misery and tension. Teresa's advice is simple (and notably close to that of St John of the Cross[4]): if visions are from God, they will do us good in any case; if from the devil, they can be turned to good, because we are always bound to admit that we do not deserve them, and so have an occasion to deepen our humility. This shames the devil into leaving us alone (8.4). If we are told to do something in a vision or locution, we must submit it to a confessor and do what he tells us (8.5). In general, since we (and women especially, Teresa thinks) are quite capable of generating hallucinations for ourselves, unaided by God *or* devil, we are to take time to digest and reflect on any 'preternatural' episode lest our enthusiasm deceive an inexperienced confessor into taking us too seriously (8.7–8). It is essential for a superior to provide sensible guidance for each individual, trying to find a confessor who suits and understands each one (8.7); and she must also make sure that visionary experience is not treated as a superior attainment. She should praise only those virtues that can properly be aspired to by *all* (visions and so forth depending entirely on the unpredictable gift of God), and must discourage the eager gossip about extraordinary visitations that can so easily throw the life of a community off balance (ibid.).

Here then, in these five chapters of the *Foundations*, we see how Teresa's sense of the possibilities for delusion and fantasy in the life of prayer is sharpened by the experience of having responsibility for a large number of volatile and often disturbed souls in the new communities of the Reform. She has become more suspicious of the extraordinary, though she retains all her impatience with those who simply refuse to deal with it, and are apparently so petrified of anyone claiming any experience in prayer beyond a mild access of devotional feeling. She retains, in other words, a clear conviction of the disorienting force of encounter with God at a certain depth, and so of the high probability of 'abnormal' phenomena being experienced. She refuses to be a programmatic sceptic, or to disapprove of visionary episodes; but she has acquired a good deal more detachment about them than she had had ten years earlier, and has discovered the dangers of bringing them into the forefront of the imagination in the confined psychic space of a small religious community. The themes already articulated in the *Way* have become more deeply rooted and more clearly expressed, and the enemy has been brought more fully into focus — that turning from the movement of God into the world towards the religiosity of a private self. *The Interior Castle* is Teresa's final attempt to mark out the path by which this betrayal may be avoided.

TOWARDS THE CENTRE: WHAT WE CAN DO

Why the metaphor of the soul as 'castle'? We have a number of slightly differing accounts of how and when Teresa first thought of it,[5] but these are of little help in grasping Teresa's intention in using it as she does. It is common enough practice to talk about the soul 'entering into itself' in prayer (C I, 1.5), and about God dwelling within. But Teresa is alert to the ambiguities of going 'within' to find God. If the soul is a home for God, it is a home with an enormous abundance of rooms, and we shall need to know where we are if we are not to be deceived and think we have encountered God when we have not. God is within, but at the *centre* (I, 1.3): the journey inward is a journey to the place where God's love meets and mingles with the life of the soul, and thus we need to keep moving through the rooms until we find the middle of what sounds remarkably like a maze.

There are many dwelling places: 'some up above, others down below, others to the sides' (I, 1.3): suggesting that we are repeatedly faced with choices about which direction to take. We have already been told (I, 1.1) to think of the castle as transparent ('made entirely out of a diamond or of very clear crystal'); and although this is primarily meant to excite our wonder at the beauty of the soul, there is, in the first chapter of the *Castle*, a kind of subtext which indicates a less benign element in this language. The castle is made of diamond or glass: thus we can see through it. We can see enough to know that God is there. Yet there are many chambers; and if their walls are transparent, we cannot know very securely how many separate us from the deceptively visible centre. This may be to press the metaphor too hard, but, as we shall discover, Teresa is constantly anxious to remind us that we are liable to mistake at least some of the 'mansions' for the central and final one. We do not know where the boundaries are if we never move forward and walk into them.

So the 'interior castle' is an image of the richness and variety of the soul considered as the dwelling place of God; but it also points at the teasing and even perilous character of the inner world, where we cannot instinctively find our own way. There is, of course, an initial 'cleaning of the glass' to be done by turning away from the mortal sin that can darken the soul, though it can never extinguish the fountain of light at the centre (I, 2.1–3). But once we have begun the journey, we see that 'the sun that is in the royal chamber shines in all parts' (I, 2.8). We must grasp what this light first shows us, the sheer size and variety of the soul's chambers, and then explore the rooms, never staying in one corner. We need to know what we are capable of, positively and negatively. Teresa's imagery, as usual, gets a little out of control. Self-knowledge is, at one level, what entry into the castle means, and there are countless different routes by which to enter (I, 1.8, 2.8 and 12); at the same time, there is a specific 'room' of self-knowledge, and, instead of wandering aimlessly, we should attempt to find this room and 'orient' ourselves from there (I, 2.8–9). What she seems to be driving at is that the soul's knowledge of its spaciousness and capacity is not simply a gathering of information. The soul's self-awareness must be organized around the awareness of its true relation to God: it must acquire self-knowledge understood as humility and repentance. If the soul takes its stand here, on the recognition of its creaturely dependence and fallibility, it may from this vantage-point see the full range of its capacities and the different gifts it may receive from God as 'existential' possibilities in its process of growth, not just as 'states' of life or consciousness in the abstract. It will see the many rooms of the house as possible paths for it or for other souls, not as disconnected aspects of the soul-in-general.

The self-knowledge of humility is a condition in which we know ourselves by looking at God; we see the neediness or the wretchedness of our state when we see the abundance and beauty of God. And to see our miserable state in this light is to be given some impetus to move, whereas the dead and false humility that simply presents us with our wretchedness can lead to self-indulgent and self-excusing despair (I, 2.10–11). We shall have problems in this early phase of self-recognition because, although the light of God is shining clearly through the crystal partitions, the outer chambers — even when cleaned from sin — are overcrowded. As we enter the castle, we are liable to bring with us a whole host of creatures from the insalubrious moat that surrounds the castle — lizards and snakes and so on. These are the self-regarding habits and preoccupations that normally keep us from any kind of self-awareness; and even when we have embarked on self-discovery, they still crowd around us (I, 2.14). In the community the sisters are delivered from some of the most obvious external problems to do with money and status and the like. But they are still profoundly vulnerable to 'spiritualized' versions of materialistic anxiety. They may *want* holiness in the way the world wants property, and to press on with penance and mortification in a way that is in fact wholly self-regarding; or they may identify their own purity and honour with a high standard of perfection in the community and become fiercely intolerant of the failures or even just the mild quirks of others (I, 2.16–17). All of this destroys community life, and chokes self-knowledge. By directing the mind to the perfection of the self as an object in its own right it keeps one *bound* to the self; whereas, strange as it may sound, the point of real self-knowledge is to become free of the self (I, 2.12).

Here is one of Teresa's most striking clarifications. We are inclined to think of self-knowledge as the accumulation of ever more detail about our interiority. The modern reader will instinctively think of this in terms of the analytic and therapeutic processes we are so used to. But Teresa is, in effect, saying that the mistake is to confuse self-knowledge with being *interested* in yourself. She wants a self-knowledge that is far more like the habitual and tacit knowing involved in knowing how to ride a bicycle or bake a loaf of bread — that is, a practised familiarity with certain constraining facts, so that we unreflectively adjust out behaviour in accordance with them. To try to ride a bicycle while enumerating the principles of riding bicycles is a recipe for falling off. So knowing oneself is being familiar with the facts of creatureliness and fallibility and need, and the supreme fact of the creator's reality sustaining, penetrating and drawing our lives together. To know about our personal histories in depth, to know our blocks, our injuries, our neuroses, to know therefore the possible paths ahead to some extent, and to know something of what we can and cannot expect of ourselves — none of this is unimportant or wrong, so long as it is held within the basic, undramatic awareness of being a creature on the road to full life with God by the help of his grace. It is this underpinning awareness that guarantees we know what kinds of relation and behaviour are futile or destructive, so that we never use our knowledge about ourselves as a weapon or a defence against others, or a justification for lack of concrete communal charity ('I have special needs because of my great sensitivity'; 'I can't be expected to put up with the behaviour/taste/conversation of people like that' . . .). In short these last sections of C I, 2 can usefully be read in conjunction with the discussion of pseudo-spirituality and melancholy in the *Foundations*.

The Interior Castle is among other things an attack on interiority as an ideal in itself, and this opening emphasis on self-knowledge should alert us to this fact. We enter the castle and, if our eyes are open, what we actually see is God, radiating love from the 'centre' which is the centre of our creatureliness. By seeing God we see more clearly what we are — muddled, distracted, frustrated, but in motion towards the love of God. If the ordinary habits of self-assertion are so powerful that we come to see our muddle and frustration as more interesting and compelling than God, we are on the way out of the castle again, and are in serious spiritual trouble. The first 'mansions', then, are the place where we are struggling to break free from obsessive and defensive concern with self: where we have begun, however ineptly, to turn our attention to God in thought and prayer (even if only a few times in a month: I, 1.8). As usual, Teresa refuses (ibid.) to play down the importance of vocal prayer, uttered with sense and conviction, in keeping this attention active. As I, 2 makes clear, however, she is not just addressing the semi-worldly and the formally devout, the barely converted, but a much wider class of people, including those who consider themselves unworldly or converted.[6] The first mansions are a place we are liable to discover in ourselves at various stages of our growth; hidden by the acquisition of new words or habits, it may suddenly reveal itself again as a room where we have never really stopped living.[7] 'You musn't think of these dwelling places in such a way that each one would follow in file after the other' (I, 2.8). There is no deliverance from the subtly overcrowded first mansions but by honesty and a consistent desire (never mind the rate of success) to keep your eyes on God.

Teresa says that she is going to deal with the second mansions only briefly, since she has written at length about them elsewhere (II, 1.1). She does not, unfortunately, specify where, but we can probably take it that she has in mind the descriptions in the *Life* (9–11) of the profoundly uncomfortable stage at which we have been given a conspicuously clearer vision of God, and so feel much more acutely the tensions of our existence, the irrevocable choices that have to be made.[8] Not surprisingly, the attractions of the 'unconverted' life are thereby brought before our minds in very sharp focus (II, 1.3–4). The intellect has a useful job to perform here (for once) simply in reminding us of the objective superiority of what God promises to anything the pleasures of the world can deliver (II, 1.4). This is a place in which what is called for is simply active moral constancy: seeking and doing God's will in the context in which we find ourselves. There is, Teresa says, nothing extra to discover about this (II, 1.8). We may expect setbacks, and indeed God allows such setbacks so that we may learn more about our besetting temptations and guard ourselves more carefully (ibid.).

We suffer more in this second stage than in the first simply because we have fewer defences against God. God has taken us at our word: if we have turned Godward, God will be eagerly desirous of bringing us closer still (II, 1.2), and we shall find ourselves less able to deceive ourselves about our need and weakness. We *know* more clearly what we are meant for (*wanted* for, as in L 9), how far we are from this, and how deep-rooted are our evasions and self-delusions. Thus, although we shall feel some kind of affective warmth here, the primary *emotional* colouring of this stage is a sense of fear or despondency at the conflicts which seem to be intensifying all the time. In a way, it would be quite easy to slip back (II, 1.4); but we only do so at enormous moral cost, because that would involve something like a denial of the truth about God and ourselves that is in front of our noses. We have to hold on to the fact that increased conflict is a sign of increasing clarity of understanding: we see more plainly what our peace or our wholeness might be as we see more plainly our own lack of it (II, 1.9). We have to be ready repeatedly to begin all over again, to do without the sense of 'doing well' at our prayers. One of the crucial features of the second mansions is a fuller consciousness of what our efforts can and cannot do. We are to carry on looking for God's will—which for Teresa *always* means the life of practical charity in community—and doing the prosaic things this demands of us, against a background of painful tension within. This tension we *cannot* resolve: God alone will do that, and we do not know and cannot dictate when or how (ibid., 7, 8, 10).

We cannot resolve, but we can deny, by trying to get back to the first mansions, or repress, by building up a solid carapace of religious practice that may for a time persuade us that all is well. The third mansions could be said to describe a 'double bind'. We need the felt security of routine, and we need the practices of sound community life to become second nature to us. Equally we must be clear that real security means moving on (and thus moving into new *insecurities*) and avoiding complacency (III, 1.1–2).[9] Naturally we *want* to be in a situation in which penance, recollection, kindness to others, natural moderation and good judgement come without much effort ('Who will say that he doesn't want a good so wonderful, especially after having passed through the most difficult trial? No, nobody will'—III, 1.6). But wanting to stay there is a temptation to be fought. Teresa recalls the rich young man of Matthew 19: he starts off confident of his virtue, yet knowing he lacks something that he cannot quite put his finger on. This obscure unease is what matters most in the deceptively smooth waters of this stage (III, 1.6–7): when we feel dryness or frustration in our prayers, despite the admirable regularity of our lives, that is a saving grace, did we but know it. Other and harder things may also keep alive a proper uneasiness here—depression, illness, misunderstanding. The great danger is in supposing that our regular and controlled lives give us some sort of claim upon God, so that we become bitterly resentful if God is apparently not at home to us in the way we should like (III, 1.6). If we continue steadily believing ourselves not to deserve anything at God's hands, we shall never lose sight of the truth that God is consistently giving to us and 'serving' us (III, 1.8); and if our inner unsettlement is not buried by religious self-congratulation we shall be able to keep this in view.

Teresa finds it alarming that practised and devout souls are so easily thrown off course by unexpected setbacks: 'It's useless to give them advice, for since they have engaged so long in the practice of virtue they think they can teach others and that they are more than justified in feeling disturbed' (III, 2.1). They will interpret the purely emotional turmoil they experience as a martyrdom, not as a sign of unresolved problems within: 'they canonize these feelings in their minds' (*canonizan . . . en sus pensamientos estas cosas*: III, 2.3). The risk, as Teresa goes on to explain, is of dramatizing one's losses or setbacks out of a still persisting sense of what is due to one's dignity. Loss of worldly goods (short of actual destitution) is a relatively minor problem (III, 2.4), though loss of reputation is more unpleasant — and, alas, easier to turn to selfish effect, grieving over the imperfections of others (III, 2.5). Teresa pointedly leaves her sisters to draw the moral for convent life (III, 2.6). Basic to much of what she says here is the gulf between the suffering we can choose and control ('penance') and that which takes us by surprise. We may believe we have great qualities of endurance because of what we *choose* to give up or put up with: we never really put ourselves at risk, however. Calculating reason is still very much in control (III, 2.7–8). But God calls us to cope with what has not been planned, what we are not confident of having strength or resource to meet, and it is our response to this that shows whether or not we have been deluding ourselves.

The third mansions 'seem the normal state of most good people', which is why Teresa is so determined to analyse it fully.[10] Goodness, in this sense, is a very long way from holiness: most of all, perhaps, because it rests on the abiding basis of a fearful and anxious self-regard or self-protectiveness and is not therefore instinctively generous. 'It is very characteristic of persons with such well-ordered lives to be shocked by everything', Teresa remarks tartly (III, 2.13). 'We have clear ideas of how devout people should act and if they don't conform to these they are open to censure.'[11] To be 'good' without humility is to be condemned to a really wretched life, 'weighed down with this mud of our human misery' (III, 2.9): as in the first mansions, we are made more and more the prisoners of ourselves. We are committed to the strenuous job of constant repression, projecting our own fears and uncertainties on to others and showing aggressive zeal for their improvement. Teresa would have had no difficulty in understanding the shrill censoriousness of modern Christian zealots for the moral reclamation of society; she might have had equally sharp words for the self-consciously consistent radical Christian, obsessed with the creation of an uncompromised lifestyle. As she herself patiently repeats, it is good to know where you stand and to have a measure of control over your life; not to feel at the mercy of intolerable inner tensions all the time. But we need to see the sensation of stability as a *gift* that is given to help us forward, not a possession or acquisition. We are being given strength for a longer journey; which is why we must on no account push away those things, internal or external, that break into our peace and contentment, our sense of order or safety.

God will, in this stage, give *contentos*, 'consolations', but not much in the way of *gustos*, 'spiritual delights' (III, 2.9). The distinction is to be fully explained in the fourth mansions, and we can also defer a fuller account until we come to look in detail at this next stage. In essence, Teresa means that the third mansions are not without emotional warmth: our regular lives, especially when rooted in genuine humility, will produce some genuine enjoyment of God. But, although there *may* be touches of something deeper, we are still on the near side of the great chasm that crosses the Christian path, the disjunction between effort and grace. So far, we have been dealing with (roughly) the first and part of the second water of the *Life* (although attempts to map the mansions on to the waters have usually been rather disastrous,[12] we can at least see where the important break or change of emphasis comes in both schemes). The gradual process in the second water by which the irrigation of the ground through the water-wheel and buckets becomes more and more regular and almost automatic is what the well-ordered piety of the third mansions represents—but how much more aware Teresa has become of its dangers! And although Teresa has not exactly changed her mind about whether we should desire exceptional (preternatural) gifts from God, she is quite clear in the *Castle* that we must want to move on: that is, to receive God's grace more directly. It is not enough to wait in the anterooms of conventional piety until forced out: we must from the first recognize that they are places of transit.

TOWARDS THE CENTRE: WHAT GOD DOES

'Supernatural experiences begin here', says Teresa of the fourth mansions (IV, 1.1). How is the transition actually made from the third to the fourth mansions? Well, in one sense this is up to God alone, and can only be so; but the account of the third mansions does suggest very strongly that we can at least know our readiness to face our inner incompleteness and to respond to external pressures, to take more risks or make new departures, is the condition on our side for God's being able to push us across into the qualitively different territory of the last four mansions. The transition is marked by a new kind of experience of God's beauty and this is where Teresa's novel distinction between 'consolations' and 'spiritual delights' comes in. Consolation, she explains (IV, 1.4), is what we feel in a wide variety of ordinary human situations: it is—to paraphrase—what we experience when events fit expectations ('when we suddenly see a person we love very much; when we succeed in a large and important business matter and of which everyone speaks well') or, we might add, when a laboratory experiment has come out right, or when we have given a good performance in a concert or play. It may or may not be a sense of achievement, but it is certainly a sense of 'fit'; perhaps what Eliot meant when he spoke of the experience felt by the poet 'when the words are finally arranged in the right way . . . a moment of exhaustion, of appeasement, of absolution'.[13] Consolation is a blend of happiness, being at ease: with, Teresa suggests, a strong element of emotional draining. We are enjoying our feelings of 'appeasement' or homecoming, and we can be rather trapped by this very enjoyment. So in prayer: consolation begins with us and ends in God (IV, 1.4), Teresa claims: that is, although the object of consoling feelings is God, their cause is what we are or what we are doing. All being well, they may go on being directed Godward; if they do, this is because they arise from a genuine awareness of God's love, and so they are still gifts of God, even if their proximate cause is our own temperament and history (IV, 1.6). But they will undoubtedly cause emotional exhaustion, particularly a shedding of tears that drains and tires us (IV, 1.5–6).

Teresa sums up the difference between consolation and delight by referring to a text from Psalm 119:32: *dilatasti cor meum*, 'Thou hast enlarged my heart'. Consolation has the effect of constraining the heart, says Teresa, it brings a sense of *pressure*,[14] however pleasant or 'releasing' it is in other ways; 'spiritual delight', which begins in God and ends in us, is a liberation from pressure quite different from a release of tension (IV, 1.4–5). She returns, after a digression on distraction and temptation, to speak of this in more detail, and makes an explicit identification between this 'delight' and *quietud* in the fullest sense. The imagery of irrigation reappears: consolation is filling a trough through a planned system of conduits; delight is filling a trough by opening it to a spring, so that the water wells up silently from inside (IV, 2.2–3). If the heart is 'enlarged' in this experience that is because something deeper in us than the heart is filling the heart to overflowing—and that source is God at the centre (IV, 2.4–5). When we experience spiritual delight we are simply perceiving the fact that God is at work with greater depth and directness at the root of our being; we are 'absorbed' and stilled by the flow from the centre. This, however, is not properly called *union*: Teresa carefully corrects the terminology of the *Life* (IV, 2.6, though she wavers later on in the *Castle*) so as to underline the difference between union as the comprehensive and established state at the end of the spiritual paths, when the soul's action is completely bound in with God's action, and the temporary sense of being 'held' in closeness to God in such a way that the soul's faculties are prevented from engaging with any specific object. It is appropriate here to recall her brief remarks on 'union' in *Foundations* (5.13): the state of absorption is *not* itself union, though it may go along with that more fundamental union of our will with God's that is achieved by obedience and humility.

As elsewhere, Teresa is not completely clear as to whether the experience of *gustos* is for everyone, whether it is a proper thing to want. The main point of her discussion seems to be that the *essential* fact is God's greater freedom to act in our souls; and the *gustos* represent the degree to which we become aware (in thinking and feeling) of this. In IV, 2.9, she goes over quite familiar ground in insisting that the favour of spiritual delights should not be something we struggle to achieve; indeed, she says, she knows people who beg God not to give them *gustos*, because of the danger of pride. Yet it *is* right to desire 'this prayer' (IV, 2.8), because it confirms the will's union with God and so brings forth good fruits. In other words, Teresa has still not fully shaken off the confusion between *state* and *experience*; she is far clearer about it than in her earlier writings, especially where union is concerned, but here the muddle persists. Certainly, if 'this prayer' is really a matter of God being more free to act in the soul and to sanctify the soul by equipping it for works of love, it would be ludicrous to pray not to have it. But it might make sense to pray not to have an excessively vivid awareness of God's working, so as not to make us overconfident. Ruth Burrows comments, with her usual perception, that Teresa blurs together three things: the grace of God's new freedom to act in and through us, the intermittent awareness of that action, and the 'upsurge of psychic energy' that such awareness may generate.[15] The *gustos* belong mostly with this third element. Teresa is right, both theoretically and phenomenologically, to distinguish them from 'consolations': there is an important gap between the sense of something fitting our expectations and the unexpected advent of beauty—the 'freshness' celebrated in the poetry of Hopkins, which may leave us shaken but not exhausted. But they remain phenomena in the sphere of human perceiving, and it is not all that helpful to treat them, in themselves, as special gifts of God. The gift is God's act itself, pervading our selfhood at new depths: if we find ourselves being held or stilled when the mind turns to God, absorbed as we might be by a sudden sight of beauty, yet not able to discern any particular object that causes this, we may see thereby that God is more intimately with us, and may perhaps feel an access of joy, a sense of hope or of homecoming. But the intimacy of God is not *necessarily* perceived like this: it may not be directly 'perceived' at all, except in our awareness of a strengthened will to go forward, and an incapacity to distance oneself sufficiently from God to form any clear ideas about God or God's dealings with us.

'Something is happening in the evolving soul that manifests itself in the quality of its Christian commitment, but its germinal point cannot be caught hold of and looked at.'[16] Ruth Burrows's summary of what is going on in the fourth mansions puts the emphasis precisely where it ought to be. It also helps us to make sense of what Teresa has to say here both about distractions and difficulties in prayer and about 'recollection'. The fourth mansions are not always a comfortable place to be: the intermittent *gustos* are accompanied by frequent and distressing consciousness of distraction, roving fantasy (IV, 1.7–8), and this may tempt us to depression or despair. We put it down to our own failings, and this can lead to great harm: we may want to give up prayer completely because of the humiliating unhappiness involved (IV, 1.9). Teresa's counsel depends in part on redefining terms for our mental life. Despite her dismissal in the *Life* (18.2) of sophisticated distinctions between 'soul' and 'spirit', Teresa admits here (IV, 1.8) that she needs to differentiate in some way between the soul as such and whatever it is that is bound up in distractions and chaotic mental images. Encouraged by a *letrado* (possibly John of the Cross), she separates 'mind' or 'imagination' (*pensamiento* or *imaginación*) from 'understanding' (*entendimiento*): the imagination can run loose even when the intellect or understanding is in touch with God. This is important because it marks Teresa's recognition that what is before the *conscious* mind in this stage of growth may tell us relatively little of what is going on in the depths of the self. She is in fact recapitulating what she had tentatively worked out in L 17.5–7, in discussing the 'third water', about the memory's efforts to capture the intellect and lead it back to its ordinary ways of functioning. But the emphasis here is rather different: in the *Life* she envisages a state in which the intellect is undergoing a specific experience of being silenced and stupefied by God while the memory throws up distracting images in (as it were) a neighbouring apartment. Here in the *Castle*, she is apparently thinking rather of a state in which the understanding capacities of the soul are habitually but unspectacularly turned to God while the conscious mind (not *just*, I think, what produces disconnected images, but a kind of reasoning, connection-making faculty) remains occupied with unprofitable or unholy thoughts. In fact, the conventional threefold division of the soul is breaking down in the *Castle*: instead of the three faculties on the same plane enjoying differing degrees of 'union' with God, the intellect's absorption standing alongside the imagination's mess, Teresa is looking for a model that allows her to talk about different *levels* of a more integrated mental-spiritual action: 'the soul is perhaps completely joined with them in the dwelling places very close to the centre while the mind is on the outskirts of the castle suffering from a thousand wild and poisonous beasts' (IV, 1.9). What we are *aware* of is the disedifying noise of *pensamiento* (very like the *logismoi*, chains of thought, described by writers in the Greek monastic tradition[17]); what we *know* is that God's presence is committed to us, and if we are lucky we may from time to time experience that knowledge emerging into conscious awareness, with the effect already described of stilling and holding us so that we cannot 'think' in any ordinary sense at all.

So we can expect — just as in the second mansions — that the more the presence of God is given space and freedom in our souls, the more we shall notice our conflicts, our compulsions, our sheer inner fragmentariness: bits and pieces of desire and fantasy, vanity, lust, resentment, normally kept in the margin of things by the ordinary activity of the conscious mind, will come much more clearly into conscious focus when the understanding, at its deepest level, faces the divine reality that it cannot conceptualize. The intellect in these depths cannot do its usual job of keeping the flow of ordinary reasoning going. When we stop doing other things to try and address ourselves to God, there is a kind of vacuum: the intellect, without any specific experience *necessarily* coming into consciousness (an experience of 'absorption' or whatever) is stuck with the unmanageable fact of God and can offer no help in the shape of pious thought or virtuous plans, and so the field is left open for the superficial or marginal operations of the mind to take over. Because we, quite reasonably, do not waste time and energy trying to blot out these operations (which would give them a disproportionate significance), they are always around. The best we can do is to carry on with prayer: that is, giving time to God, and not allow ourselves to be discouraged. As Teresa sensibly says, the painfulness of this is the result of not knowing well enough how the different levels of mental activity work (IV, 1.9), and of obscure impulses to self-depreciation and self-punishment (IV ,1.13).

IV, 3 discusses the vexed question of 'recollection'—practically the only place in the Teresian corpus where the saint actually sits down to think this through.[18] From the vantage point of the prayer of quiet, the holding of the soul by God, we can look back and identify what has helped to lay the foundations for it, humanly speaking (IV, 3.1). God wants to summon us into the castle, and calls 'Like a good shepherd, with a whistle so gentle that even [the sheep] themselves almost fail to hear it' (IV, 3.2); if we *are* to hear, we must dispose ourselves for listening. Teresa sticks to her lifelong conviction that it is not up to us actually to *stop* the intellect working (IV, 3.4, where she confesses that her view is controversial, and claims that Peter of Alcántara is on her side—though in fact the book she refers to is by Luis de Granada), and warns that the surface mind, the *pensamiento* or imagination once more, will 'become more restless through the effort made not to think of anything' (IV, 3.5). Stopping the mind is like holding your breath—unnatural and hard work (IV, 3.6)—and the effort concentrates attention on us, not God. Proper recollection, then, must be a matter of quietly slowing down mental activity, restraining the 'rambling' of the intellect and of the *pensamiento* (IV, 3.7) by using few and simple words. God's presence is being given, and all we have to do is enjoy it, uttering brief aspirations of love, rather than struggling for some complete suspension of activity (ibid.). But the more the will becomes absorbed in loving God, the more the 'holding operation' of simple acts of love, brief forms of words, tends to fall away, leaving (so to speak) nothing between the inner silence and wonder of the soul and the superficial mess and noisiness of the imagination (IV, 3.8). Teresa's terminology is more than usually muddled here, as she seems to have forgotten the distinction between intellect and imagination that she has just been drawing; but her general meaning is clear. 'Recollection' is the state in which the inner gaze of the soul is becoming more and more steadily fixed on God's self-giving, and that steadiness of regard finds expression in simple patterns of words;[19] as this deepens and simplifies, God's activity engages us with greater completeness, and our deepest 'mental' activities are reduced to silence, leaving the *impression* of greater interior confusion. Thus recollection stands on the frontier between the third and fourth mansions, between human and divine activity—a temporary but crucial condition. If we have not done something to quieten and discipline the busy and efficient flow of religious activity typical of the third mansions, we are not likely to open our depths to God in the way the fourth mansions presuppose. Teresa at last tackles how the essential transition to receptivity happens *other* than by the access of very tangible and dramatic graces. Brief as this treatment is, it represents a very important redressing of balance in respect of the *Life*—made possible largely by the fact that her agenda in the *Castle* is not 'political' or tactical in the way it was in the *Life*.

The remainder of IV, 3 returns to the problems of the prayer of quiet. It requires a good deal of care in respect of avoiding situations of temptation: the important thing is to go on putting oneself in the position where grace can be received, like a child at the breast,[20] since to fall back from this point is specially dangerous (IV, 3.10). Teresa implies that someone with this degree of familiarity with the life of prayer can have an enormous influence for evil in being able to speak with authority about some aspects of this life as though they were the whole: they can become a great teacher of false spirituality. And, very naturally, she adds some remarks on that particular manifestation of false spirituality so sharply treated in the *Foundations*, the self-indulgent absorption of the lazy or over-susceptible soul.

The fifth mansions mark the beginning of union properly so called. In speaking of the prayer characteristic of this phase, Teresa again uses language of the soul's ordinary capacities being 'asleep', as in the third water (V, 1.4), but cautions against deducing from this that we should expect it to be a 'dreamy' stage. Real sleep is not a condition of vagueness or woolgathering, but a time when our ordinary consciousness simply goes underground. For Teresa, it seems as if this is a phase in which, while we are in it, we can find *nothing* to say about the 'life of the spirit'. We have lost any way of formulating what is happening in us. The soul is divorced from the body (V, 1.4) in the sense that it is too numbed to attend to the ordinary stimuli transmitted by the physical senses. The distinctive prayer of the fifth mansions is thus a very brief spell in which there is no identifiable awareness of physical state or surroundings (V, 1.9) and perhaps also some slowing or even arrest of certain physical functions (V, 1.4). Eastern Christian writers in the 'hesychast' tradition have sometimes spoken of a perceptible slowing of the heartbeat and breath in certain states of prayer,[21] and it seems likely that Teresa has something like this in mind—the involuntary by-products of a general slowing-down of our rhythms of thought and speech. The gentler pace of being set up in the fourth mansions, with the stilling of our inmost mental life, here overflows perceptibly into the life of the body.[22]

This is something Teresa is happy to call *a* 'union', but it is not the final, pervasive condition to which the whole story is moving. If the fourth mansions increase our awareness of inner confusion, the fifth can be a stage of enormous restlessness and unhappiness. The experience that Teresa treats as typical gives a tantalizing hint of what is to come, and, emerging from the 'underground', the soul is made wretched by the obligation of ordinary material and social life (V, 2.8). It wants death: although it knows that God's will is that it should live and perform its earthly duties, 'it is not entirely surrendered to God's will' (V, 2.10). It is also tortured by the rejection of God that can be seen in the world around—apostasy, heresy and what Teresa thought of as plain heathenism (Islam): this is a pain that tears the soul apart (V, 2.11); but it is a mark of favour, the impress of God's seal (V, 2.12), since it reflects Christ's own desire, expressed at the Last Supper (L 22.15), to leave the world. Teresa wrestles with this rather more strenuously than she had done in the *Way* (W 42), though this passage echoes that in the *Way* quite closely—especially in its insistence that Jesus' knowledge of future human sin must have been a greater torment to him than the prospect of the cross. Wanting to die because of the pain of present circumstances is obviously an ambivalent thing, a sign of imperfect resignation to God; but the *sensation* of wanting to die because of the moral and spiritual horrors of the world, because of the compulsive self-destructiveness of human beings, can be a grace, since its impulse is bound up with charity and compassion. Christ longed to be away from the world of sin and rejection; yet the very same love of souls and of his Father that made his life so painful was also what made the pain bearable, since his living and dying in the world was to be for the world the 'one release' from its imprisonment (V, 2.13). So we, as best we can, must 'want' (i.e., assent to) the suffering we endure from 'wanting' (i.e., feeling a longing) to die: the love from which this comes is Christlike, and the acceptance of the tension and agony is Christlike.

Teresa is still casting around here, and these paragraphs are far from lucid. But what she has done is to abandon her earlier rather uncritical assumption that wanting to die is *of itself* a mark of grace and of spiritual advance. By introducing here a distinction between the soul's misery at having to perform mundane duties and its hypersensitivity to humanity's unfaithfulness to God, she manages to get some critical perspective on the restless unhappiness of the fifth mansions; and this perspective is shaped by the incarnational interest that increasingly pervades her mature reflection. As in *The Way of Perfection*, what matters is the taking-up of our will and our emotion into the single stream of love flowing through Christ from the Father.

The fifth mansions are explicitly associated by Teresa with the text from Colossians, 'You have died and your life is hid with Christ in God' (Col 3:3). Hiddenness is the keynote of this phase. The celebrated image of the cocoon and the butterfly developed in V, 2 is meant to underline this central feature of the fifth mansions. In the dumb and objectless stillness which characterizes our prayer at this point, we are in fact spinning a cocoon around ourselves: by emptying the self we 'build' Christ around us. When we are reduced to emptiness and silence, dead to all external stimuli and all internal prompting, what is left is the presence of Christ around us; and out of that emerges the butterfly, the transformed soul, fragile and restless, but beautiful as it was not before (V, 2.1–7). As usual, Teresa vacillates rather about whether her focus is the state of absorbed prayer described at the beginning of the fifth mansions or the entire phase of which this experience is typical but not exhaustive or definitive. When she speaks of the means by which we weave the cocoon of Christ's presence (V, 2.6), she refers to the continuing disciplines of the Christian and monastic life, as if the 'burial', the obscurity and silence, were a process extending over a period. But then, disconcertingly, she goes on almost at once (V, 2.7) to describe the condition of being dead to the world purely in terms of the experienced 'union' (which 'never lasts for as much as a half hour'). V, 3.3 contrasts the 'delightful union' of transient experience in prayer with the fundamental union of will that it presupposes: if we have the latter the former is really neither here nor there. It is important, she says, not to give the impression that 'supernatural' gifts (meaning, in Teresa's not very strict terminology, preternatural exceptional effects) are coterminous with being in 'this place', this set of mansions.

It seems, then, that once again we have an underlying condition which may or may not be manifested in specific experiences in prayer. The condition is one in which (as already noted) the sort of consciousness of the spirit's life that we might expect is radically obscured, not only by the experience of absorbing blankness in prayer, but more generally. Other writers suggest that this may be a phase when the ordinary language of theology or devotion comes to sound nonsensical or even repellent.[23] Nothing is adequate, nothing feels truthful; the words habitually used in and of prayer are unrecognizable. There is only an obstinate conviction of being drawn closer to the truth or reality, an unwillingness to revert to easy words or images of the way of Christ. This is no less a silencing, a cocooning, an underground life, than the empty, dark yet intense suspension of mental activity Teresa knew in her prayers at this point. There is here what Eckhart and others (Bonhoeffer, perhaps, in his remarks about living before God as men and women who can get along without God[24]) have spoken of as letting go of God for God's sake.

Yet this phase can also be called the beginning of 'spiritual betrothal' — when God and the human spirit make a conscious mutual commitment (V, 4.4). We know with new clarity who it is with whom we have to do — though this knowing is certainly not a matter of expressible conceptual clarity. Perhaps it is simply the stubbornness of our conviction that, whatever else is going on, we are at least no longer in danger of mistaking ideas and words about God for God, or confusing our own sense of doing well with the grace of God. We have been brought up against that sheer *difference* of the creator from the creature, about which we can finally say nothing satisfactory. But the betrothal is not yet formalized and finalized (we should remember that Teresa's society treated betrothal as a major ceremony): all we have is a declaring of intentions (V, 4.5). Our *sense* of stubborn adherence is still deeply vulnerable; it is not *itself* the reality of lasting union, and we may still deceive ourselves, especially as the devil is now more than ever eager to hold us back. We may develop attachments to 'little things' we have scarcely noticed (V, 4.8): protected as the (monastic) soul is from obvious and dramatic temptations, it can still be undermined by faults in the prosaic matters of common life, and so needs more than ever to be aware of whether or not it is growing in plain human charity and willingness for ordinary tasks (V, 4.9).

This is the more important because severe and bewildering upheavals still lie ahead for those with the will to move forward, as the betrothal is finally sealed and celebrated.

HOMECOMING

The sixth mansions occupy nearly a third of the whole work: Teresa seems to bundle into these chapters her reflections on nearly all the most controversial topics in the life of prayer. This is presumably because this is the stage at which discernment is most obviously needed, since it is the stage of greatest disorientation. It is here that she offers her fullest analysis of visionary and other exceptional experience, and her maturest reflections on the place of the human Jesus in the soul's reflections. The whole of this section presupposes the problematic situation set out in the first chapter (VI, 1). The 'butterfly' that has come to birth in the preceding stage is, as we have seen, vulnerable, restless and confused; so the sixth mansions are, even more than the fifth, a place of quite acute trial and suffering. We find here the language of the 'wound of love', so important in the imagery of John of the Cross (VI, 2.2): the deeper touch of God creates a sense of longing that is excruciatingly painful, yet also a source of pleasure. Unexpected and inexplicable reminders of God make the soul shiver (ibid.). There is a pervasive awareness of something begun, something promised, and the requirement to wait for it to come to fruition is agony. It is also a time of external trial: unfriendly gossip, accusations of spiritual arrogance or self-deceit, unwelcome praise (even worse), physical (possibly psychosomatic) illness, nervous and unimaginative spiritual directors. Furthermore, because of the loss of clear and plausible words for the life of the spirit that has occurred in the fifth mansions, the soul does not know how to communicate its experiences to confessors and others, and is liable to feel itself quite at the mercy of the vagaries of the imagination. Not even reading helps: the intellect is still stupefied by God's presence and cannot engage with words *about* God (VI, 1.9).

The profound union of will initiated in the fifth mansions is the hidden sustainer of the soul in the vicissitudes of the sixth (VI, 1.2), though the transitory experience of the 'wound' can help. About this, Teresa believes, we cannot be deceived, since the devil cannot counterfeit this peculiar fusion of pleasure and pain. This is an interesting criterion: the authenticity of the experience lies in its paradoxical character, in the fact that it will not fit a ready-made category of 'consoling' or 'upsetting'. But other experiences are more ambiguous. From VI, 3 to VI, 11, Teresa engages with precisely the kind of experiences that had so marked her own journey, especially at its crucial moments of transition, and attempts to discover the standards by which they are to be judged.

Throughout this discussion, she is quite clear that extraordinary visitations that are described as if they were physical experiences are the most suspect of all. The depressive or the hyper-sensitive, 'imaginative' soul is quite capable of manufacturing pseudo-physical illusions: that is, as we should say, simple hallucinations (VI, 3.1; cf. 9.4 and 9). Such a soul may be convinced that what is in the mind's eye is literally present, and this claim to see with the eyes of the body is what ought to make the superior or director very wary indeed: it may be necessary to stop such a person practising mental prayer at all (VI, 3.3). Basically, Teresa's criteria for the authenticity of exceptional experiences have to do with the presence or absence of two features: one is the sense that what the experiences convey is a gift, a moving of things on to a quite new level in the soul; and the second, obviously arising from the first, is the sense that what is conveyed exceeds what can immediately be understood or spoken about. Thus a putatively 'material' vision is one that must be looked at carefully, since it may well be only the recomposition of elements from existing experience; it does not immediately challenge the adequacy of our categories.

Teresa discusses three main categories of what she would call 'supernatural' phenomena: locutions, ecstasy and visions. We have already noted some of her advice about locutions,[25] and here she sums up earlier remarks and systematizes them, adding some intriguing phenomenological observations about what she regards as authentic communications. We hear again (VI, 3.5) of the idea that God's words to the soul 'effect what they say': a divine locution does not convey information primarily; it conveys the loving act of God. It creates assurance and peace. We know that it is from God because we become aware (not necessarily all at once) of a difference having been made in the depth of the self over and above any decision or movement on our part. So too (VI, 3.6), an increase in peacefulness and in eagerness to praise is a reliable test; and so is the clarity and persistence of the words we hear (VI, 3.7). What comes from our imagination or from the devil cannot produce these results: at best, we shall simply be telling ourselves what we secretly want to hear.

True locutions are clear, instantaneous, unexpected, rapid and pregnant with unforeseen material for further meditation (VI, 3.12–16): they say more than we could have *planned* to say, and we cannot refuse to listen (VI, 3.18). Teresa seems to be describing a sensation not uncommon in dreams, or in a semi-wakeful state (despite her proper insistence at VI, 3.10 and 12 that this is not a dreamlike condition), the sensation of hearing words distinctly and quite rapidly spoken that are only very imperfectly intelligible. 'True' locutions are the equivalent of this in a fully wakeful condition: something presented quickly and firmly to the mind, with no preparation. The difference is that the detail of the utterance can be clearly remembered, even if it is not perfectly understood.

Chapters 4 and 5 go on to look at ecstasy of various kinds, and Teresa here begins (VI, 4.5–6) to discuss the difference between kinds of vision—a subject to which she will return in more detail. Her categorization draws distinctions among the following: a brief experience of being stirred by a word or idea about God in such a way that all else in the soul is kindled into a loving absorption or suspension (VI, 4.3); a more dramatic suspension of physical faculties, as in the fifth mansions, but more powerful and disturbing (VI, 4.13); and 'flight of the spirit' (VI, 5.1), a sudden loss of ordinary mental awareness, frightening and irresistible, when the water that has been slowly filling the soul from within (IV, 2.2–5) suddenly surges up and carries the soul into another realm of awareness entirely, quite oblivious of the body and the outside world. The test for all these is much the same as with locutions—the presence of peace and acceptance, even in the midst of the tortured and obsessive yearning that may be more superficially felt as a result of these rapturous episodes (VI, 5.10, 6.1–2). That yearning is of itself a risky thing, and should not be deliberately fostered or intensified, especially not in a person of weak or suggestible constitution, as it is in danger of becoming a purely natural and self-regarding passion (VI, 6.6). And this is particularly important in thinking about the 'gift of tears' at this stage: there can be self-indulgent, exhausting fits of weeping, quite unlike the gentle overflow of tears given by God (VI, 6.7–9).[26] At the same time, a sort of causeless joy may be present (VI, 6.10), and there may be real discomfort in holding this back—since you will probably be assumed to be mad if you give it free reign.[27]

In such a condition, where the soul is more and more taken up in a kind of objectless sensation of love, is it not a regression of some sort to continue to reflect on the human Jesus (VI, 7.5)? Teresa records the opposition to her own views which she has experienced from those who insist that the formless divinity is the soul's proper object in this advanced state, but is quite unrepentant. She may be wrong, she says, or she may really be saying the same thing as her opponents, but what she is certain of is that for her the prompting to leave off consideration of the sacred humanity came from the devil. She proceeds to clarify her grounds for insisting on the necessity of keeping not only Jesus but the saints before our eyes; and in so doing reveals a great deal of what she thought central to her own theology and devotion. She repeats—with much increased lucidity—earlier remarks about different senses in which Jesus may be an 'object' for the mind, and freely grants that formal meditation on the life of Jesus is probably going to be impossible for anyone who has reached the sixth mansions (VI, 7.10–12). But there are two points to be borne in mind. First, our fervour is by no means consistent, and will need kindling from time to time, so long as we have not yet reached complete union in the seventh mansions; and so we need to make ourselves aware of who Christ is, how we make him suffer, and what we owe to him. These simple facts require no massive efforts of imagining or thinking; the more we are caught up in God's love, the more it will be enough for the intellect to dwell or gaze on a single image, a single event or saying, with no detailed discursive activity at all (VI, 7.11). This simple gaze may itself issue in the 'suspending' or blanking out of the intellect, but it is still a necessary preliminary. The second point (VI, 7.13–14) is that we do not ever get to a state of uninterrupted enjoyment of quiet: 'Life is long, and there are in it many trials', and for the bearing of such trials we need human support. Equally important, it is good for us to put aside the delights of absorption and to remember Christ's cross with sorrow. 'Jesus is too good a companion for us to turn away from him and his most blessed mother.' Because Christ is generous enough to share our human pain, we not only need his help in our own suffering, but owe it to him to share in his. We should remember here Teresa's reaction to the image of the suffering Christ: we are needed by the human Jesus, and on the awareness of that need grows the beginning of a belief in our human worth.

We are not angels, Teresa repeats (VI, 7.6), but bodies; we learn as bodies, and we need to have companionship with those who, in the body, have served God. Unbroken contemplation is not and cannot be our destiny (VI, 7.7). And if, in the seventh mansions, we do not need our devotion kindled in the same way by reflection on Jesus, this is because the human life of Jesus is now being mirrored and lived out in our bodily humanity (VI, 7.9). Some have quoted John 16:7 ('it is to your advantage that I go away') in support of abandoning reflection on the sacred humanity,[28] but Teresa turns the flank very forcefully. If the apostles *needed* Jesus to go away, their faith must have been very weak and muddled: for the really mature in faith, Jesus' presence cannot be a danger or hindrance (VI, 7.14). Spiritual maturity, in other words, is here seen as not wanting to stop being flesh and blood: Mary, who bore Jesus in the flesh and knew him as both human and divine, is the paradigm of this maturity; and the abiding presence of Jesus in the Eucharist should warn us off the *corrupt* 'spiritualism' into which Satan wants to lead us (ibid.). As Teresa has hinted in VI, 7.9 and goes on to underline in VI, 8.1, the 'inward' journey through the castle is the journey of the Son to the Father, *through* history and flesh — an insight wholly congruent with her striking idea, discussed in Chapter 3, of the Eucharist as Christ coming to the Father who waits within the soul. These pages on the humanity of Jesus are informed by the same radically incarnational theology as *The Way of Perfection*, and look forward to her final statements about the acceptance of the temporal and material in the seventh mansions.

The implication of what she has been saying is spelled out in VI, 8.1: visions and the like are meant to show us Christ accompanying us on our fleshly journey, and ultimately for no other end. Teresa explains that for her the 'visionary' experience first dawned in the form of a sense of Christ's presence alongside her that had no visual content at all (VI, 8.2); and, given what she has said about Christ as companion, this makes perfect sense. Only in very special circumstances and for a very particular purpose would we expect to see Christ 'facing' us. The movement of our prayer is in Christ to the Father; Teresa's Christocentrism is not a cult of Jesus. The 'intellectual vision' of simple awareness of Christ may last for a very long time without interruption, whereas 'imaginative' visions — a specific picture before the inner eye — are much more short-lived (VI, 8.3). At the same time, an imaginative vision *can* be more beneficial (VI, 9.1) because it is 'in greater conformity with our nature'. To see the human Jesus (or Our Lady or one of the saints) in a determinate shape, however briefly, is closer to the way in which our minds ordinarily get to know things. Teresa has in fact set up an intriguing dilemma for herself here, as the incarnational impulse moves her in two different directions at once. The imageless awareness of Christ's nearness is in some obvious ways better, safer, more normal: it does not make Christ an object in himself (thought of course at one level it is possible and proper to *address* Christ) but presents him to the mind as the power that moves us along the road to the Father. In so doing, it keeps our attention on the earthly, mortal road we must walk with Jesus. But our earthly and mortal knowledge comes from impressions, images, ordinary sense impressions: to 'see' Jesus, to see the historical form of the holiness into which we are being led, seems again to keep us bound to what we are as fleshly beings, even if this is not a matter of seeing with fleshly eyes. There is no point in trying to resolve the dilemma as to which is 'preferable' overall (it did not worry Teresa greatly); but it is important to see how both types of vision are understood within the Christocentric framework she has developed.

The good confessor, once again invoked here (VI, 8.8–9, 9.11–13), must be a man who is not so anxious about the possibility of diabolical illusion that he fails to see how even illusion can be turned to profit if we respond with humility and reverence. Teresa, as the *Life* records, had been advised by one confessor to greet her visions with a vulgar gesture of abuse, and this caused her enormous strain;[29] in VI, 9.12–13 she recalls this again, and commends the advice of more sensible directors—which is to venerate any likeness of Christ, whatever its source, and to beware of thinking about imaginative visions as if they were a reward for piety or virtue. VI, 9.15 repeats and elaborates advice given elsewhere on the folly of wanting visions: the person who desires these experiences will be in grave danger of fabricating them unconsciously, and does not realize that they go together with enormous sufferings and trials. God will give them to the truly humble, and he will also give strength for these trials. To be humble, to know that you do not and will not *deserve* visions, to resist the urge to seek (and manufacture) 'special' experiences—this is the best defence against delusion, the best guarantee against self-deceit or diabolical fraud, and the best grounds for complete honesty with a confessor: if you are genuinely surprised or troubled by a vision (of whatever kind), that should make you *more* ready to share it with a confessor, since your confusion will make it clear that this is not simply something sought or projected.

VI, 10 touches on a point to which Teresa returns in VII—a different form of intellectual 'vision' that is simply an unexpected and compelling insight into some doctrinal truth; and in 11 she returns to the pains of unfulfilled longing in the sixth mansions, and the real dangers of bodily hurt in the weaker or more sensitive body (11.4 mentions the slowing of the heartbeat as a symptom which makes a person in ecstatic prayer comparable to one on a deathbed). But the main issues have been dealt with.

We may still, though, ask what exactly *is* the sixth phase? Teresa has discussed problems and phenomena that crop up at earlier stages, and it is hard to see completely clearly what is distinctive in this phase: that is, what is *theologically* distinctive over and above an intensification of peculiar phenomena. The answer, I think, is two-fold. First, this is the point at which our relation with God becomes fully established in its direction: because it is characterized by such agonizing restlessness and impatience with words and formulae, it necessarily looks beyond itself. In some sense, it has become impossible to slip back, even if mistakes are made, and damage can still be done. Second, it is a stage in which the conscious, planning ego has completely lost control — whether this finds expression in the absolute lack of convincing, honest-sounding religious language for what is going on, or in the violent onset of paranormal phenomena, or both (as Teresa herself seems to have found). Those who have assimilated the sixth mansions to St John's 'passive night of the spirit' are surely right.[30] Some kind of decisive surrender has been made, the surrender without which final union would not be possible. In the fifth mansions there was still the residual danger of concentrating on our own faithfulness rather than God's; but the sixth draw our attention away once and for all from the resources of our will, and drive us forward in urgent longing that is more and more consumed and determined by its object — the God at the centre whose presence has become irreversibly pervasive in us and compelling to us.

The seventh mansions are 'spiritual marriage' (VII, 1.2), complete union. Teresa hesitates to say too much about it for fear 'others will think I know about it through experience' (ibid.), but it is clear enough that she does know from experience at least something of what ultimate union can mean. It is a state higher than and distinct from 'rapture' (VII, 1.5) — a direct retractation of L 20.1, it seems. At earlier stages, in the fifth and sixth mansions, God unites the soul to God, but in such a way that the ordinary exercise of mental life, ordinary self-awareness is taken away: but here the soul knows what is going on (VII, 1.6). It is given 'intellectual' vision of the Trinity, so that it grasps both the unity and the distinctness of the divine persons (compare T 13 and 51); and, as with other such visions, this is not something that competes with normal visual perception, but endures, in this case lastingly, as an awareness that accompanies our day-to-day experience (VI, 1.6–8). Thus the soul is *active* in this state: united with God, it now does God's work. The intensity of the soul's awareness of the Trinity within will vary greatly, but there remains an unshakeable and fundamental *conviction* of God's companionship (VII 1.9). This prompts Teresa to qualify her earlier brisk dismissals of the idea of distinctions within the self; she needs a word for whatever is united with God at the root of the self, and a word for what it is that remains vulnerable in its feelings and thoughts. Trials and pain persist, and the mutable surface of the soul may complain 'as Martha complained of Mary', objecting 'that [the depth of the soul] was there always enjoying that quietude at its own pleasure while leaving [the conscious self] in the midst of so many trials and occupations that she could not keep it company' (VII, 1.10). She seems to settle (VII, 1.11) for using 'soul' itself for the depth of the psyche, and 'spirit' for the active and conscious faculties (cf.VII, 2.10; T 25); but almost at once, in VII, 2.3, she reverts to identifying them. She is not particularly interested in establishing a consistent terminology, since all she needs to do is signal the all-important distinction between the state of final union itself and any particular experience. Being wholly and abidingly bound to the life of God in Christ, living the life of Christ (now that the 'little butterfly' has given up its life to Christ: VII, 2.5) is compatible with a whole range of emotional states, and with a persisting vulnerability to conflict, trial and pain (VII, 2.9–11).

However, although the sense of joy in union will sometimes well up in words of praise and gratitude (VII, 2.6), the fact that the soul is anchored in God at its centre means that extremities of affective experience become a thing of the past. The trials of the 'spirit' do not produce darkness or dryness in the 'soul', and the desire to serve God and the confidence of God's favour remain unchanged (VII, 3.6, 8, 10). On the other hand, there is no more restless longing for tangible signs of God, 'consolations or spiritual delight' (VII, 3.8), and no experience – or hardly any – of 'rapture' (VII, 3.12). The anxiety that attends the emotional heights and depths of the sixth mansions, not least the fear of making a fool of yourself in public, is allayed; we no longer have to worry about straining our constitution and doing ourselves damage (ibid.). 'The cross is not wanting but it doesn't disquiet . . . For the storms, like a wave, pass quickly' (VII, 3.15).

It is still quite possible, then, to be depressed about one's sin or laziness or feebleness, still possible to wish one were dead — at the level of passing reactions to things (VII, 2.9, 3.14, etc.); there may even be an unrelieved (if transient) sense of one's *natural* helplessness in the face of the lizards and vermin from the castle's moat (VII, 4.1), so that we do not lose sight of our creaturely frailty. Nor is the soul in the spiritual marriage delivered from venial sin (VII, 4.3). But the definitive reality is our being in Christ and, through Christ, in the Father (VII, 2.7) in such a way that we no longer find our state of mind obsessively interesting: there may be joy or misery, weakness or resolution, but the soul registers all this with 'strange forgetfulness' (VII, 3.2), interested only in finding what will serve the honour of God and the needs of God's human creation (VII, 3.2, 4–6; 4.6, 10–15). The point and purpose of the whole process of the soul's transformation is 'the birth always of good works, good works' (VII, 4.6): not unbroken repose, but apostolic activity on the basis of inner stability (VII, 4.10). She is careful to deny that she is teaching the doctrine associated with the *alumbrados*,[31] that the soul in this state absolutely cannot slip back, but, although we must maintain a concern not to offend God (VII, 2.9), the main thing is that we are set free from worrying about satisfying God, or about risks and pitfalls in the 'inner life'. Indeed, it would not be far from the truth to say that for the soul in the seventh mansions the 'inner life' does not exist as an independent object of examination and concern. Attention is wholly on God and the world.

The soul is willing to suffer, but not miserable if it cannot (VII, 3.4); it is not afraid of death (VII, 3.7), and, as we have observed, may occasionally feel it wants death, but is fundamentally resolved to *live* so as to do whatever God wants.[32] In some sense the prospect of the joys of heaven is neither here nor there (VII, 3.6). If there is a basic acceptance and a basic joy or gratitude in the present moment, there is no cause for those exhausting yearnings for death that have characterized earlier stages in the journey. We must accept that we are now committed to growth in love realized in the obligations of mission and service: 'love . . . cannot possibly be content with remaining always the same' (VII, 4.9). 'Martha and Mary must join together in order to show hospitality to the Lord' (VII, 4.12): Teresa is sceptical about the pious excuse that Mary is said to have 'chosen the better part', since Mary's own contemplation follows on the work and apostolic witness involved in her conversion (VII, 4.13). And if it is said that the life of Carmel affords no *real* apostolic opportunities Teresa remarks that we should remember that the sisters are called both to prayer and to sanctification through the prosaic business of living together in love: 'sometimes the devil gives us great desires so that we will avoid setting ourselves to the task at hand, serving our Lord in possible things' (VII, 4.14). 'Being a contemplative' is simply not, for Teresa, the exhaustive definition of *anybody's* vocation: what is definitive is our identification with Christ's offering to the Father, which is wholly directed at once to God and to the life and healing of the world (VII, 4.15).

So, with her well-loved fusion of the supposedly distinct vocations of Martha and Mary established as the guiding principle of the highest stage in spiritual growth, Teresa ends her most mature and self-critical work. The speed of its composition[33] and one or two major interruptions in the process give it a superficially disjointed look, of which Teresa was well aware. But the speed, fluency and confidence of composition also confirm what a more careful reading will reveal: that she is writing out of an unprecedentedly coherent and synoptic vision of the growth of the spirit towards union. For all the remaining fascination with the 'technicolour' of preternatural phenomena, Teresa is here, as was suggested at the beginning of this chapter, undertaking a kind of 'demystification' of what moderns tend to refer to as mysticism (not a word in her vocabulary). Her personal journey, her deepening awareness of the perils of false interiority, above all the growing comprehensiveness, nuance and resourcefulness of her vision of the incarnate Christ enable her to draw together themes from the whole of her work in something like a synthesis. The movement is ultimately one of 'homecoming', coming to oneself. If God is at the centre, we can only live and act from the centre of our reality (and so live and act with integrity) when we let that central action of God that holds us in being have free play in us. 'It is only when God has been able to love us in fullness that we are wholly *there* . . . Only when we are God-filled are we truly human.'[34] Until we reach God we are discontented with ourselves, our limitations, the duration of time, the pressure of our bodies: the paradoxical conclusion of the *Castle* is that union with God—the wholly and sovereignly 'unworldly', the utterly free and different—is the only thing that will stop time and mortality and the flesh feeling alien or insulting or frustrating. It is as united with God that we learn to be where we are in the world.

Teresa's history is—not surprisingly—vividly present in her thinking about the Christian life. A story that is full of discontinuities, frustrations, false starts and risks will inevitably generate a theology that stresses how hard and how strange a thing it is to 'be where we are in the world'. She assumes that we are likely to be strangers to ourselves and that we (like her beloved Augustine) need a measure of divine violence to be brought home: it is not natural to us to be natural. But this means that all the records in Teresa's work of violent and disorienting episodes are misunderstood if read simply as a characterization of something called 'mystical' experience: the question to which she is finally seeking an answer is how a self compulsively at odds with its own real good and liable to produce any number of self-justifying and self-flattering fantasies may come to *belong* in the single movement of God's love, making and affirming and renewing the concrete world of bodies in communication. The seventh mansions of the *Castle* are probably her clearest testimony to the possibility—and the joy—of that belonging.

Notes

1 See above, pp. 8, 32–3, 43.

2 As it was for John of the Cross: see the recollections of John of the Cross by Madre Magdalena de Espíritu Santo, printed as an appendix to Allison Peers's translation of the saint's works: *The Complete Works of St John of the Cross* (London, 1943), pp. 320–1.

3 Kavanaugh–Rodriguez III, p. 419. On the treatment of melancholia, see also *Letters* I, 59, p. 148, where the depressed nun is advised to 'go where you can see the sky'.

4 In, for example, *The Ascent of Mount Carmel* 2.17–19, 3.13.

5 See Kavanaugh–Rodriguez II, pp. 267–9.

6 Ruth Burrows, *Interior Castle Explored* (London and Dublin, 1982), p. 18.

7 Cf. John of the Cross, *The Dark Night of the Soul* 1.1–7, which makes very much the same point: there are highly spiritualized versions of all the most elementary vices and sins.

8 See Noel Dermot O'Donoghue, *With Inward Glory Crowned. A Guide to St Teresa of Avila's Interior Castle* (Manchester and Dublin, 1981), pp. 16–17.

9 See Kavanaugh–Rodriguez II, pp. 486–7 note 2 on Gracián's problems with Teresa's apparent willingness to assert some kind of assurance of final salvation—a highly controversial point in the aftermath of the Council of Trent. Teresa is in fact quite careful in her phrasing, assuming that there is objectively such a thing as a secure path to salvation, but that there can be no guarantee that any individual will indefectibly remain on it, given the unpredictable vicissitudes of this life.

10   Burrows, *op. cit.*, p. 28.

11   Ibid., p. 33.

12   Trueman Dicken describes one such influential attempt: *op. cit.*, pp. 203–5.

13   T. S. Eliot, *On Poetry and Poets* (London, 1957), p. 98.

14   Including, in certain circumstances, physical pressure: see IV, 2.1.

15   Burrows, *op. cit.*, pp. 50–1; cf. Rowan Williams, 'Butler's *Western Mysticism*: towards an assessment', *Downside Review* 102 (July 1984), pp. 197–215 – esp. pp. 203–6 on the question of 'substantial touches' in John of the Cross.

16   Burrows, *op. cit.*, p. 17.

17   See *The Philokalia*, trans. G. E. H. Palmer, Philip Sherrard and Kallistos Ware, I (London, 1979), pp. 50–1, 141–3, 162–4, etc.

18   Trueman Dicken, *op. cit.*, ch. 7; esp. pp. 191–2, 196–203, on the difficulties of sorting out Teresa's ideas about 'recollection'.

19   Once again, it is worth comparing this with Augustine Baker, *Holy Wisdom*, section 4, ch. 2 (on 'aspirations' in prayer).

20   See Chapter 3, note 12 above.

21   See Kallistos Ware, *The Power of the Name. The Jesus Prayer in Orthodox Spirituality* (Oxford, 1974), esp. pp. 18–22.

22   The principle here is expounded by John of the Cross, though in a rather different idiom and context: *The Living Flame of Love*, 2.12 (recension A), 2.13 (recension B).

23   See, for example, John Chapman OSB, *Spiritual Letters*, ed. R. Hudleston (London, 1935) for some pointed comments on this.

24   Dietrich Bonhoeffer, *Letters and Papers from Prison* (enlarged edn; London, 1967), p. 360.

25   Above, pp. 72–4.

26   An excellent study of the whole phenomenon of tears in prayer is Maggie Ross, *The Fountain and the Furnace. The Way of Tears and Fire* (Mahwah, NJ, 1987).

27   The parallel with Ignatius Loyola's notion of 'consolation without preceding cause' (*Spiritual Exercises*, 330) may be worth exploring – one of several points of contact between the very distinct idioms and frames of reference of these two writers. Teresa's sympathy with the Jesuits she knew in Avila, and theirs with her, is something that should qualify any glib opposition between 'Carmelite' and 'Ignatian' spiritualities; though Teresa's *Vejamen* suggests a certain wariness of the *Exercises* as a requirement for spiritual beginners.

28   Who? The text is not in fact used by either Osuna or John of the Cross in their discussions of the humanity of Jesus.

29 29.5-6; the priest in question was probably Gonzalo de Aranda, a friend and associate of Daza, Salcedo and their circle; he later became a firm ally of Teresa's.

30 For example, O'Donoghue, *op. cit.*, p. 34.

31 And, presumably, Protestants by this date; cf. note 9 above.

32 Teresa in her *Spiritual Testimonies* 17 and 37 (both almost certainly referring to the same experience in July 1571) identifies a moment of breakthrough in this connection, related to an earlier locution (mentioned in T 28), in which Christ tells Teresa that she is now his friend in the same way as Mary Magdalene was during his earthly life. Reflecting on the demands of this friendship, Teresa is determined to live and serve her friend.

33 She wrote about half of *The Interior Castle* (as far as V, 2) in just over a month; and, after a delay of a little over four months, completed the remainder between the beginning and the end of November 1577. For a vivid description of her absorbed and rapid writing, during the period following her Communion each day, see the testimony of Maria del Nacimiento in the introduction to the Kavanaugh-Rodriguez translation, II, p. 267 and note 13.

34 Burrows, *op. cit.*, p. 112.

5

Mysticism and incarnation

DEFINING MYSTICISM
Some false starts

Throughout this book, the word 'mystical' has been used almost exclusively in the sense that Teresa herself would have found intelligible: as a designation for the sort of knowledge of God that is obscure to the intellect. The root meaning of 'mystical' has to do with hiddenness, closed doors; and until the sixteenth century, Christian usage of words deriving from the Greek *muō*, 'to close up' or 'conceal', stayed close to this primitive sense. When the anonymous fifth-century writer we know as Denys the Areopagite wrote a treatise on 'mystical theology', he was writing about the way in which Christian liturgy displays the 'mysteries' of God's action in relation to the created order—the mystery of God going out from the depths of the divine nature to create and then to become incarnate in our nature, God binding creation together in communion and drawing creation back to its divine source. To understand this divine movement is to receive it into yourself in such a way that you are taken beyond all words and signs; and this openness or passivity to God's movement ('suffering divine things') is what 'mystical theology' means.[1] Exposure to the hidden unity of God's going forth from and returning into the ultimate hiddenness of the divine life-in-itself is, of course, very much what Teresa, in her quite different idiom, understands to be the essence of our prayer in particular and our sanctification in

143

general; and in this sense alone she might have been persuaded to call her experience as a Christian 'mystical'. More specifically, the mystical ('mystical theology', as in L 9.1) begins when the self is *surrendered* at a radical level to the activity of God, so that it can no longer be thought of as acting from a centre separated from God. The mystical is the 'supernatural' (C IV, 1.1), and both mean simply the state in which what we are doing coincides — more or less — with what God is doing; or, in theological terms, it is the formation of our created selfhood in the likeness of Christ.

'If such is the case we finally understand why mysticism was never reduced by the Fathers to the level of a psychological experience, considered merely, or primarily, in its subjectivity. It is always the experience of an invisible objective world: the world whose coming the Scriptures reveal to us in Jesus Christ, the world into which we enter, ontologically, through the liturgy, through this same Jesus Christ ever present in the Church.'[2] Louis Bouyer's summary of the classical meaning of the mystical expresses very clearly what is central to Teresa's understanding — though he continues to use the word 'mysticism', which, I want to suggest, has some problematic aspects. The way Bouyer phrases his judgement draws our attention to the difficulty involved in speaking today about mysticism and the mystical. From being a word bound closely to the hidden continuities of God's purpose with the world, 'mystical' has become an adjective characterizing particular religious states of mind; and 'mysticism' is defined by *The Oxford English Dictionary* as involving 'belief in the possibility of union with the divine nature by means of ecstatic contemplation; reliance on spiritual intuition or exalted feeling as the means of acquiring knowledge of mysteries inaccessible to intellectual apprehension'. Mysticism has come to be opposed to the rational and the institutional aspects of religious life, and it is very frequently regarded as a form of experience common to all religious traditions and representing a level of unity in the religious apprehension of reality deeper than the merely historical and linguistic diversities between faiths. We can identify a phenomenological core to 'mysticism' that has some real coherence; we can map out subdivisions and variations within a single overall pattern. This approach was given classical expression in a number of influential studies from the early decades of this century in Britain and Germany especially,[3] and is still alive and well in many departments of religious studies (and occasionally in departments of psychology as well).

To discuss in detail how mysticism and the mystical have come to be defined would need another (and longer) book. It is enough for now to note that they have become words associated with a specific range of states of consciousness, states of consciousness we should be inclined to describe as abnormal or at least exceptional, with some significant analogies to conditions usually identified with mental pathology or dysfunction. Opinions differ as to whether these analogies should be pressed to the conclusion that 'mystical' experience actually *is* a mental disorder.[4] The exceptional states in question may be what we should otherwise call hallucinatory: the receiving of what seem to be sense impressions without the presence of publicly identifiable sense stimuli; or they may be experiences of the breakdown of the usual sense of personal identity and distinctness, a sense of the self merging with what is not the self (God, the ensemble of the cosmos, another person). Some writers have wanted to take the latter as somehow normative for 'mysticism', and so to contrast the claims of Christian writers on prayer and contemplation (who tend to emphasize the abiding distinction between God and the created self) unfavourably with traditions that are happier to speak of ultimate absorption into unity. Distinctions are sometimes drawn between Christian 'mystics' in terms of whether they are 'monistic' or 'theistic' in orientation, whether they emphasize unity or some sort of conscious relationship as between different subjects.[5] But what enables all the diverse phenomenological material in question to be bundled together under the one concept of 'the mystical' is finally, it seems, the judgement that ordinary consciousness is being interrupted in such a way that we are given a *direct* awareness of sacred reality, however that reality is described.

This evidently has *something* in common with what Teresa and her tradition understood by the 'mystical' (though they would not have understood a noun like 'mysticism') to the extent that what is in view is a shift from less to more 'direct' contact with the divine, a removal of certain of the obstacles that the awareness of the ordinary data of human consciousness may set up to a deeper harmony with divine agency. But the Catholic Christian understanding of this involves subordinating the study of particular abnormal states of consciousness to the evaluation of the pattern of human reflection and behaviour that is emerging through and beyond any such exceptional states. If the 'mystical' ultimately means the reception of a particular *pattern* of divine action (creative love, self-emptying incarnation), its test will be the presence or absence of something like that pattern in a human life seen as a whole, not the presence or absence of this or that phenomenon in the consciousness. What might justify a student of religious phenomenology in applying the term 'mystic' to someone would not, by any means, settle the Christian question of whether or not such a person was having what Christian tradition would call 'mystical' experience—the assimilation of their life to Christ's. And while the student of phenomenology might conclude that, say, John of the Cross had more in common with Shankara[6] than with someone like Teresa's tough peasant secretary and nurse, Ana de San Bartolomé, the Christian theologian would have to disagree. John and Ana both ask to be judged by the pattern of the Word of God made flesh and crucified.

However, it would not be wrong to conclude that Teresa's own way of presenting her particular living-out of this pattern unwittingly does a good deal to prepare the way for the characteristically modern approach to the mystical. There had been before Teresa some writers—especially in the Eastern Christian world—who had, in different ways, emphasized the experiential side of the pattern of Christian discipleship: the fourth-century Macarian homilies and the eleventh-century Byzantine saint Symeon the 'New Theologian' describe personal experiences of an exceptional character; and Evagrius of Pontus, a contemporary of the Macarian homilist, offers criteria by which such experiences may be judged (and, usually, found wanting). He is one of the earliest Christian writers to insist in plain terms that the awareness of God at its highest human point is a consciousness of no particular object, a pure wordless intuiting of a reality so pre-eminently at one in itself that it cannot be broken up into image or concept.[7] These writers would certainly merit a place in any anthology of what moderns call mystical literature. And there are also, of course, in East and West, testimonies from visionaries of one sort and another: a number of the better-known saints are credited with receiving visions (Thomas Aquinas is one obvious example), and there are the great works of visionary literature emanating particularly from female writers such as Hildegard of Bingen and Julian of Norwich. Teresa, however, is doing something perceptibly different. She presents a picture of her life as a Christian in terms of a pattern of *growth*; and the exceptional experiences she describes and discusses function to some extent as markers of the transitions between different stages. Thus she is doing more than most of her predecessors: not only recording and reflecting visionary and other preternatural episodes, but locating them on a map of the Christian life designed to be of more than individual or anecdotal interest. She is also doing more than Evagrius or those whom Evagrius criticized: she is systematizing (however awkwardly or provisionally) her 'mystical' episodes and proposing that they be evaluated not by a set of general criteria about what true encounter with God must be (experientially) like, but according to how these episodes fit into the whole movement of a soul towards Christlikeness.

This may need to be spelled out a little further. Evagrius (and the tradition deriving from him) seeks to find characteristics *in* the experience itself which will tell us whether or not it is truly to do with God. 'Prayer is communion of the intellect with God. What state, then, does the intellect need so that it can reach out to its Lord without deflection and commune with this without intermediary?'[8] This is the question with which Evagrius begins his series of apophthegms on prayer; and his answer is in terms of 'making the intellect deaf and dumb',[9] not shaping 'any image of the deity' or letting the mind 'be stamped with the impress of any form'.[10] Pure prayer frees us from all material sensations;[11] the presence of particular impressions to sense or mind is a sign at best of imperfection and at worst of diabolical interference.[12] As we have seen at several points in this book, Teresa is well aware of a tradition that commends this refusal of all images as the path to true contact with God, and treats it with suspicion. She makes it very clear that, as far as she is concerned, the criteria of authenticity do not lie in the character of the experience itself but in how it is related to a pattern of concrete behaviour, the development of dispositions and decisions. There is no one kind of experience that declares itself at once to be an experience of God; and the person advancing in the way of Christ must learn not to be afraid of the sort of highly specific and concrete perceptions of Christ or the saints that may well accompany periods of significant spiritual change. The only rule of thumb she suggests is that the closer such perception is to what we should call the hallucinatory—actually supposing the object of vision to be present to the senses—the less likely it is to be genuinely of God (above, p. 131).

But the effect of this Teresian emphasis is paradoxical and double-edged. On the one hand, the shift of *theological* emphasis away from the character of the experience itself places all preternatural episodes firmly under the standards of judgement to which all Christians are answerable. In that sense, 'the mystical' is not, for Teresa, to be opposed to the intellectual and the institutional: there is a common

Christian vocation, lived out within the historical structures of the Catholic Church, and the 'specialness' of exceptional experience is relativized. To recall the phrase used earlier: mysticism is demystified, and mystical experience *as such* is accorded no particular authority. Its authority — as Teresa implicitly argues in the *Life* — has to be displayed in the shape of the vocation of which it is part. On the other hand, if no particular experience can be programmatically ruled out from serious theological consideration, there is good reason for intensified phenomenological interest in the varieties of preternatural or paranormal occurrence in prayer, especially when (as in Teresa's case) these are to some extent organized as an ascending series. Teresa herself, as we have noted so many times, is fascinated by her experiences, and yet at the same time more and more committed to an account of the nature of Christian maturity in which they are not unimportant but, ultimately, incidental. Her growing recognition and affirmation of the different gifts that may be given to different temperaments and circumstances qualifies the impression that she is simply and crudely offering her own history as normative — though she is constantly in danger of doing just this when she is most caught up in the warmth and drama of her encounter with Christ. But if we take away or water down her Christological framework, with its corporate and ecclesial, moral and sacramental dimensions, what is left appears all too easily as a schema of psychic adventure, an unprecedentedly full and, above all, continuous record of 'mystical experience' — one of the foundational texts of mysticism in the modern sense. And, for all the enormous differences of tone and emphasis between him and Teresa, John of the Cross has suffered a similar fate at the hands of those who fail to see the theological structure within which he works and imagine that both the 'nights' and the 'union' of which he writes are clearly distinguishable, isolable states of subjective awareness, felt experience, rather than ways of talking about stages in the movement Godwards of a whole, acting and reflecting self, not strictly chronological and not reducible to special kinds of awareness.

In other words, Teresa helped to invent 'mysticism', albeit unwittingly. She had plotted her own remarkable experiences on a chart of spiritual progress and thus encouraged the student of a later generation to suppose that the charting of spiritual progress was primarily a matter of a phenomenology of states of consciousness. The final product of this supposition is the idea, given classic and authoritative shape in the work of William James, that religious experience is not so much the experiencing of the world within the framework of faith as the experiencing of special religious data — whether encounters with supposedly supernatural individuals or an awareness of 'divine' reality within the self and the world, beyond the play of passing circumstance. And beyond this lies the contemporary interest in 'religious experience' as providing possible confirmation, evidential support, for the claims of theistic language: if our immediate personal states of consciousness are the only place where real certainty is to be found, here, surely we can begin to settle the issue of what we may be sure of in religious matters. If there is a basic identifiable unity to religious or mystical experience, *that* is what we may be sure of, and the claims of particular religious *traditions* must be assessed in the light of this.[13]

Teresa and her contemporaries would have found this surprising. For all Teresa's interest in the visionary and paranormal, she is not disposed to use it as evidence for the way the universe is. 'Do mystical states establish the truth of those theological affections in which the saintly life has its root?' asks William James in the course of a discussion of Teresa.[14] Teresa herself would never have imagined that 'mystical states' could do such a job. Presented as they are by her in the *Life*, they may have a highly significant role in resolving arguments about practical and pastoral authority, but it would not have occurred to Teresa that they had any part whatsoever to play in doctrinal discussion. So far from 'mystical states' being a sort of paradigm of certainty, they have authority only within a frame of reference which is believed in on quite other grounds, and are therefore properly to be tested according to their consistency with this. Certainly Teresa considers certain of her experiences (especially locutions) to carry a kind of self-authenticating stamp upon them; but the self-authentication is, as she says, a matter of their effecting what they say (above, pp. 72–3, 131): that is, confirming the spoken assurance of divine presence or faithfulness. They do not therefore offer evidence in support of a contested claim about matters of fact. Once again, it looks as if Teresa's language, when divorced from her theology, gives some illusory support to the Jamesian approach to the question of mysticism; whereas, in its context, it is compatible with Teresa's overall assumption that 'mystical' paranormal states are *essentially* questionable. Distantly in the background stands Evagrius once more: thinking we see something is neither here nor there in constructing a truthful account of the universe we stand in or the God we stand before. Isolated perceptions, states of consciousness that can be marked off and studied as individual units, are not pieces of neutral evidence presented to the impartial tribunal of a blank mind waiting to discover what reality is like. They are part of the history of a materially identified and temporally limited self that has had to learn to 'read' the world by learning how to live in a particular human group. What we experience has sense and force, can be communicated, discussed and understood, only because we have learned to recognize and respond to the shape of the world in a way that is common to the human beings among whom we live.

If this general philosophical point is correct, the 'modern' approach to mysticism is full of difficulties.[15] The search for a core experience, for the essentially mystical, is bound to be fruitless if it assumes that there is a paradigm example of the mystical consciousness that can be abstracted from specific historical religious traditions: the exceptional, the paranormal episode in the life of a religious believer is properly understood within, not apart from, the expectations, conventions and criteria of the believer's milieu. There is, of course, an interesting, even impressive convergence in some of the language used in different traditions about paranormal episodes and unusual states of consciousness, but we should be cautious about supposing that this indicates 'the same experience' in the sense of an identical state of consciousness or a consciousness of the same object. There may be far more to be said about such convergence in quite other terms. Above all, the use of mystical experience to establish what it is in religion that we may be (empirically) sure about not only misconceives the actual way in which records of exceptional experience function in the language and the debate of a tradition, but begs the major philosophical question of whether we can *ever* talk of experience that is not already shaped by the *shared* consciousness that human communication establishes and embodies. To understand Teresa, we must try to get rid of most of what words like 'mysticism' have come to mean, and follow her own example in relating her experience to her tradition.

A new model

In a provocative study of Buddhist spirituality some years ago, an American scholar suggested that the 'mystical' states of consciousness that appear in some kinds of Buddhism are more or less designed to illustrate the Buddhist world-view: 'Rather than speak of Buddhist doctrines as interpretations of Buddhist mystical experiences, one might better speak of Buddhist mystical experiences as deliberately contrived exemplifications of Buddhist doctrine'.[16] This formulation, of course, at once raises some problems: 'deliberately contrived' appears to rule out, more or less programmatically, any significant element of the unexpected in mystical experience, and to contradict anything like Teresa's insistence that her paranormal episodes came unsought. It is to place the whole realm of exceptional spiritual experience in the domain of the will to a degree which the records of such experience, Christian and non-Christian, hardly justify. But it would perhaps be a mistake to take the observation in too strict a sense. Its main thrust accords with the points raised already in this chapter — that we should be suspicious of any theory that presupposes innocent and empty consciousnesses receiving, the world over, experiences of much the same kind, and then translating them into a particular religious dialect appropriate to the locality. What happens to the self in the states we call 'mystical' must, on the contrary, have some intelligible connection with the language and tradition in which that self is formed. To that extent at least, doctrine cannot properly be described as an interpretation of mysticism.

But what exactly is the relationship? The development of a new religious movement ordinarily involves an experiential moment in which words and perceptions are reordered in a way that the parent tradition cannot ultimately accommodate. This is certainly not reducible to a specific 'mystical experience'; all kinds of further factors enter in, and in the developed accounts of the origins of innovative, separatist religions (Christianity, Islam, Buddhism) some allusion to *transitional* moments of experience in the life of a founder or his first disciples is normally built in (Jesus' baptism and temptation, the resurrection appearances and Pentecost, the dictation of the Qur'an by the archangel, Gautama's enlightenment). In other words, religious traditions for which a datable historical origin is of some significance tend to think in terms of a cluster of transitional events in which one important element is the decay and recomposition of available models of religious meaning. Jesus 'hears' the words of God addressed to Israel and Israel's kings addressed to himself, marking out for him a vocation continuous with that of his people, yet not fully provided for in their existing frame of reference. The first disciples discover, because of the resurrection appearances, that the divine promise to be with Israel through the Law and the

Temple has taken a new shape in Jesus' continuing to be with them. Mohammed retells the history of God's involvement with the world as a history of the prophetic summons to obedience, so that submission to the transcendent unity of the creator — as expressed in the divine will for a single, just community — overrides both social particularism and ecclesiastical piety — both the limitations of Israel and the blasphemous Christian attempt to obscure the unity of God by misplaced devotion to the prophet Jesus. Gautama struggles for insight through the contemplative disciplines of India and discovers what those disciplines both presuppose and conceal — that there are no real subjects, divine or human; only a hunger for illusory solidity that prevents the transient play of mental activity finding its place *in*, not outside of, the interlocking process of things. In each case a religious tradition has created a structure and discipline that, in certain historical circumstances, generates a revolution in patterns of speaking and acting that can claim both to 'fulfil' and to go beyond that tradition.

Other kinds of religious tradition, like Judaism or the various styles of Hinduism, do not look to this kind of germinal moment of transition and remaking, but rest their understanding on a different kind of foundational story. Here there are no 'founders': religious practice rests on the communication of a timeless pattern of wisdom, a way of doing things and living together that participates in a precosmic order. For Judaism this communication is anchored in a history (exodus and covenant) but is nonetheless concerned with the imparting of a supra-historical order: orthodox Jews continue to think of Torah as manifesting the eternal mind of God. For some Hindus, there is a primordial revelation to the first sages of the Vedas; for others simply the everpresent possibility of contact and merging between the self within and the self without; and for yet others there is the communication of love and grace to the devotee from a personal 'lord'. But, absurd as it is in many respects to assimilate Judaism and Hinduism (both of which are deeply unsatisfactory designations anyway), both see the mediation to human beings of sacred meaning and power as *not* bound to a particular human biography in which some kind of paradigm transition takes place.

All religious traditions, not just the so-called 'higher' religions, are conscious of the passage of time and the possibility of forgetfulness of what is generative of their language and practice. The proposal for redefining 'mysticism' is that it is whatever in a religious system is thought to enable a re-establishing of contact with that generative element, over and above the ordinary ritual means of recollection or reappropriation.[17] Each religious tradition sustains—though often with a high degree of strain and conflict—roles, practices and conventions, positions to be taken up, methods for breaking down and reconstructing perception—other than the regular practice of corporate ritual—that are believed to go on giving access to whatever lies at its supposed origins. And each tradition thus trains personalities to be potential critics or reformers: if the person who takes up these roles and practices can establish that what she or he sees from their position is credibly related to the foundational realities of the tradition, or holds together its distinctive concerns with more plausibility than certain of its current intellectual or institutional manifestations, they will properly acquire considerable authority as a touchstone of the tradition's integrity. Their lives become a kind of classical exegesis of the tradition's basic texts and stories: something like what used to be called a *règle vivante* in monastic communities—someone from whose conduct you could reconstruct the text on which it was based. But, more than this, such a life becomes a point of *access* to a truth in danger of being overlaid by the passage of time.

The sort of people who tend to be called mystics must, in other words, be understood as having a clear function *within* a specific religious tradition; and if we want to generalize about mysticism, we should concentrate more on this comparability of *function* than on any supposed comparability of the content of *experience*. Where the latter is marked or significant, we should be looking for what it is in the systems and traditions involved that is convergent or comparable, instead of opposing convergent experience to divergent doctrine. The person who takes up the role of a non-ritual or non-priestly 'holiness' (proximity to the source of meaning or grace or creativity) by exposing himself or herself to disciplines for the reshaping of the consciousness so as to open it up comprehensively to the central myth or narrative of their tradition—such a person seems to be necessary to corporate religious practice, whether they are found among the prophets of Israel, the shamans of Asia and the Americas, the *sangha* in Buddhism (especially the monastic groups of Mahayana Buddhism), Hindu *sannyasins* or Christian contemplatives like Teresa and her sisters. All such persons can intelligibly be said to set out to 'exemplify' their doctrines, to internalize their myths in the pattern of their mental and imaginative lives.

They are necessary, but also dangerous. 'Deliberate exemplification' sounds controllable, but most traditions of exposure to the generative sacred reality involve (deliberate) risks — a stepping beyond some conventional religious expressions and behaviour-patterns, a 'dismembering'. It is always possible that what finally emerges is no longer containable within the tradition. Thus the 'mystic' is not only a potential critic but a potential destroyer; religions with a highly-developed sense of orthodoxy and its limits, of the boundaries of acceptable diversity, normally have a rich literature of anti-'mystical' reaction and critique. This is certainly true of all three of the major Western Semitic faiths: Judaism, Christianity and Islam. The uncontrolled and unpredictable elements in the vocation to this kind of holiness are both the most valuable and the most suspect of its contributions. For a religious tradition to foster and sustain the forms of non-ritual access to the sacred is for it to take a necessary and calculated but still quite genuine risk.

So, returning to the rather crude typology of religions sketched a little earlier, it is possible to see something of how the religious phenomena we know as 'mystical' fit into the varied patterns of religious expectation and practice. Exceptional, perception-changing experience in Judaism and Hinduism is generally conceived as a recapitulation of the basic relationship established between the divine and the world. Jewish mysticism, from at least the early centuries of the Common Era, develops two themes above all: the gathering-up of what the act of creation has made manifold and diffused — sometimes conceived as the ascent of the soul 'back' through the levels of emanation; and the soul's participation in the angelic liturgy of the highest heaven, where the created spirit comes to bear God's name and be permeated by God's glory, a created mirror of the divine life. Increasingly, and partly under gnostic influence, Jewish mystical cosmology evolves the doctrine of the self-splitting of the divine presence (*shekhinah*) into a glory 'above' and a glory 'below', with creation seen as the exile of divine glory from heaven, and the holy life on earth — the keeping of the Law — understood as the leading out of exile of that scattered glory. Exodus and covenant themes are thus woven into esoteric cosmology. Hinduism, as usual, resists generalization; but we can discern two main strands, 'gnostic' and devotional, in Indian literature about the soul's progress, corresponding to the monist cosmology of some of the classical texts, especially the Upanishads, and the personalized mythology of other works like the *Gita*. The self may seek an undifferentiated union with the cosmic self, or a well-ordered life in the world sustained by love and loyalty to a loving divine master. Which one is sought depends on which of the two focal notions or images of classical Indian religion predominates: the ultimately illusory nature of the world of manifold appearances, or the uncontrollable, even playful, fecundity and generosity of the divine.

Traditions that focus more directly on historical points of transition look to the possibility of recapitulating that transition. The Buddhist holy person aims at 'enlightenment' such as Gautama received: that is, an insight into the nature and source of that attachment that dooms us to the cycles of the world—an insight potent enough to spring us free from the traps of consciousness. This may be pursued through the shock tactics of some forms of Zen, or through the heavily mythological meditations and rituals of the Tibetan schools, or the techniques of concentration and abstraction, the focusing of mind on its own utter contingency, practised in Southern Buddhism; but the goal is the same, a step towards the realization of what Gautama realized. Popular, 'lay' Buddhism practises rituals whose existential significance is being incarnated in the life of the ascetic, and in this sense, Buddhism has integrated the mystical practitioner into its institutional identity more profoundly and successfully than any other major tradition: the holy is to be found in the life of the meditator, the monk, and there is, strictly speaking, no *priesthood*. Islam has had a more chequered relationship with its 'mystics'. Because it is more systematically grounded even than Judaism on the ideal of a universally accessible and universally applicable holy Law, Islam is inevitably suspicious of the religious need to identify persons whose access to the sacred is unusual or exemplary. Still, it has had to come to terms with an irrepressibly fertile 'mystical' strain, influenced (or contaminated?) by both Christian and Hindu sources: the imagery of an absolute, ecstatic submission to the divine command merges into an erotic idiom and sometimes a strong current in the direction of monism. But insofar as we can identify the distinctively Islamic in Muslim mystical literature, it lies in the clear affirmation of response to the divine unity, expressing itself in the unification of the created soul in its self-giving to God. The soul is brought back to its original state as an idea in God's mind, existing simply as the manifest effect of a particular command of God: it *is* obedience, and nothing else. This is always sailing close to the monist wind, and the rhetoric of some Sufic writers about identity with God has done nothing to allay suspicion;

but there is a recognizable Islamic pattern here. The 'mystic' *is* what the tradition seeks to create: perfect response, absolute obedience.

Because Christianity has a rather more complicated foundational story, its mystical literature can be expected to be more diverse and in some ways more problematic than that of Islam. There is the story of God's becoming human, the story of that humanity itself, and the story of the establishing of the community of faith in Easter and Pentecost. What is it that needs to be recapitulated? The movement out from heaven and back to it? The pattern of the incarnate ministry? Jesus' path to the cross? The disciples' experience of the resurrection? In some sense, all of these; but no single life is likely to be able to manage this range. What is more, an exclusive focus on one of these elements at the expense of others produces a damagingly distorted picture of what is actually focal in Christian language. Thus, for some strands in the Christian tradition the moment of outgoing and return represented by the incarnation and the bringing-back of creation to the Father predominate in a way that leads to treating the incarnate human life of Christ as purely instrumental to the task of bringing us to the contemplation of the heavenly identity of the Word. We must begin where the journey of God towards us was completed, but mount beyond to where that journey began. In this model, we internalize our foundation story and complete its direction by *reversing* it.

As Teresa insists again and again, this is not good enough: it carries the hidden assumption that, since our salvation lies in abandoning our material modes of knowing and understanding, we ought not to be material and finite. But there are also problems with concentrating on the recapitulation of the pattern of the earthly life and passion. Following Christ's example in his ministry has little to say directly to the project of reconditioning perception, as opposed to the reformation of behaviour. And, to the extent that the believer identifies *undialectically* with the suffering Christ, the transformative meaning of the cross can be obscured in a self-indulgent dolorism or even masochism. The search for encounter with the risen Lord can produce a distortion in the opposite direction: that is, a devotional relationship with a divine figure whose particular history, both in incarnation and passion, has practically ceased to be understood as the potential form that the believer's own history must take.

The history of Christian spirituality amply records all these possibilities. There is a powerful tradition that is—as we have noted—hostile to reflection on the human Jesus beyond a certain point.

There is a revulsion of feeling away from over-subtle or over-abstract accounts of interior life, towards a prosaic and serious moralism, focused on the virtues of Jesus: for example, the *Imitation of Christ*, the moral theology of Jeremy Taylor and other Anglicans of the seventeenth century. There are many varieties of passion-mysticism: the phenomenon of the stigmata is the most dramatic external sign of this; and we have in our own century the very remarkable writings of Adrienne von Speyr, describing regular experiences of participation in the dereliction of Jesus crucified and of Jesus going down into hell on Holy Saturday.[18] We have instances—from Richard Rolle in mediaeval England to Tilak in nineteenth-century India—of ecstatic devotion to the person of Jesus as exalted Lord, and a strong tradition in evangelical pietism of regarding this as the normative form of internalized religion. We have also, in the last two decades, an unexpected resurgence of the language of a 'new Pentecost'—the ecstatic recapitulation of what is believed to be primitive Christian experience in the Charismatic Movement. Representatives of all these schools are to be found among the saints of the various Churches, and it is impossible to say that one style alone is authentic—though there is a powerful pull in this direction, for some groups in particular. In recent years, both charismatics and anti-charismatics have fallen prey to this.

Perhaps, though, what gives particular greatness to those figures whose work and life have been seen as classical and authoritative in Catholic tradition is their capacity to see the unity of all these different aspects of spirituality because they see the unity of the divine act underlying them. Any one such figure may in practice concentrate on or have an *attrait* towards a particular style, but will be able to set it in the context of a coherent theology—and sometimes at least to acknowledge also the proper and legitimate diversity of spiritual paths. We have seen in these pages that Teresa becomes ever more conscious of the unifying themes of her basic theology, and—perhaps consequently—less passionately attached to the normative authority of her own experiential patterns, though she never wholly casts off this tendency. In other words, she succeeds in 'internalizing' an unusually full range of Christian themes, myths, or images. The same could be said of very different figures like Gregory of Nyssa, Augustine, Julian of Norwich, John of the Cross—and perhaps in our own day Edith Stein, Thomas Merton or Dorothy Day. These figures, in written texts as well as the 'text' of their lives, serve (as I have argued the so-called mystic must serve) as points of orientation, touchstones of integrity, for the language and hopes of other believers precisely because they witness to so broad and comprehensive an access to the 'sacred source' of Christian commitment, the action and passion of God in the *whole* event of Jesus Christ. The contour of divine movement towards the world manifest in this event becomes once again present and potent in a life whose contours follow out that primary movement. The shape of the fundamental story becomes the shape of this human biography in a comprehensive way—comprehensive enough to create the kind of profound disturbances and disorientations of consciousness that the 'mystic' characteristically describes.

Teresa, like the other figures just mentioned, and many more, represents and embodies an 'open door' for the Christian community into the world of its own first formation. She herself presupposes something very like this: both the *Way* and the *Foundations* were written with the assumption that part of the indication of the life of Carmel is its character as *manifestation*, a making concrete of the possibilities of Christlikeness, showing what it means to live within the movement of God's love towards the world. We do her less than justice if we concentrate on her 'mysticism' as an individual phenomenon alongside other phenomena of religious psychology.

TERESA AND THE WAY OF CHRIST

Throughout this book we have seen how Teresa's vision of her calling is consciously informed by a theology that lays special stress upon God's desire to be present with the creation—the desire that causes God to abandon divine status and to become defenceless, dishonoured and unprivileged. Teresa's Christmas carols are almost all focused on this: Christ is poor and held in contempt and needs the shepherds—and us—to guard him; he has come from his native land, his *tierra*, to save us who have been made exiles from *our* land by sin (*el pecado nos destierra*).[19] The Christchild is God almighty, and at the same time the kinsman (*pariente*) of 'Bras and Menga and Llorente'.[20] The shepherd lass (*zagala*) who gives birth to Christ is so radiant that the shepherds ask 'Is she some relation to the magistrate [*alcalde*]?' and are answered that she is of higher lineage, 'a daughter of God the Father'.[21] Conventional Christmas pieties in one sense, but a vivid reminder of Teresa's theology, particularly as expressed in the *Way*—God's carelessness of safety for our sake,

God's willingness to suffer so that we may become members of the divine kindred.

For Teresa, the act of commitment to the (reformed) religious rule was the primary means of imitating the second person of the Trinity, in incarnation, ministry and passion all together, because it was a repudiation not only of our selfish will (F 5.2–12, as well as many chapters of W: 13.6, 32 *passim*, 33.1, etc.) but of our honour (see, above all, W 27.6). And this imitation is also to be found and followed in the detail of discipleship *within* the community and within the path of prayer itself. Several sections of chapter 5 of the *Foundations* spell this out very clearly. The union that matters is union with the divine will, not an experience of absorption (5.13); we must be ready to abandon solitude and the conscious enjoyment of God's presence so as to carry our love for God into the everyday world. 'Through obedience we in some way give up enjoying God himself. And yet, this is nothing if we consider that he came from the bosom of his Father out of obedience to become our slave' (5.17). The imitation of the pattern of incarnation is shown in not isolating and privileging 'the spiritual life' over the entirety of a life lived in the power of Christ.

Here Teresa stands, surprisingly, close to Meister Eckhart. There is not only the famous dictum ascribed to him, 'If a man were in rapture like St Paul, and knew a sick man who needed some soup from him, I should think it far better if you abandoned rapture for love';[22] there is also Eckhart's well-attested fondness for turning the classical interpretation of the Martha and Mary narrative upside down—most obviously in sermon 86,[23] but also, by implication, in sermon 2 of the German works.[24] In sermon 86, Eckhart argues that Martha *must* break into Mary's absorption in the overwhelming grace of God, because Mary must learn to serve God in God's absence, as it were, away from the manifest consolation of Christ's presence. 'Martha . . . feared that [Mary] would remain stuck in this pleasant feeling and would progress no further.'[25] Martha, on the contrary, possesses everything of temporal *and* eternal value: she acts in works of love and service with full awareness of what she does. 'We have been put into time for the purpose of coming nearer to and becoming more like God through rational activity in time.'[26] The 'care' shown in the doing of works of love, the trouble Martha is aware of, means that her active involvement strips her of consolation; but by bringing her to inner nakedness and simplicity in this way, it unites her to God. She is care-full and troubled, but not '*in* care', drowned in egoistic anxiety.[27] This is to follow the example of Christ, who in his earthly life is at once wholly united with the divine life, yet vulnerable to the pain of temporal existence.[28] Mary *alone* cannot be a complete or perfect soul because we never free ourselves from temporal human responsibility while we live in time. Mary presupposes Martha: the mature contemplative is someone who has learned Martha's way, and the attempt to be Mary without this learning process is a mark of immaturity.[29] So in sermon 2, the soul that is spoken of throughout is *Martha*'s: both virgin and wife, both free and fertile, stripped from ego-centred attachment and pregnant with the Word.[30]

Teresa certainly did not know Eckhart, and would just as certainly have found many aspects of the Dominican mystic deeply problematic (not least his attitude to the role of the humanity of Jesus in contemplation). But their agreement here is striking. For both of them, intimacy with God is conceived as assimilation to a God whose life is itself a movement, a 'mission'. God is not God except as the one who sends the Son. Eckhart's model remains in many ways quite deeply marked by the Neoplatonic structure he seems to take for granted: being itself is naturally a movement of outflowing and return. Teresa's approach is more obviously anchored in the Bible and the pattern of incarnation itself. Both speak about the need to learn prayer and its consolations for the sake of service and love, but it is, characteristically, Teresa who links this with the Son's leaving of the Father for our sake. The Son comes in search of the lost, and our service of him is therefore identical with our service of others, insofar as that is linked to their eternal interest. So, like Martha, we provide him with 'food': 'His food is that in every way possible we draw souls that they may be saved and praise him always' (C VII, 4.12).

The paradox of Christian mysticism — at least on Teresa's account — is that there is *no* detached divine absolute with which to take refuge. We may and must detach ourselves from all that keeps us from God: our sin, our fearfulness and false humility, our pride of race or family; but the God with whom we are finally united is the God whose being is directed in love towards the world, which we must then re-enter, equipped to engage with other human beings with something of God's own wholeheartedness because we have been stripped of certain modes of self-protectiveness: of an understanding of our worth or loveableness as resting on prestige, achievement or uniformity. The way of perfection leads back to taking our active place in the human community. Just as for Eckhart (despite his wholly different idiom), the nearer we are to God in stillness and emptiness, the nearer we are to the point of pure generative love from which the everlasting Word comes forth, and whose overflowing is the making of the world. In an important sense, then, there is no single or static experiential terminus for Christian 'mysticism'. Even if, like John of the Cross, the imagery of progress and ascent is pervasive, the goal is simply a state in which we enact the action of God through our growth into faith, hope and love—though John's doctrine of a return to the created order is far more muted than Teresa's.[31]

This is not to ascribe to Teresa an optimistic activism, a 'worldly holiness' of the bland sort popular in some styles of modern spirituality. Teresa and John (and the Christian tradition in general) agree in assuming that love of the world, missionary presence in the world, leaving the bosom of the Father in search of the lost, is the hardest thing any human being could presume to undertake. We have made ourselves strangers to the world by sin, and strangers to God. We must, in Teresa's language, simultaneously learn friendship with God and each other; and that process involves becoming strangers to ourselves, or ourselves as we have conceived and constructed ourselves. We must become strangers to the tyrannies of honour and dignity: the ascetic life in a community of equals initiates this process, and teaches us a new solidarity with the dispossessed and powerless.[32] And the extraordinary upheavals of psychic and physical life, the ecstasies and the acute pain and disorientation so vividly described by Teresa, serve precisely the same purpose, of making us strangers to ourselves so as to become friends of the world and God. Because of the deep disorientation involved, we may *think* we are more than ever strangers to God and the world, and will long for dissolution and rest—hence the torments of the sixth mansions. But the end of this particular exploration is indeed 'to arrive where we started / And know the place for the first time':[33] that is, to make friends with our existence as creatures in an unpredictable world. It is *because* the world (including ourselves) is not a place where God is clearly and immediately to be seen that we undertake the journey to the soul's centre; and for us to act in such a way that God is at work in our working requires a discipline that will often seem to lead away from action, or to expose us to shocks and stresses that threaten to interrupt our active lives. But from at least the time of Augustine onwards, Christians had agreed that it is hard to be 'natural', to live in the world as creatures bearing God's image.

So Teresa's interest as a chronicler of the dramatic phenomena of 'mysticism' is a fruitful source of misunderstanding for the modern reader. The strangeness and the drama are part of a movement whose culmination is the almost prosaic apostolate of the seventh mansions — though we should not forget that this is a prose fired by intensities of love and commitment far beyond the ordinary. Behind the competent practicality of the person living in union is a continuing experience (so Teresa sees it) of living on the edge of ecstasy, undergoing moments of piercing intimacy and seeing into the heart of theological mysteries. The point is that such intensity and such perception are no longer alien to the soul that has completed its journey, and so no longer interrupt the flow of thought and action. To be actively in the world and at the same time wholly exposed to the reality of God is something most of us cannot imagine: we use activity as a defence against exposure to God; or we use the claims of God (as we see them) as a defence against the risks of action and apostolic faithfulness in a 'world in flames'. That life which fuses these inseparably together is Christ's.

One further reflection on Teresa's Christological scheme may be appropriate here. I have suggested that the greatest Christian mystics are those whose lives and writing demonstrate something of the integral *unity* of the Christian story; but I have noted also that all sorts of factors may determine the particular way in which that unity is organized and represented in a life. We have been made more attentive than ever in recent years to the extent to which context (rightly) sets the agenda for the enterprise of Christian reflection. Teresa's case is no exception. For her, the unity of the story is, as we have seen, centred in the twofold sense of God as wanting our company and God as the enemy of human systems of status. If Teresa's family and social world had been different, this would not have been so manifestly the focus of her thought. As we saw in the first chapter, she was in several ways an anomalous person, not an insider. Thus the unifying thread she perceives is to do with the God who is hidden within the diversities of human life (the King in the centre of the castle), who is 'anomalous' in refusing to stay within the proper hierarchical structures of a well-ordered universe, and whose action is *essentially* at odds with the quest for personal security and legitimacy on the basis of good behaviour. 'God at the centre' is consistently set in opposition to a 'centre' of social order and power and purity — the centre from which Teresa, as a woman and a Jew, is distant. Turning to God within is a very familiar strategy in religious protest; when the approved centre of public existence is not accessible, it is necessary to relocate the centre in the inner life. But what makes Teresa so interesting in this respect is that this shifting of the centre is conceived as God's own characteristic movement: God *is* a reality moving away from a centre of self-possession towards being-in-another. And so the moving of the centre of meaning that is involved in turning from external ambiguity to inner clarity is saved from being simply a move into the private sphere by its association with God's journey into creation. The rejection of the world's standards is also a claim on behalf of God's will and ability to penetrate the world and to remake it in self-abandoning love.

CONCLUSION: TERESA'S LEGACY TODAY

The more clearly and freely we see a figure like Teresa against the background of her age the more we may appreciate the possibility of a 'conversation' with her. If she is made simply a mouthpiece for would-be timeless pieties, she becomes remote and eccentric, inviting the ill-informed scorn of an age uninterested in those pieties. If she is conscripted into the service of typically twentieth-century causes, she becomes only a sounding-board for our own preoccupations. If we look in turn at three areas of contemporary interest arising in connection with Teresa's work, we may discern some of the dangers of modernizing Teresa, and so perhaps begin to have some sense of how she might, in her very difference from us, have something of weight to say to us. The three areas I shall look at briefly are: (1) the role of women in the Church, (2) Church and society, and (3) authority.

(1) Teresa is not, of course, a feminist: the term would be an anachronism for almost any woman in the pre-modern period. She assumes, when she bothers to think about it, what her Church and society meant her to assume about being a woman, and when she thinks about it, it rather depresses her (L 10.8; W 1.2). Like earlier writers in the ascetical tradition, she speaks of the mature female saint as an honorary man (W 7.8). She plays the part of a dutiful daughter of the Church, and is fully aware of what her environment tells her to identify as the characteristic weaknesses of women. At the same time, she does *not* assume that all this is directly ordained

in revelation. She is conscious of some tension between the voices of patriarchy in her day and the narrative of Jesus, as she is conscious of the same tension between the way 'public' authority operates and the authority she discovers for herself.

Is her quite sincere and articulate determination to be a loyal daughter of the Church simply a piece of false or distorted consciousness? This is not a simple question. Reading the *Life* it is hard to escape the impression that she felt she had betrayed her father in some way — failing him in his spiritual need, deceiving him about her own spiritual state. Her urgent insistence on getting her spiritual fathers to recognize and evaluate her experience, her insistence on telling all to her confessors, can be read as an attempt to make reparation for evasiveness and untruthfulness with her fleshly father. But what must qualify this rather pat psychological judgement is the manifest fact that she is not content with a purely daughterly role, dependent on a father's approval. As we have seen, her anxiety about her experience is at least as much to do with a more deeply-rooted sense of her tendency to hide from herself; and she is able, both for herself and others, to demand that the paternal authority appealed to should justify itself by its fruits, and allow itself to be exposed to a critique based on the living-out of the gospel's standards. Reconciliation with the father is undoubtedly a motif in Teresa, but it is inseparably interwoven with the desire for the father to be a participant in dialogue and debate. Not everything depends on paternal approval.

She returns several times to the theme of Jesus' accessibility to women, irrespective of their status and achievement (as in the *Vejamen*), and Jesus' readiness to be helped and comforted by women (W 3.7). The friendship of Jesus cuts across any rigid account of the spiritual or intellectual capacity of women; and it is the voice of Jesus himself that brushes aside a bald appeal to the Pauline prohibition of women teaching in the Church ('"Tell them they shouldn't follow just one part of Scripture, . . . and ask them if they can by any chance tie my hands"':T 15). Just as — in the popular Spanish culture of the day (see Chapter 1) — the king was the focal point of the code of honour and so (in a way) the touchstone and the guarantor of honour, so, for Teresa, 'His Majesty' did not necessarily feel constrained by how the code operated at lower levels, and could honour whomever he wished. The invitation of Jesus to women does not overthrow the status patterns and structures of the Church, which are in some vague sense derived from God; but it prevents us from supposing that in any specific case the will of God can be directly read off from them. Christ gives spiritual understanding where he wills (S 1.2), even where this understanding is not the kind bound up with the (male) vocation of teaching and preaching; and even so, one of the trials of the sixth mansions for a woman is the longing to communicate what is understood. 'She has great envy of those who have the *freedom* to cry out and spread the news abroad about who this great God of hosts is' (C VI, 6.3). Thus the egalitarian action of God honouring the friends of God stands in tension with facts in Church and society that Teresa believed to be simply given. God's practice is to be witnessed to, therefore, in the construction of a community that both is and is not part of the Church's structure: it is obedient to the discipline of the Church, but because its members are in any case outside the power system of the Church, as women, they have the rather paradoxical freedom to display the priorities of the gospel in a simpler way.

Teresa is thus an eloquent witness to essential elements of internal conflict in Christian tradition. She does not want to overthrow the continuity of the Catholic Church, to reinvent it or recover a more authentic pattern for it as a whole; she has no conception of what the Reformation is about. But she is nonetheless conscious of the gospel narrative — and the narrative of God's whole 'mission' in creation, of which this is a part — as providing some critical perspectives on the Church's contemporary reality. On the place of women in the twentieth-century Church, Teresa has no conclusions to offer us. We live in a situation in which far less is taken for granted about women, and in which a radicalized religious life is no longer the only obvious way of witnessing to the freedom of the gospel in the Church. But, by expressing in her struggles for a particular kind of community her own sense of the questions put by the practice of Jesus to the assumptions of Church and society, she keeps those questions vividly present to later generations — more vividly than if she had raised the issue of 'the status of women' in a coherent theoretical way.

She lends little support to the idea that female spirituality is characteristically passive or receptive. We have seen that she disliked the idea of *seeking* passivity, and believed that women were especially prone to illusion and fantasy if they tried to empty their minds; better to work hard, physically and mentally. Like the male theorists of her age she assumed that women's mental activity was more mixed up in their physical being than was the case with men;

so that the control of mental and physical functions belonged together. If a woman *tried* to suspend mental control it was a short step to physical profligacy. This was part of the folklore of the Catholic establishment, fed by stories of the excesses of *alumbradas* and *beatas*. Teresa generally goes along with this, but is concerned to defend the possibility of *God*'s bringing the mind to passivity: if it truly is God who is at work, then, despite the physical and psychological disturbance involved, the spirit will not want to do anything displeasing to God. The threat of the uncontrolled female body is outflanked by insisting on God's union with the female will; characteristically Teresa both meets and relativizes the requirements of Catholic obedience.

This does not remove the ambivalent elements in her bridal and erotic imagery for relation with God: William James, in the discussion of Teresa already referred to,[34] spoke of a kind of flirtatiousness, an immature emotionalism, in this language; and some more recent writers, particularly feminist critics, have echoed this, and deplored the self-humiliation carried in such an idiom when used by women.[35] There is some weight in this. As we have noted, Teresa does undoubtedly take on the conventions of her time as regards the relations of male and female, and this clearly included a strong expectation of submissive rhetoric from the female side. Passivity to God may translate uncomfortably accurately the passivity of woman to man in social and sexual relation. But it is important to balance this with a number of other factors in Teresa's writing. There is the manifest fact that Teresa understands passivity to God as a moment in the process of assimilation to the divine liberty—the assimilation to which her parallel images of Christ as kinsman and friend point. There is her own highly critical assessment of the unfreedom of the married woman, most vividly expressed in the striking passage in *The Way of Perfection* (26.4; cf. 11.3) where she describes Christ, the spiritual husband of the Carmelite religious, as obediently responsive to her moods. And there is the theology underlying this that understands the incarnation as God's movement into the receptive or passive position, into need and dependency. Teresa's spirituality is not to be reduced to a simple pattern of 'female' contemplative receptivity to God: there is a more complex interrelation of action and passion in both God and the female self before God.

(2) Teresa is not a social reformer. Despite her own mockery of obsessions with dignity, titles and precedence, and her confession of

ineptitude in the finer points of etiquette (W 22.1), she accepts without question the facts of social inequality. Within a few paragraphs of her satirical comments on etiquette she can say (in connection with giving proper attention to the saying of vocal prayers), 'we must not approach a conversation with a prince as negligently as we do one with a farm worker' (W 22.3). She mixes freely with the leading families of Spain, and unashamedly uses their influence to gain her ends; she appeals to the king to cut through the knots of ecclesiastical bureaucracy and corruption, begging him to intervene on behalf of John of the Cross in 1577 (*Letters* I, 204). She is clearly in full support of Philip II's imperial policy in the Americas and regards him as a defender of the faith: a slightly suspect tradition[36] may imply that she transmitted to the king a 'message' from Christ exhorting him to show no mercy to the Muslim remnant in Spain—though the interpretation of the supposed locution is far from clear. We do know that she regarded death in battle when serving with the armies of the Catholic king as death for the sake of the Christian faith (*Letters* I, 11a).

She is certainly critical of aristocratic self-indulgence and neglect of the needs of the poor (W 33.1; S 2.8): wealth is a trust from God, which must be regularly and systematically used to relieve suffering: occasional almsgiving is not enough. In her report in 1562 on the state of her soul she notes that she has acquired a new level of compassion for the poor: 'if it were up to me I would give them the clothes off my back'. Dutiful almsgiving has been replaced by visceral feeling and real longing to relieve them; she feels no disgust about talking to them or touching them: a significant development for a gently-nurtured lady of the sixteenth century. But her critique of the wealthy remains firmly in the framework of a rather individualized understanding of social virtue—the wealthy doing their duty to the needy with no questions raised about the means of acquiring wealth and no suggestion that the problem of the poor is powerlessness. Much of what she says here belongs with what is said by compassionate Christian moralists from St John Chrysostom in fourth-century Antioch to Edward Bouverie Pusey in nineteenth-century Oxford. The wealth of the wealthy is taken for granted: the question is whether it can be used with humility and generosity.

In an age in which economic analysis, in the terms in which we understand it, was practically non-existent, this is a good question (as far as it goes); but it is not here that we find Teresa's most authentically radical vision. As we have noted in the opening chapter of this book, 'honour' was not, in sixteenth-century Spain, a minor issue about social manners; it was a question of how people *belonged* to society, how they were connected with each other. To criticize the conventions of honour was implicitly to challenge the secular basis of social unity. Honour, for Teresa, is not innate by virtue of birth; it can be discarded without damage to the person. Communities can exist with other bonds — that is, friendship with each other and with God; for the Christian the existence of such communities is an essential witness to God's own saving disregard for honour, human and divine. Honouring God overrides all other considerations; and if the community life that honours God requires of us a share in 'dishonourable' manual labour, the bread-and-butter work of daily life, this is all to the good (*Constitutions* 22, among other examples). The small community, in its modest premises (W 2.8-10), is one where all must collaborate in daily work which will contribute to sustaining the community financially (*Constitutions* 9). There is no sense here of the unacceptability of earned income — something that would have been taken for granted by most religious communities of the day, as it was in aristocratic Spanish society at large.[37] It has been suggested that Teresa's encouragement to her brother Lorenzo to acquire 'honour' for his family by buying a farm (*Letters* I, 158) reflects a similarly high estimate of honest labour, but this is more than doubtful: Lorenzo plainly means to live off his rents.

All in all, then, Teresa identifies a point of tension, rather than providing any resolution — just as she does in her views of women. The system that holds together human society independently of the grace of Christ is absurd and often damaging; witness her scathing remarks in F 20 and elsewhere about impoverished noble families living in rural isolation and consumed with anxiety over marrying off their poorly dowried daughters. F 10 (mentioned in Chapter 1 above) with its startling story of a girl pressured into betrothal to an uncle so as to avoid the loss of property and family dignity, shows Teresa's particular awareness of the price paid by women in an honour-dominated culture. The society established by kinship with Christ is wholly different. Teresa does not restrict her sense of the demands of the gospel to the religious community alone, though this is the major focus of her attention; she is quite generally critical of secular vanity and dignity among the clergy. Thus the Christian society, the religious house above all, manifests to the world a specific model of social relation, centred upon friendship, a belonging together of equals. If it does not actively seek to transform the whole of society into this pattern, at least it offers a practical release for some from social bonds of hierarchy and status, and puts a standing question to the idea that the existing forms of social belonging are natural or inevitable. In a society that had no clear concept of planned social change or of the possibility of a population taking corporate political decisions, it would be unrealistic to expect more: but we, in a radically different environment, may take her questions about the foundations of social unity as suggesting an agenda affecting more than the monastic world alone.

(3) Teresa is not a defender of the rights of individual conscience or judgement as such. She never questions the right of the Inquisition to pursue its task[38] or the right of bishops and nuncios to oversee and discipline her work, however much she protests at and resists some aspects of their activity. She is manifestly and vocally horrified by what little she knows of the Reformation. Her desire to be, and to be seen to be, a loyal Catholic is quite sincere, and she cannot easily be claimed as a proponent of the authority of experience. She is genuinely not an *alumbrada*. That men and women deceive themselves about their awareness of God is axiomatic for her; indeed, it is one of the things that her own experience, in the widest sense, impresses upon her — through her work as a nourisher of souls and through her memories of the unsatisfactory early years of her convent life. Individual experience, however vivid and compelling, has no authority as such: it is to be rigorously tested, with friends and confidantes, and with those officially charged with conserving the Church's teaching, the *letrados* among the clergy.

But Teresa's independence appears in her insistence that those in authority in the Church be clearly answerable to the reality, the incarnational movement of God, that directs her own prayer and action. Her own 'mystical' experience is in an important sense validated for her by being demonstrably a deeper penetration into the fundamental narrative of the Christian Church — the act of God that is daily enacted in the Eucharist. We have noted, too, at several points, her willingness to appeal to the practice of Jesus and the apostles as recorded in the gospels. In other words, she accepts an authority beyond her experience, the authoritative action of God, which, as we noted in Chapter 2, she understands and encounters as an overriding interruption of her own self-serving religiousness; but this is an authority to which the official authority of the Church is no less subject than she is. The Church is, for Teresa, the indispensable mediator of the saving action of God in Christ; there is no hint of an appeal *from* the Church to a 'pure' Christianity outside it. But the Church's mediation is performed through the sacramental action which witnesses to God's unchanging commitment; the Church presents Jesus, sacramentally and in its retelling of Scripture, as the way for all people to find their way to the knowledge and love of God and to have their will and desire bound to God's. The Church, in short, guards and transmits those possibilities that Teresa and those like her realize. If the contemplative radical like Teresa questions the Church's practice, even in some respects the Church's methods of exercising authority, she does so in the name of what the Church itself 'authoritatively' does and says. If Teresa reposes what often seems like an overgenerous trust in the authority of theologians, especially theologians who know something about prayer, it is because she assumes that the theologian—unlike the plain pastor or administrator—will have a deeper grasp of the shape and logic of God's action in Christ; and even with theologians, she is at times prepared to ignore their expert advice in favour of her own sense of that logic—as with her struggle to establish the principle of poverty and self-sufficiency in her first foundation. 'I didn't want to benefit from theology if it wasn't conducive to my following my vocation'; such was her response to the cautions of Fray Ibáñez (L 35.4), who was in fact subsequently moved to change his mind.

Looking at all these three areas of tension in Teresa's writing and experience—her feminine identity, her social perception and her understanding of authority—something of a general conclusion begins to emerge. If 'mysticism' is about the personal appropriation of the patterns and icons of a tradition, that appropriation is inevitably a risky affair from the institution's point of view. But within the major religious traditions this does not lead to the simplistic opposition between institution and individual spiritual liberty that a liberal religious studies perspective might expect. A profound and prolonged immersion in the fundamental images and stories of the tradition may well generate, as in Teresa, a new degree of awareness of the points of strain, ambiguity and irresolution in the tradition as it is handed on. Such an awareness is going to be essential for any tradition that is not content to settle simply for ritual and ideology, any tradition concerned to *continue* the process of discovering and maintaining its integrity. We saw earlier in this chapter how the 'mystic' offers a way into the generative realities underlying everyday religious practice; more specifically, we can now say that the life of someone like Teresa not only opens up a comprehensive sense of what Christian identity involves, but also alerts the tradition-conserving institution to 'unfinished business', and prevents it being too easily ready to suppose that it has mastered its own resources. We might expect Teresa to show us tensions and unclarities in the areas discussed, if it is indeed true that Christianity is a faith marked in its very origins by unsettling new perspectives on human unity and equality, on the nature of community and the exercise of power. Studying Teresa reminds us of some of these disturbances built into the Church's story, those awkward and still unresolved challenges to our systems of hierarchy and separation, arising from the narrative of a God who will not stay in a safe and predetermined place; she reminds us that we do not yet know what it would be like if the community of Christ's friends let themselves be fully taken up into God's self-imparting act.

When your Father does what you ask him by giving us his kingdom here on earth, I know that we shall make your words come true by giving what you give for us. For once the earth has become heaven, the possibility is there for your will to be done in me. (W 32.2)

Notes

1 Andrew Louth, *Denys the Areopagite* (London, 1989), pp. 100-9.

2 Louis Bouyer, 'Mysticism. An essay on the history of the word' in Richard Woods (ed.), *Understanding Mysticism* (London, 1981), pp. 42-55; quotation pp. 52-3.

3 The works of Ralph Inge, Evelyn Underhill, Baron von Hügel and, on the Continent, Friedrich Heiler and Rudolf Otto may be mentioned here; a discussion of some of the issues raised may be found in Rowan Williams, 'The Prophetic and the Mystical: Heiler revisited', *New Blackfriars* 64 (1983), pp. 330-47.

4 See the various articles in Woods, *op. cit.*, Part III, particularly Kenneth Wapnick, 'Mysticism and schizophrenia', pp. 321-37.

5 See, for example, Deirdre Green, *Gold in the Crucible* (Shaftesbury, 1989), ch. 2, where John of the Cross and Teresa are contrasted as 'monist' and 'theistic' types.

6 Thus Green, *op. cit.*; the assimilation of Eckhart to Shankara implied

here goes back to Rudolf Otto, *Mysticism East and West* (London and New York, 1932).

7 See the works of Evagrius in *The Philokalia*, trans. G. E. H. Palmer, Philip Sherrard and Kallistos Ware, I (London, 1979), pp. 29–71.

8 Ibid., p. 57.

9 Ibid., p. 58.

10 Ibid., p. 63.

11 Ibid., p. 68.

12 Ibid., p. 64.

13 William James, *The Varieties of Religious Experience* (London, 1925), p. 428.

14 Ibid., p. 415; see pp. 346–8 for his further evaluation of Teresa.

15 This is the burden of Nicholas Lash's excellent recent study, *Easter in Ordinary. Reflections on Human Experience and the Knowledge of God* (London, 1988); chs 3 to 8 provide a thorough critical discussion of William James.

16 Robert Gimello, 'Mysticism and meditation' in Steven Katz (ed.), *Mysticism and Philosophical Analysis* (London, 1978), pp. 170–99; quotation p. 193.

17 See Williams, *op. cit.*, pp. 340–44.

18 See Hans Urs von Balthasar, *First Glance at Adrienne von Speyr* (Eng. trans.; San Francisco, 1981), esp. pp. 64–8.

19 Kavanaugh–Rodriguez III, pp. 387–8.

20 Ibid., pp. 388–9.

21 Ibid., p. 391.

22 *Spiritual Instructions* 10.

23 Bernard McGinn (ed.), *Meister Eckhart: Teacher and Preacher* (New York and Mahwah, NJ, 1986), pp. 338–45.

24 E. Colledge and Bernard McGinn (eds), *Meister Eckhart: the Essential Sermons, Commentaries, Treatises and Defense* (New York, 1981), pp. 177–81.

25 Sermon 86, McGinn, *op. cit.*, p. 339.

26 Ibid., p. 340.

27 Ibid., pp. 341–2.

28 Ibid., p. 343.

29 Ibid., pp. 343–4.

30 Sermon 2 (above, note 24) deals with a text (Luke 10:38) in which Martha alone is named).

31 John's positive appreciation of the created order comes out most clearly in certain passages of *The Living Flame* and in the *Romances* (his cycle of short lyrics on the eternal purpose behind the incarnation).

32 *Spiritual Testimonies* 2.4.

33 T.S. Eliot, *Little Gidding*, 241–2.

34 See note 14 above.

35 Sara Maitland, 'Passionate prayer: masochistic images in women's experience' in Linda Hurcombe (ed.), *Sex and God. Varieties of Women's Religious Experience* (London, 1989), pp. 125–40; pp. 134–5 on Teresa.

36 Stephen Clissold, *St Teresa of Avila* (London, 1979), pp. 143–4.

37 See the introduction to the *Foundations* in Kavanaugh–Rodriguez I, p. 40.

38 See the remarks to Gracián recorded in Efrén de la Madre de Dios and Otgar Steggink, *Tiempo y vida de Santa Teresa* (Madrid, 1968), p. 584. See also pp. 32–4 above.

Index

175

(This index does not include modern authors)